John Hick and the U

'John Hick's contribution to religious studies has had a profound effect on modern Western theology. Chris Sinkinson's thoughtful and robust assessment of Hick's work is urgently needed. As we face the continuing challenges of religious pluralism, this book will enrich and encourage a new generation of orthodox scholars and believers "to contend for the faith once for all entrusted to the saints". Highly recommended.'

—Steve Brady, Principal, Moorlands College, Christchurch

'If you've heard of just one philosopher of religion, it may well be John Hick. Even if you've never heard of any philosophers of religion, you can almost guarantee you'll have come across ideas about religion prevalent in our culture that have been influenced by Hick's thinking. He really is the godfather of religious pluralism.

'In Chris Sinkinson's excellent book, the author not only describes Hick's pluralism but crucially excavates Hick's early commitments on the theory of knowledge which set the trajectory for his later radical theological revisionism and his interpretation of religion. Chris's analysis is a very clear and salutary reminder of how philosophical roots inimical to a Christian doctrine of revelation leads to a theological vision and a Jesus unrecognizable from healthy historically orthodox Christianity. I highly recommended this book.'

—Dr Dan Strange, Academic Vice Principal, Oak Hill College, London

'I am delighted to see this fresh edition of Chris Sinkinson's critique of John Hick's work. Clear and readable, yet based on comprehensive research, it makes complex philosophical arguments simple, so that we not only "get the point", but also see "where it leads" in terms of Christian faith and other faiths. With surgical skill, Sinkinson exposes the illogicalities and contradictions within the pluralist ideology, and indeed the arrogance that hides behind its popular plausibility. This book will be enormously helpful as a resource to Christians who choose to engage with the dominant pluralism in our culture, enabling them to do so with insight and understanding as well as grace and courage.'

—Christopher J.H. Wright, Langham Partnership

'A vigorous, respectful, demanding and rewarding investigation of John Hick's philosophy and in particular his epistemology. Chris Sinkinson offers a helpful study of the embeddedness of all religious beliefs in tradition-specific cultural contexts. An important and prolific pluralist writer is, paradoxically, found to be insufficiently pluralist.'

— Howard Peskett, Former Vice Principal, Trinity College, Bristol

'Readers will learn from this lucid, rigorous and challenging work. Whether they agree with his conclusion or not, they will have to rethink many issues regarding Christianity and other religions in the light of this book. Sinkinson's argument, approach and his epistemological investigation, makes this book an important contribution to Reformed theological approaches to other religions as well as a profound and persuasive argument against the pluralism of John Hick.'

—Gavin D'Costa,
Department of Theology and Religious Studies, Bristol University

John Hick and the
Universe of Faiths

A Critical Evaluation of the Life and Thought
of John Hick

Chris Sinkinson

Paternoster:
thinking faith

First published 2016 by Paternoster
Paternoster is an imprint of Authentic Media Ltd
PO Box 6326, Bletchley, Milton Keynes MK1 9GG.
authenticmedia.co.uk

British Library Cataloguing in Publication Data

A catalogue record for this book is available from the British Library

ISBN 978-1-84227-918-2
978-1-84227-919-9 (e-book)

Cover design by David Smart smartsart.co.uk
Printed and bound by CPI Group (UK) Ltd., Croydon, CR0 4YY

Contents

To my wife Ros, who has made faith and
life a great adventure

Preface

As a first-year undergraduate student in philosophy at Southampton University, John Hick provided a lifeline. I came across his slim volume, *Philosophy of Religion*, in its distinctive purple cover in the university bookshop and knew I had to read it. In comparison with many of the textbooks we had to read, this book had one remarkable quality: crystal-clear clarity. Hick had great understanding of his subject but also wrote with personal interest and a desire to clarify rather than confuse.

I read all of Hick's works that I could find and ended up pursuing a doctorate related to his work with Gavin D'Costa at Bristol University. One theme stood out above all others. Hick was writing on the crucial issue of the Christian response to religious diversity, and in multicultural Southampton and Bristol it was hard to see a more pressing issue for Christianity.

I shared with Hick a personal conversion story as a late teenager but had never found his path to pluralism attractive. This book explains why. The more I considered his philosophical position the less attracted I was to it as a Christian. To really understand the problem in Hick's theology of religions we need to understand its roots. It grows not from his convictions about Jesus but from a certain kind of western philosophical tradition. As we consider Hick's life and development we find his pathway much less revolutionary than some think.

In trying to understand why this is the case, there is an opportunity to reflect on much more than the thought of a single scholar. In the growth of Hick's thought we can see a microcosm of the growth of much contemporary western theology. We move from an evangelical orthodox faith, through a liberal modernist view to a more radical minimalist religion. The roots of Hick's thought lie deep in the soil of Enlightenment thinking. As we chart the course of his development we find a map of the development of western theology.

Critics may complain that I have committed the cardinal offence of subjecting Hick's philosophy to a theological critique. Such critics wish to keep theology and philosophy quite distinct. It is unfair to launch a cross-disciplinary enquiry or so it is claimed. However, such an objection is a smokescreen. Hick clearly subjected theological ideas to philosophical analysis. Why should we not subject philosophical ideas to theological analysis? Who has the right to grant priority to one over the other? In reality there is no sharp distinction between theology and philosophy of religion, but they both dialogue with each other. This book is a dialogue between the history of theology and philosophy as they speak to each other in the work of John Hick.

In the opening to Hick's textbook on the subject he writes, 'Philosophy of religion is thus a second-order activity, standing apart from its subject matter' (*Philosophy of Religion*, pp. 1–2). Is this really possible? It depends on what the 'subject matter' may be, but if the subject matter is our most important loyalty, our fundamental convictions, then surely not.

I remain convinced that Hick is one of the most important scholars of the twentieth century. Always helpful and stimulating, he was both capable as a writer and generous as a person. He certainly asked many of the right questions. The relationship of Christianity to the universe of faiths remains an urgent issue. But I think Hick provided the wrong answer. In my attempt to show why, I want to also point to other ways to try to explain the universe of faiths. Against the tide of contemporary culture it will be increasingly necessary for Christians to demonstrate that clear convictions are entirely compatible with respect and love. The resources for such a response to pluralism do not require a revision so much as a return to the roots of the Christian faith.

1

John Hick's Religious Journey

The world religions pose a challenge to all Christians. From school religious education lessons to ethnic diversity in the workplace no one can live in the western world without being well aware that the Christian faith is but one option among many. What should a Christian make of this plurality? Are all other religions false? Are those who follow other religions facing the certainty of an eternal hell? Or might other religions offer a path to salvation, or at least some sense of the true God?

The twentieth century saw an enormous upheaval in the western world. Church attendance and personal Christian faith have declined by most measures. However, this has not translated into the extinction of spirituality or religious diversity. Secular atheism has vocal representatives but it has failed to capture the soul of the west.[1] The real change has been the growth of liberalism within all religious traditions. Christians, along with adherents of other faiths, have become less dogmatic about the truthfulness of their own religious persuasion. Most religions in the West have generated more inclusivist attitudes towards people of other faiths or none.

While Christianity has not died, it has undergone radical review. It is no exaggeration to say that what are considered examples of Christian theology today would have been barely recognizable as Christian at the beginning of the twentieth century. A major factor in the transformation of Christian thought has been engagement with religious diversity. Of course, secularism and developments in modern science have had an influence too. The Big Bang cosmology and evolutionary theory are clearly developments that Christianity has had to grapple with. But the awareness of religious diversity has dramatically shaped Christian self-understanding.

In order to understand these changes and to evaluate new definitions of Christian thought, we shall explore, in detail, the position of one particular thinker. John Hick grew up and developed his religious faith through the twentieth century. Having come to an evangelical Christian faith as a young man, his outlook changed over the course of the decades until he came to commend a version of Christianity that many would consider heretical. His thought was philosophically erudite and expressed with simple clarity. Hick considered the plurality of faiths at both academic and pastoral levels. He engaged with both religious thinkers and pressing political issues during his lifetime. His influence on Christian thought has been enormous. No academic study of the Christian response to religious diversity is complete without interaction with his work. No university religious studies syllabus can avoid some engagement with many of his ideas.

By studying the work of John Hick it is possible to study a much greater meta-narrative. It is to study the development, reformation and, to many, the decline of orthodox Christian thought. In Hick's work we can analyse an attempt to respond to the challenge of religious pluralism that has serious fault-lines. Not only can we engage critically with Hick's ideas but also we can assess wider problems in Christian theology. How do we respond to religious diversity? What is the fate of the unevangelized or those who belong to other religions? I am convinced that Hick has asked many of the right questions. But the answers that he gives reflect a deeply problematic version of Christian theology. This is not simply a problem in Hick's own personal work. It is the fundamental problem in the western tradition of theology. As we will see, since the Enlightenment, a version of Christianity has emerged that is incompatible with biblical thought. The development of Hick's own thought, from evangelical to radical, reflects this wider cultural movement. The shortcomings of the western liberal tradition can be identified and critiqued in the particular example of Hick's philosophy of religions.

Journey to Faith

John Harwood Hick was born on 20 January 1922 in Scarborough, Yorkshire. His childhood was not marked by any great interest in religion, as he found the parish church his family attended a matter of 'infinite boredom'.[2] However, he did have an interest in spiritual matters. As a child he met George Jeffreys, one of the founding figures of the Elim Pentecostal Church. Jeffreys was visiting the home of Hick's grandmother and the young John Hick attended the prayer meeting. During the course of the evening he 'felt a strong physical effect, like an electric shock except that it was not a sharp jolt but a pervasive sensation' throughout his body.[3] The experience left Hick with an intense feeling of emotional release. Nonetheless, he remained unimpressed with Christianity and felt more attraction to a western form of Hindu philosophy known as theosophy.

The Theosophical Society had been founded in 1875 by Helena Petrovna Blavatsky. Using an emblem that blended symbols from various world religions, the society used the motto: 'There is no Religion higher than Truth.' Theosophy promoted a mix of eastern religious thought, occult practice and Christian imagery to the western world. During his teenage years Hick explored these ideas; 'I was attracted by theosophy as the first coherent religious philosophy that I had met – much more so than the Christianity I knew.'[4] While he would later reject it, theosophy laid a foundation for his interest in esoteric religious ideas.

Britain in the 1930s was recovering from the First World War. With its massive loss of life on the European battlefields, many had turned to spiritualism for hope. Spiritualist churches sprang up, offering means to contact the dead and find comfort in bereavement. Hick experienced séances and other spiritualist meetings but remained unconvinced. His autobiography reveals both his openness to consider supernatural possibilities alongside his sharp critical faculties: 'On the few occasions when I have had a séance with a professional medium in London, the medium going into a trance and then a deceased person supposedly speaking through him or her, I have been quite unconvinced. But I have a strong rationalist streak and spiritualists say that this inhibits genuine communication!'[5]

This confession is illustrative of Hick's entire work. He was a man intrigued by all things spiritual, but never uncritical of what he observed. His brief interest in theosophy, during his teenage years, was a prelude to the later development of his ideas. Writing in 1939, before his conversion, Hick had commended subversive and heretical thinking as a path to truth: '"Heresy", I said, "is that salutary state of mind in which everything is seen as alive and mysterious and worth looking at". Reading all this now I see how my intellectual development has been surprisingly consistent apart from the interruption of the evangelical years.'[6]

Hick initially read law at Hull University. During his first year he 'underwent a spiritual conversion' and 'became a Christian of a strongly evangelical and indeed fundamentalist kind'.[7] His conversion brought him into association with the Inter-Varsity Fellowship Christian Union (now known as UCCF in the UK). Through this fellowship Hick identified with what he described as 'Calvinist orthodoxy of an extremely conservative kind'.[8] He had come to believe in the inerrancy of Scripture, the virgin birth and the literal incarnation of Christ. In years to come he would modify or dispense with all of these beliefs but he retained a familiarity with evangelical theology.

The Second World War interrupted Hick's studies. As a conscientious objector he refused to serve in the armed forces. Hick was not an absolute pacifist and even thought that the military struggle against Nazism could be justified. However, he felt it was important that he, among others, made a stand against the cycle of violence that mars human history. As a result of this thinking he joined the Friends Ambulance Unit. This Quaker-run service provided medical support to those in the armed forces and was organized along military lines with its own uniform.

This period of Hick's life did not see him renounce Christianity but he did come to consider the evangelical Christian Union movement too rigid and narrow-minded. For example, he felt that members were intellectually dishonest in their attempts to reconcile the opening chapters of Genesis with contemporary scientific thought.

After the war, Hick completed a degree in philosophy at Edinburgh University and graduated in 1948. With lecturers including the Kantian scholar, Norman Kemp-Smith, it is no surprise that Hick became deeply impressed by the work of Immanuel Kant. In fact, there is no single author as influential on all Hick's work as Kant. Hick claimed that most of his final year at Edinburgh was spent studying Kant's first *Critique.*

He went on to complete a doctorate at Oriel College, Oxford, under the supervision of H.H. Price. The fashionable area of study at the time was the philosophy of mind and Hick was able to engage with this by applying philosophical insights to the nature of religious faith. How do we know what we claim to know about God? He found his supervisor a tough critic and Hick felt that he did badly at his oral examination and did not expect to pass. However, he did pass, received a PhD and went on to publish the doctoral material in the form of his first book, *Faith and Knowledge.* Hick's thesis was heavily indebted to Kant's basic insight. All knowledge is conditioned by the structure of the human mind. We never see things the way they really are, but only in forms appropriate to the limitations of the human mind. Faith is a way of seeing the world in the light of a divine reality. Believer and non-believer alike see the same objective universe. But the person of faith will interpret that universe in the light of their belief in God and see a divine significance. The deciding factor between believer and non-believer is faith.

Pastoral Ministry

Despite his obvious promise as a serious philosopher, Hick's immediate career did not lie in academia but with the church. After completing his doctoral studies, Hick trained for ordination into the English Presbyterian Church, which later became part of the United Reformed Church (URC). His first pastoral ministry, from 1953 to 1956, was at Belford Presbyterian Church on the Scottish border. This would also prove to be his only pastoral charge. During this time he married Hazel Bowers. Hick seems to have functioned well as a minister during this brief time. He was no longer an evangelical in his convictions but would have taught and practised fairly traditional Christian values. Although frustrated with evangelicalism and his perception that this represented a very narrow brand of Christianity, Hick seems to have had no problem fitting into a traditional denomination. The end of pastoral ministry came with an invitation to teach philosophy at Cornell University in 1956. Hick knew that if he spent too long out of academia he would become unemployable and so he did not leave it long before embarking on an academic career.

It is important to underline that John Hick was primarily a philosopher rather than a theologian. This point colours all of his thinking. Though his Presbyterian ministry training included the study of theology at Westminster College, Cambridge, all his formal qualifications were in philosophy. His doctorate in theology was an honorary degree from Uppsala University in Sweden, given in recognition of his contribution to theology. Hick's philosophical training explains why much of his work was devoted to exploring the foundations of Christian thought and belief. Many Christians engage with Hick as a theologian. They are concerned with matters of Christology or eschatology, typical areas of systematic theology, and engage with John Hick as another theologian with somewhat radical ideas. But Hick himself was a philosopher. His primary concern was not with the teaching of the Bible or the history of Christian thought. His concern was to ask questions regarding logical coherence and the rationality of an idea.

Is this a legitimate thing to do? Of course, but there is a problem. For the Christian faith the source of truth is not philosophical speculation but divine revelation. Philosophy helps us make sense of what we mean, but it cannot determine what is true. To know what is true about God, faith and matters of eternal life we need revelation rather than speculation. In that sense, philosophy serves theology as a useful set of tools rather than dictating to theology as its master. This is not the relationship of theology to philosophy that we will see in Hick's work and we will engage with the problems that result during the course of our study.

Faith and Philosophy

As Assistant Professor of Philosophy at Cornell University, Hick was able to refine his ideas. He developed his doctoral thesis into the book, *Faith and Knowledge*. Though initially it had been hard to find a publisher the book proved to be an enormous success. It has been reprinted many times and remains a popular account of Christian epistemology. My claim in this book is that its basic arguments remained a consistent part of Hick's position throughout his life. Though his beliefs would undergo major modification, his basic epistemology would not. The explanation of faith that Hick offered was clear, illuminating and, as I will claim, deeply flawed.

Epistemology deals with the theory of how we know anything at all. The epistemology of religious thought raises all kinds of interesting questions. Beliefs of religious people can be both highly contentious and deeply profound. Hick uses the term 'faith' to describe religious knowledge. He rejects a model of faith that he describes as 'Thomist-Catholic', after the theologian Thomas Aquinas. According to the Thomist model, faith is a matter of assenting to the truth of certain beliefs, including the Trinity, the incarnation and so forth. In contrast, Hick proposes a model of faith that is to do with subjective, personal experience rather than with intellectual abstraction. Our experience leads us to interpret the world around us in the way we do. We experience the world in many different ways, often reflecting our own subjective state of mind. Perhaps we feel a sense of joy and see the world as a place of delight and wonder. Weighed down by anxiety we might see the world as a hostile and threatening place. Faith is an act of interpretation applied to the religious dimension of existence. It is not a response to verbal, doctrinal statements but to the religious significance of the world. So faith is not so much about 'what' you know, as 'how' you know it. Faith is a way of knowing the world in its religious significance.

Hick describes the traditional model of faith as Thomist-Catholic because it is most clearly seen in the Roman Catholic tradition. However, it is also a plausible description of the evangelical tradition with which Hick had parted company. Typically, among evangelicals faith was not so much an experience as a conviction about truth. Hick takes issue with this description of faith. It is too intellectual. Part of the problem lies in the confusion over whether 'faith' is a verb or a noun. In English it is almost always a noun, but this can be misleading. The stem of the Greek word used in the New Testament simply means 'trust'. As a verb form it can mean to trust, or to believe. The call to 'have faith in God' (Mark 11:22) is a demand that we trust God. However 'faith' can also describe the content of belief. Ephesians speaks of 'one Lord, one faith [and] one baptism' (Eph. 4:5). Jude 1:3 describes a faith we must contend for. Faith can describe how we trust God or what it is we trust about God.

There is both a subjective and an objective dimension to faith. Hick dispenses with the objective sense, with its emphasis on assent to doctrines, in favour of the subjective sense, with emphasis on the attitude of the religious believer. It is ironic that he labels the erroneous view as Thomist-Catholic, given that he describes his own view as best summarized by Thomas Aquinas' simple statement, 'Things known are in the knower according to the mode of the knower.'[9] We know nothing directly, but only indirectly through the way they appear to us. Hick's epistemology had already found expression eight hundred years earlier in the work of Thomas. The Thomist-Catholic model has a place for 'faith' as both noun and verb. It describes both the attitude of trust and the content of belief. Thomas Aquinas offered a very nuanced description of the meaning of faith but Hick rejects the ensuing Catholic tradition as too heavily intellectual.[10] His rejection of the Thomist-Catholic model is partly the result of his desire to separate faith as cognitive content from faith as a personal experience. Hick will place his emphasis on the latter meaning of faith at the expense of the former. Historically, these were more often considered two dimensions of the same thing.

The Character of Faith

In contrast to the Thomist-Catholic tradition, Hick proposes a model of faith that is to do with subjective, personal experience rather than with intellectual abstraction. Our experience leads us to interpret the world around us the way that we do. Faith is the act of interpretation applied to the religious dimension of existence. It is not a response to verbal, doctrinal statements but a response to the felt religious significance of the world. Hick argues for this position by making the case that all knowledge has this character. There is a pattern to knowing which is as true of scientific knowledge as it is of religious knowledge. All forms of knowledge involve personal interpretation based on other subjective factors. Hick demonstrates how this is not unique to religious knowledge but part of a more general approach to epistemology.

There are four levels or types of interpretation corresponding to four areas of our knowledge. The first is that of *natural knowledge.* At this level there is the least ambiguity in what we see and, correspondingly, the greatest extent of agreement among people on how we should interpret things. Even if someone were not sure what a lamppost might be they would probably still interpret it as a hard, perpendicular object and walk around it rather than into it.

The second level is that of *moral judgement.* Situations inviting a moral response offer a greater degree of subjective freedom. For example, the Nazi leadership of Germany probably exercised their moral judgement differently than most people would in their situations. This made the Nuremberg trials a complex affair. How do we bring criminals to account if they had considered their actions justified within the political ideology of their time? However, the assumption (or hope) that most people would think differently than Goebbels or Himmler encourages us to think that there can still be objective standards of morality. Thus, despite anomalies, there is a high degree of moral agreement around the world on issues such as murder, theft and deception.[11]

The third level is that of *aesthetics*, which allows for greater freedom still. Our interpretation of the artistic value of something we see or hear depends on many subjective factors. What makes something the finest meal or the most sublime music relies on very personal preferences. Consequently, there is much less agreement among people on what should be judged as good or bad art.

The final level of knowledge is *religious faith*. Notice how these levels of interpretation are on a spectrum. They all count as knowledge, but they are based on increasingly subjective factors and ambiguous data the higher we go. The difference between the level of religious knowledge and those previous levels lies in the fact that religious faith involves a total interpretation of the universe. Faith is not an interpretation of just one aspect of reality, but involves our relationship to reality as a whole.

The universe is ambiguous. An atheist interprets it as devoid of transcendental significance. A convinced believer is able to interpret it as having religious significance. According to Hick, both believer and non-believer may remain rational in holding their alternative beliefs. Of course, at least one person must be wrong, but both may be rational. Hick's theory of religious knowledge allows that it is possible to be rational and mistaken.

In this model, Christian faith is one form of religious faith according to which 'in the historical figure of Jesus Christ . . . God has in a unique and final way disclosed himself to men'.[12] Faith is justified by the personal experience of believers, for the universe 'seems' that way to them. This is Hick's earliest published account of faith. At this stage in his life he would have still considered himself an orthodox believer. However, very little of his account relies on any orthodox doctrine. It is true that the description of the historical Jesus reflects a high Christology (a 'unique and final' disclosure) but it is left unclear what specific doctrines this is based upon: miracles? Prophecy? The resurrection?

A Defence of Faith

This description of faith can play into the hands of the anti-religious. For example, a movement earlier in the twentieth century, logical positivism, had already attempted a demolition of religion along these lines. Logical positivism was a movement in decline by the time Hick published but its influence continued to be felt across western philosophy throughout the twentieth century. This philosophical tradition was based on empiricism – all true knowledge is based upon testable sense experience. The movement grew out of the atheist philosophy of Bertrand Russell and the early Ludwig Wittgenstein. Logical positivists claimed that for language to be meaningful it must make claims that are empirically testable. To understand the meaning of a claim we must be able to state the conditions necessary for its truth value to be tested. Statements that are tautological ('all bachelors are unmarried men') or to do with mathematics ('7 + 6 =13') are true by definition. But what about claims regarding physical reality?

A.J. Ayer offered what he termed the principle of verification as a way of distinguishing between intelligible and nonsensical claims.[13] Intelligible claims do not have to be true. But they must be testable. The claim 'all swans are white' is intelligible (even though false) because one could suggest what kinds of test would be necessary in order to arrive at a verification of the claim. Even though in practice it might be impossible to test every swan (living and dead) we would still know, in principle, how to test the claim.

However, the claim 'the universe, including everything in it, is doubling in size every minute' is meaningless because there would be no way of testing the claim. Any instruments that could be used to measure the expansion would double in size along with the universe. Claims that cannot be verified, at least in principle, are not truth claims. The best that can be said of them is that they are emotive statements that express how we feel rather than telling us anything about the universe in which we live.

The real agenda of the logical positivists was to dismiss metaphysics and religious language. Ayer argued that religious language is neither true nor false, but merely expresses how someone feels. 'God is love' or 'Jesus is divine' provide no information content about the real universe but only indicate the state of mind of the believer.

Responses to logical positivism were wide-ranging and, ultimately, fatal to its cause. What was left for any language regarding love, beauty or purpose? How coherent was a movement that promoted a criterion that could not itself be tested? This was a fatal objection. As a claim about reality, the principle itself was strictly untestable. So what was its status? Was Ayer simply expressing his own emotional state when he presented the principle of verification? The principle was subjected to heavy criticism and revision through which a weaker but more useful principle of falsification was devised. In a famous interview late in his life, Ayer pointed out that the most important weakness in his theory was that 'nearly all of it was false'.[14]

Despite the many problems in the principle of verification, Hick felt its force and sought to respond to it. It set the agenda for the postwar period in British philosophy and anyone engaged in the philosophy of religion had to reckon with it. One approach might have been to accept the terms of the debate laid down by the positivists and seek to show the empirical evidence in favour of faith – the resurrection of Jesus, the historical nature of biblical events, confirmed predictive prophecy. However, this could not be Hick's route. After all, his own epistemology recast religious statements as expressions of our experience of an otherwise ambiguous universe. Hick was willing to concede to the atheist critic that as far as empirical evidences are concerned there was no fact that could settle the dispute either way.

Nonetheless, Hick accepted the principle of verification and sought to show how Christianity is verifiable. The principle of verification does not establish if a claim is true, it merely provides the conditions for a test. It may be that we do not have the resources or ability to actually carry out the test at this present time. So, in order to establish that religious claims are genuine truth claims, Hick only had to isolate one claim that would be verified through empirical, sense experience.

Hick's answer is known as *eschatological verification*. Religion makes claims about the future. Expectations concerning the future will be confirmed or disconfirmed at some point in the future. For example, if I claim that there is intelligent alien life in the universe then that claim can obviously be confirmed if one day we make contact or find remains. But notice that the claim is asymmetrical. There is no situation in which we could disprove that there is alien life. The only relevant evidence would be that which confirms the claim.

Hick uses the example of language describing the afterlife and a future state of bliss. In a parable of two travellers, Hick describes two people who hold different beliefs about their destination while walking the same road.[15] One believes it leads to a celestial city, whereas the other believes it leads nowhere. As the road itself remains ambiguous, providing no conclusive evidence either way, both travellers must be content to recognize that their beliefs about the destination of the road are matters of opinion. However, their division of opinion is over a matter of fact. Either there is a celestial city or there is not. One event in the future would verify the claim of the celestial-city believer: rounding a corner and arriving at the city. Hick's parable illustrates the position of the religious believer who makes true, verifiable claims about reality.

A post-mortem encounter with God would be a real, sensory, mental experience that would verify the Christian claim. On dying and entering a world beyond the grave the Christian has verification of their belief. Admittedly, the claim is asymmetrical. If there is no after-life then nobody will be around to disprove the claim. But this is beside the point. The challenge of the logical positivists has been met. Religious truth claims are demonstrably meaningful because they deal in matters that are open to experiential confirmation.

Hick's proposal of eschatological verification was a useful response to the atheists of his day. Their attempt to dismiss religious language as meaningless was dubious in any case but Hick provided a specific example that met their challenge. However, it is important to notice how Hick's epistemology and description of faith steers him away from more obvious apologetic responses. Traditionally, Christians have made more of the bodily resurrection of Jesus, the historical reliability of the Bible, the evidence of design in creation or miracles in order to defend the faith. All of these areas involve empirical evidence. Even if the evidence were shown to be faulty they would demonstrate that a Christian passes the challenge of the logical positivist. A Christian is making claims about the physical universe and not simply making emotional statements about their subjective state of mind. Hick does not take this approach. He cannot because his description of faith is that it describes a total subjective response to an otherwise ambiguous universe. Faith is not belief in God on the basis of this or that event or evidence.

Hick's epistemology has much to commend it and his influence among Christians owes much to this early work. In certain respects he shares in the tradition of Reformed epistemology, which emphasizes the self-justifying nature of faith. Faith has a personal-subjective quality and this provides the context in which we form a world-view. Notable proponents of a similar epistemology in the Reformed tradition of Christianity include Alvin Plantinga and Nicholas Wolterstorff.[16] However, as Hick's work develops we notice how passing this resemblance turns out to be. The Reformed thinkers ground their epistemology in an orthodox view of creation, revelation and God. This was never the case for Hick. Though holding an orthodox faith at this point in his work, Hick's epistemology is compatible with any religion or none. Faith as a form of interpretation describes the epistemology of atheists, Hindus or Christians. It does not require any particular doctrinal commitment. At this stage we should simply note that Hick is certainly providing an epistemology for his position, but it is not clear that he has really described Christian faith. An epistemology is a theory of knowledge and he discusses this in neutral, philosophical terms. Faith, simply meaning 'trust', is used in a religious context to describe convictions about certain beliefs (faith 'in' Christ). While we may want to point out that atheists, Hindus and Christians all have 'faith' in something we are also aware of how important that *something* is. To discuss Christian faith in isolation from the specific, creedal content of that faith is misleading, as we will find in the work of Hick.

At his stage in his life and ministry, Hick considered himself a mainstream, orthodox believer. His first published journal article was a critique of an account of the incarnation. D.M. Baillie, a Scottish theologian, had argued in a 1948 publication that the incarnation can be understood as the supreme form of the 'paradox of grace'. While written in terms that sound familiar to readers of Karl Barth, Hick identified Baillie's work as describing the incarnation as a form of adoptionism. This heretical teaching had been rejected at the first Council of Nicea (*c.* AD 325) on the grounds that it undermined the true divinity of Christ. Jesus was truly a human but only adopted by God for a dwelling-place on account of his sinlessness. Having identified this implication in Baillie's position, Hick was able to salvage something of value but reject the heretical implication.[17] Hick never doubted that he was correct in his description of Baillie's work but, ironically, would one day come to think 'that this radical departure was a right move!'.[18]

A Legal Challenge

After a brief period in pastoral ministry, Hick took up an academic post at Cornell University from 1956. Hick taught the philosophy of religion and proved to be a popular lecturer (in typical humble style he put this down to his exotic English accent!). Cornell had a significant philosophy department but after three years he moved to teach in a theological environment.

While more liberal institutions showed interest, Hick actually pursued an opportunity at the more conservative Princeton Theological Seminary. On his arrival in 1959 an important controversy flared up. Not only teaching in their seminary, he also wished to transfer his ministerial credentials from the English to the American Presbyterian Church. This would provoke a dispute among Presbyterians and probably lead Hick to some soul-searching of his own.

Technically, Hick's position at Princeton and in the Presbyterian Church assumed adherence to the 1647 Westminster Confession of Faith. However, few members of faculty and ordained ministry would have subscribed to its every word. John Hick's appointment became a test case for whether the confession still had authority.

When questioned about his position on the confession he expressed doubts over 'the six-day creation of the world, the predestination of many to eternal hell, the verbal inspiration of the Bible and the virgin birth of Jesus'.[19] Hick saw himself as still holding to a conservative theological position. Indeed, in Church of England circles Hick probably would have still been more at home among conservatives. The British church was generally more liberal than churches in the States. However, to his American observers, Hick was a radical.

His liberal stance, particularly on the virgin birth, led to a number of church leaders attempting to prevent the transfer of ministerial membership. In the end this failed, and Hick retained his teaching post at Princeton. However, this theological controversy was only the beginning of what lay ahead. Hick continued to hold a resentment toward the American Presbyterian Church throughout his life. In one of his last writings he castigated the church, which had 'still today so far as I can tell barely progressed theologically since then'.[20] This might actually pay a compliment to Presbyterianism but that would depend greatly on one's own theological perspective! As for Hick, his interest in defending biblical Christianity was on the wane. Certainly, in comparison with the very radical theologies that were emerging in the 1960s, Hick's theological position was still fairly mainstream. But he was clearly no evangelical and he would have no interest in returning to a position he would now dismiss as fundamentalist.

2

Questioning Orthodoxy

The Problem of Evil

Hick returned to England in 1963 where he lectured at Cambridge University. This came about through his receiving a fellowship that would allow him to write on the problem of evil. Making use of the vast library resources of Cambridge, Hick immersed himself in the study of various theological attempts to explain the existence of evil. This was eventually published as his second major work, *Evil and the God of Love*. It has been reprinted many times and some would hold it to be his best work.

The book provides a sustained treatment of various Christian attempts to reconcile the existence of a good God with the reality of evil and suffering in the world. Hick compares two alternative traditions as rival answers to a problem that has occupied theologians throughout church history. The major, mainstream solution to the problem finds magnificent expression in the work of St Augustine (AD354–430). God created the universe and Adam and Eve were originally good. Through a rebellion against God, Adam and Eve fell from this state of grace. Since then, redemptive history has been the story of God's restoration of a paradise lost. Augustinian theodicy emphasizes divine predestination, human sinfulness and a historic fall.

In contrast, Irenaeus (AD130–202) described the human struggle against evil and suffering as part of the process of developing the spiritual nature of men and women. According to this model, the 'fall' in the Garden of Eden, as recorded in the book of Genesis, was a necessary step toward God rather than a catastrophic falling out of favour with him. It was necessary for Adam and Eve to recognize their weakness, finitude and imperfection. In leaving Eden they began a process of learning morality, love and courage through life in a world of pain.

God's creative work had to include the permission of evil and suffering in order to prompt the necessary growth in men and women towards an increasing likeness to God. According to Augustine, evil was a disruption of the good. God did not create evil, but evil is a distortion of the good that God had made. In contrast, Hick uses the work of Irenaeus to describe suffering as part of God's original intention for creation. God never intended creation to be pure bliss, because he wanted creation to be a testing ground in which we could grow through struggle. Ultimately, suffering will have been justified because it will have served a purpose in helping humanity toward a higher, noble goal.

If we had to choose between a world without pain, and a world with pain we would probably choose the former. But what if the choice was not between worlds but between roads? Might we not choose a road of pain if we knew the road led to somewhere much better than where we had started? This is the greater-good defence. Where Augustine saw the fall as a disaster, Hick describes an adventure. The creation account of Eden is a myth describing choices that we made that will lead us to greater maturity in the end. Pain can bring out the best in us. Evil forces us to make moral decisions. Without suffering we would have no saints. In contrast, an Augustinian theodicy can only see evil as a privation of the good, not as part of the good.

Crucial to the Augustinian view is the assumption that Genesis describes a historic fall. Augustine was well aware of the hermeneutical issues in the interpretation of Genesis, but still maintained that the account of creation and fall must be understood as in some sense historical events.[1] This was an interpretation that we have already seen Hick had little time for. He took it as read that the account of creation and fall must be considered mythological, and this had implications for our theodicy: 'Because we can no longer share the assumption, upon which traditional Christian theodicy has been built, that the creation-fall myth is basically authentic history, we inevitably look at that theodicy critically and see in it inadequacies to which in the past piety has tended to blind the eyes of faith.'[2]

If the fall was not a temporal event then it is to be understood as a myth. But if there were no historic fall then no theodicy that requires it to have actually happened can be tenable. Happily, according to Hick, the Irenaean alternative does not require a temporal fall. We have arisen from primitive simplicity and moral naivety and are on a journey towards moral and spiritual maturity. A literal fall is not required, though as a spiritual parable it may have some value.

What Hick's theodicy does require is a life after death. In the case of children dying in infancy or those suffering at the hands of murderous regimes it seems untenable to point out any spiritual benefit this side of the grave. Hick makes the point that the logic of his theodicy requires eternal life. Not only that, but if all suffering is redemptive then the concept of hell is incoherent, 'Misery which is eternal and therefore infinite would constitute the largest part of the problem of evil.'[3]

However, the hope of a universal salvation where all are saved does provide compensation for present suffering. How will universal salvation be possible? Hick describes God as like a grandmaster chess player taking on a novice, allowing his opponent personal freedom but always guiding the moves towards a desired outcome, 'Although we cannot foresee the detailed course of the game, we know that, whatever moves the novice makes, the master can so respond as sooner or later to bring the game to the conclusion that he himself desires.'[4]

With this analogy, Hick believes he can hold together faith in a universal salvation with the fundamental reality of our own freedom in belief and behaviour. The Irenaean theodicy is a better fit for contemporary understanding than the classic Augustinian approach.

Hick's explanation of these two approaches has been enormously influential. In fact, the term 'Irenaean theodicy' is commonly used in academic literature as shorthand for John Hick's ideas. The UK school syllabus will introduce Irenaeus to students only by way of Hick's Irenaean theodicy. The problem is that when reading

Irenaeus it proves rather more difficult to find this theodicy. Mark Scott persuasively demonstrates that a far better representative of Hick's position is Origen (*c.*182–254), rather than Irenaeus. Origen envisages creation as a schoolroom for the soul.[5] There are two particular features of Origen's theology that are foundational for Hick's own work. Origen supports an allegorical reading of the account of creation in Genesis, and defends a universalist view of salvation.[6] The features most important to Hick are clearly evident in the work of Origen, but much less plain in Irenaeus. In fact, Scott points out that Irenaeus directly refutes two key ideas in Hick's work.

Irenaeus has a reputation for literal exegesis of the text. He uses the pattern of creation–fall–redemption and clearly describes what he considers a literal event, 'For along with the fruit they [Adam and Eve] did also fall under the power of death, because they did eat in disobedience; and disobedience to God entails death.'[7] Irenaeus clearly affirms a doctrine of hell and eternal punishment. His language on this, as with the fall, is not so dissimilar to that of Augustine. Regarding life after death he states, 'Has the Word come for the ruin and for the resurrection of many? For the ruin, certainly, of those who do not believe Him, to whom also He has threatened a greater damnation in the judgement day than that of Sodom and Gomorrah.'[8] On the key themes of the fall and future judgement Irenaeus sounds much more like his supposed opponent Augustine than like his interpreter Hick. As for the idea of this world being a place of 'soul-making', such a claim has always been included as a part of the orthodox tradition, 'Consider it pure joy, my brothers, whenever you face trials of many kinds, because you know that the testing of your faith develops perseverance' (Jas 1:2).

The thought of Origen is a much more natural fit with John Hick's ideas. Among the church fathers he was much more comfortable with offering allegorical interpretations of Scripture than were his contemporaries. Assuming the pre-existence of souls, Origen denies that Genesis describes a literal beginning of creation. The process of soul-making does not stop in this life, but continues beyond the grave.

Origen speculates about the continuing process of soul-making in 'the endless world'.[9] Most importantly, Origen is generally acknowledged to have held to a universal view of salvation and is probably the closest exponent of something like universalism in the early church. All of these features make Origen's work a much better fit with that of Hick than that of Irenaeus.

This raises an interesting question. Why did Hick attribute so much to Irenaeus and practically ignore Origen? Scott, an enthusiast for Origen's speculative theology, suggests that Hick simply failed to read Irenaeus closely, 'Hick's specious appropriation of Irenaeus stems from his lack of engagement with the Irenaean corpus. Rarely does he actually cite Irenaeus, and even less does he carefully exegete his work.'[10] This explanation is possible. Hick was not a trained historian or even theologian. His expertise lay in philosophy and it may well be that he read Irenaeus only in so far as it provided fuel for his own ideas. However, this seems highly unlikely. As a scholar always interested in detail there may be another reason why Hick chose to identify his work with Irenaeus rather than with Origen.

Hick was writing this material in the immediate aftermath of the investigation into his orthodoxy. It is clear from his writings that he was hurt to be charged with heresy. He described himself as mainstream liberal rather than theologically radical. He continued to identify himself as a philosopher in the orthodox Christian tradition. Irenaeus was considered an orthodox church father. Origen was not. Though a Christian leader and thinker of some standing and one who would face martyrdom, his ideas were never accepted by the wider church. His bishop disowned him. Even friends dismissed his ideas. A number of later church councils condemned his work as heretical. On many key themes his theology clearly owed more to Greek thought than to biblical exegesis. In the light of this history it seems clear why Hick would have invested more heavily in finding hints of his own ideas in Irenaeus while ignoring Origen. He knew he was following a highly speculative path but wanted to present it as mainstream, Christian orthodoxy. To have argued for an 'Origenian' theodicy would have been fatal.

Expanding Horizons

In 1967 Hick took up the H.G. Wood Professorship at Birmingham University and began a phase that would lead to a revolution in his thinking. The most powerful challenge to his theology came not from academic circles but from the city of Birmingham itself. Birmingham had then, as it does now, a large multifaith community including substantial numbers of Muslims, Sikhs and Hindus along with the well-established Jewish community.

Hick became familiar with the world religions in a way that he had not been before. Apart from friendships and functions, he became involved with an inter-religious movement set up in Birmingham to counter racism and in particular the violent extremism of the National Front. Attendance at mosques, synagogues and gurdwaras presented Hick with a simple insight, 'It seemed evident to me that essentially the same thing was going on in all these different places of worship.'[11] The cultural forms were very different, but Hick felt there was a common experience. He was challenged by the quality of life, morality and spirituality evident in the lives of devout religious people from other traditions. He writes, 'Thus it was not so much new thoughts as new experiences that drew me, as a philosopher, into the issues of religious pluralism, and as a Christian into inter-faith dialogue.'[12]

These new experiences led to the next stage in development of his thinking. However, Hick had already come to believe in universalism. He was not interested in evangelism or encouraging personal conversion from another faith to Christianity. Hick held that we are all on the journey towards salvation. The new challenge for Hick was to understand how other religions could offer their own valid pathways to salvation. As we will see, it would not require a major shift in theological thinking for Hick to incorporate the insights of other religions.

In 1970 Hick began work on a major book that would exemplify his new way of doing theology. The book was a consideration of eschatology and the afterlife. In many ways it would naturally follow

Evil and the God of Love. However, the structure, style and data of the book would represent a significant shift. Hick's previous works were written self-consciously from within the Christian tradition. *Evil and the God of Love* assumed the existence and relevance of a personal, loving God revealed in Jesus. The book also engaged with a range of Christian theologians down through the centuries. His new work would step outside the tradition and explore religious themes in the context of the world religions.

The eschatology of *Death and Eternal Life* relates ideas about the afterlife from Christianity to those found in Hinduism and Buddhism. Rather than setting two early church fathers side by side and comparing their theology, he would explore the concept of the afterlife in Christianity, Hinduism and Buddhism. Hick spent significant time in India and Sri Lanka during his research towards this book. Furthermore, during this period he was writing a number of short articles arguing the possibility that Christianity was not the one true religion, nor even necessarily superior to any other religion. He was about to undergo a revolution in his thought. In order to do so one key Christian doctrine would have to be substantially modified. By the time he came to publish *Death and Eternal Life* in 1976 he had already made a profound theological shift.

The Essence of Faith

The most significant change in Hick's position was clearly established in his collection of essays published in 1973 as *God and the Universe of Faiths*. The book brings together succinct statements of Hick's position on epistemology, theodicy and other religions. Regarding epistemology and theodicy, Hick clearly summarizes his work thus far and they offer no new ideas or arguments. However, regarding the world religions, Hick takes a radical new road.

Three of the essays were originally a series of lectures given at Birmingham University in 1972 and formed a single argument. The titles given to the printed lectures were 'The Essence of Christianity',

'The Copernican Revolution in Theology' and 'The New Map of the Universe of Faiths'. They form a simple and yet powerful argument for what is now known as the *pluralist hypothesis*. This hypothesis would be developed in the course of Hick's later career. It becomes such a dominant theme in his work, and so influential on the study of religion and theology, that it is the main topic dealt with in this book. We will see important revisions and developments introduced by Hick. But first it is worth pausing and considering this early statement of his new theological position.

By the 'essence' of the Christian faith Hick wanted to identify what mattered most to religious believers. His stated aim was to identify such a foundational theme that it would provide a key to interpreting all the world religions. This necessarily guided his selection of the essence of Christian faith. It had to be something that would provide a general approach to all religions.

Hick's stipulation of what would count as the essence of faith is revealing. He writes, 'It is this that we want to compare with the essence of other faiths, rather than any historical peculiarities of the Christian tradition which lie away from its religious centre.'[13] From the outset, Hick sought to identify the essence of Christianity as something not unique to it. After all, if the essence were not 'universal' then the project of finding a common essence to religion would not get off the ground. Hick rules out such 'peculiarities' as the incarnation, atonement, Trinity or resurrection because they would not provide a basis for comparison.

In effect, Hick is arguing that whatever will facilitate inter-religious comparison must determine how one goes about identifying the essence of Christianity. Whatever is unique, special or contingent to a historical context must 'lie away from', in Hick's words, the essence of faith. Ruled out, a priori, is the possibility that what might matter most to religious people, of any tradition, is a historical event, unique person or particular doctrine.

The obvious Christian answer to the question of the essence of their faith would be something to do with Jesus Christ and salvation through him. Hick does allow that as a starting point for his excavation of the essence of faith but certainly not as its conclusion. He follows the New Testament description of salvation as a 'way' and concludes that the essence lies not in right belief but in right behaviour. Salvation is not about coming to hold certain doctrines as true but about living life in a certain way.

According to Hick, what is distinctive in the Christian approach to this way is the fact that it is tied to a particular historical figure: 'The life, death and resurrection of Jesus of Nazareth, his influence upon those who responded to him in faith, their memories of him and of his words, and their experiences of a new quality of life in a new relationship with God and with one another.'[14]

The essence of Christianity is, then, a practical way of living inspired by the Christ event. However, this does not seem promising as a universal essence. The Christ event sounds like a historical particularity, but it is not. Hick denies that the incarnation is an event in public history, preferring to describe as an event in the experience of a believer. Hick is convinced that the actual Jesus of history is now beyond recovery by any normal methods of research. Therefore, all that we really have is an atemporal experience of Christ. This less specific focus fits well with his desired aim to identify an essence that does not rely on historical particularities. To be a Christian today is to have an experience inspired by certain images, rather than being a deliberate response to the historic claims of the unique personality called Jesus of Nazareth.

Hick's formulation of the essence of Christianity is really an attempt to continue the classic liberal project of disentangling the Christ of faith from the Jesus of history. He postulates that a process set in very quickly after the death of Jesus whereby the community of people living the new 'way' exaggerated the character of their founder until, within two generations, he was thought of as God. Hick explains this elevated respect for Jesus as simply the way first-century Jewish believers struggled to express their vivid experience in a Judeo-Greek metaphysical framework. Using the language and concepts of Greek culture, their articulation of what their experience meant to them was increasingly abstracted from the real historical life of Jesus. A very different explanation of the same experience would have taken shape in a different culture: 'In eastern terms he [Jesus] was a *jivanmukti*, or he was a Buddha, one who had attained to true knowledge of and relation to reality.'[15]

The categories in which followers sought to make sense of their experience of Jesus were relative to their culture. Had the historical Jesus ministered further east, or had the early church been born in India, then Hick is sure that Jesus would have been described in eastern terms. The doctrine of the incarnation would not have got off the ground. Many of the early church debates that led to their councils and creeds simply reflected the philosophical categories available to them.

We will return to the theme of Christology later. The doctrine of Christ is crucial in any Christian attempt to make sense of pluralism. However, it is worth noting here how this discussion fails to take into account just how significant the early Christology of the New Testament really is. A high Christology was compatible with the Jewish monotheistic background but would clearly lead to conflict between Christians and their Jewish compatriots.[16] On the other hand, among the pagans, the Christians would have to develop new vocabulary in order to describe what Jesus meant to them. The very earliest traditions within the New Testament present the highest Christology. If they had not intended to imply an ontological incarnation then Jewish and Greek thought gave them many other conceptual resources in which to express themselves. It would not have been difficult for the New Testament writers to express some sense in which Jesus was a divine being or, even the Messiah, without implying divinity. It is hard to understand why the early Christians got into such trouble with Jewish religious leaders, Roman government and Greek scholarship if it all hinged on misunderstood vocabulary.

Hick pushes the significance of the doctrine of the incarnation to one side as a later, complicated and controversial development. Prior to such doctrinal gymnastics lay the simple experience of Jesus as an expression of divine values. The essence of Christianity must be found in this experience, not in a doctrine.

Salvation Outside the Church

Having established the essence of Christianity in a particular quality of experience, Hick continues his comparison of Christianity with other faiths. This leads him, in the second essay, to his famous call for a *Copernican revolution* in theology. Hick is well aware that for much of Christian history the church has sought to maintain an exclusivist stance on the question of salvation. Salvation requires a personal faith response to Christ or some kind of personal connection to the church. This was expressed strikingly in the Roman Catholic papal pronouncement *extra Ecclesiam nulla salus*, meaning 'Outside the church, no salvation'. Though the origins of the phrase are found in the words of Cyprian (*c.* AD 200–58), it appears as a doctrinal formula in various official statements of the Catholic Church including the Fourth Lateran Council (*c.* 1215).[17] In various other forms it expresses an exclusivist understanding of salvation. Not only is it true to say that salvation is found in Christ but it also follows that outside Christ there is no salvation, 'No one comes to the Father except through me' (John 14:6). Given a very particular definition of salvation, there is a logic to this implication. For Roman Catholic and Orthodox traditions this is directly associated with the historic institution of the church as the means through which this salvation is made available. If salvation is defined as being visibly joined to the historic institution of the church, then the pronouncement is little more than a tautology. Outside God's saving work (the church), there is no salvation.

Hick joins with many others in expressing repugnance for this exclusivist view of salvation: 'Can we then accept the conclusion that the God of love who seeks to save all mankind had nevertheless ordained that men must be saved in such a way that only a small minority can in fact receive this salvation?'[18] Such rhetoric allows Hick to brush off a range of theological positions that seek to maintain the exclusivist stance without compromising the doctrine of the love of God.

The range of theological positions are often categorized under the three headings of exclusivism, inclusivism and pluralism.[19]

Exclusivism maintains that salvation is exclusively through Christ. Traditional evangelicalism has been seen as exclusivist, though many are unhappy with a label that carries connotations of elitism or racism. It is worth highlighting the great breadth of positions catalogued as exclusivist. Karl Barth is generally considered an exclusivist theologian, even though his soteriology is often considered universalist. Barth could never have been taken to imply that all people are saved through their own religious traditions. Salvation is solely through divine decree. But God is able to elect all to salvation if he so chooses. A universalist tone is evident in a number of Reformed theologians.[20] At the other extreme would be the restrictivist account of salvation represented by Loraine Boettner. In *The Reformed Doctrine of Predestination* Boettner sees the death of the unevangelized as evidence that God had never intended their salvation: 'When God places people in such conditions we may be sure that He has no more intention that they shall be saved than He has that the soil of northern Siberia, which is frozen all the year round, shall produce crops of wheat. Had He intended otherwise He would have supplied the means leading to the designed end.'[21]

Had God intended to save someone living in unevangelized lands, missionaries would have arrived with the gospel. This form of exclusivism is better described as restrictivist. The emphasis is on salvation being restricted to those who consciously hear of and respond to the saving work of Christ, but this is not the only form of exclusivism.

Inclusivism agrees that salvation is through Christ but draws attention to other ways in which this salvation may be mediated through general revelation or other religions. While theological liberalism has tended towards an inclusivist view its most rigorous formulations are probably found in Roman Catholic teaching. Hans Küng and Karl Rahner both provided inclusivist explanations of salvation. These were highly influential in Roman Catholic theology during the late twentieth century.

Küng described two ways of salvation, an ordinary way and an extraordinary way. The ordinary way of salvation would be the religious traditions in which someone was born, whatever they might be. The extraordinary way would be the revelation of God through the church.[22] Karl Rahner also sought to develop an inclusivist position by describing adherents of other faiths as 'anonymous' Christians. Rahner describes degrees of church membership from explicit faith and baptism to 'non-official and anonymous Christianity which can and should yet be called Christianity in a meaningful sense, even though it itself cannot and would not describe itself as such'.[23] Such a person is saved through Christ and belongs to the church even though they do not themselves realize it or acknowledge it.

Hick repeats his challenge to exclusivism many times throughout his work.[24] He is aware of attempts to modify the implications. Not only are there inclusivist theologies like those of Hans Küng and Karl Rahner but even the more exclusivist models offer some hope for those who die unevangelized. The hardline, though quite logical, position of Boettner is not commonly held among evangelicals. While some evangelicals adopted a largely inclusivist theology[25] most have simply expressed a confidence in salvation exclusively through Christ while admitting agnosticism as to how this may apply to those dying in ignorance.[26] Even the most conservative evangelicals make exceptions for various categories of people who are physically prevented from expressing explicit faith in Christ.[27] None of these modifications impresses Hick who sees them as attempts to sidestep the logic. He draws upon a scientific debate of the sixteenth century to illustrate how the current religious dispute is unfolding and why he will, in the end, be proven right. The scientific debate lay behind the Copernican revolution in astronomy.

The Copernican Revolution

Prior to the revolutionary work of Copernicus, the Alexandrian astronomer Ptolemy (*c.* 90–168) had established a picture of the universe that had later been understood as harmonious with the biblical account. According to the Ptolemaic picture, the earth existed at the centre of the universe with the stars, planets and sun revolving around it in concentric circles. However, it was found to be increasingly inaccurate as a way of predicting the positions of the planets. The moon, the sun and the stars all followed a predictable pattern and seemed to confirm that the earth was the fixed centre of orbits. A planet ('wandering star') could also be observed moving position night after night against the background of fixed stars. But rather than simply moving across the sky from east to west a planet could appear to stop and, on subsequent nights, move in the opposite direction. Consequently, astronomers introduced what were known as 'epicycles' to accommodate these irregularities. The planets moved in smaller supplementary cycles during the course of their larger orbit of the earth. With the explanatory value of these epicycles, astronomers sought to maintain the Ptolemaic picture of the universe.

Tycho Brahe, one of the outstanding observational astronomers of the sixteenth century, compiled a revised form of the geocentric system taking these epicycles into account but modifying how they functioned. According to Brahe the sun, the moon and the stars all orbited the fixed earth. The five known planets orbited the sun, which was in turn orbiting the earth. This explanation seemed to explain the observational anomalies. But Brahe's complex system never took on in the astronomical community. The reason for its failure will be a key to the success of Hick's own theological proposal. A Polish astronomer, Nicholas Copernicus, had already proposed a far simpler and more useful model.

According to Copernicus, the sun was at rest in the centre of the celestial system and 'epicycles' were no longer necessary to explain the movement of the planets. It was the sun that lay at the centre of the universe, and not the earth. Copernicus' model was very simple but had great explanatory power. It required the scientific community to shed unnecessary assumptions in order for there to be a simpler explanation of astronomers' observations. However, shedding those assumptions would prove a more difficult task for many. For emotional and psychological reasons it would not be easy to shift from a geocentric to a heliocentric view of the cosmos.

The Copernican revolution was essentially a change of perspective on our position in the universe. Hick, writing as a Christian thinker, and not nearly as unorthodox as he would later become, calls for such a transformation on the part of the church: 'It involves a shift from the dogma that Christianity is at the centre to the realisation that it is God who is at the centre, and that all the religions of mankind, including our own, serve and revolve around him.'[28]

Hick draws upon this account as an analogy for the development he describes in Christian theology. The older theological picture of salvation as exclusive to the church or to the Christian proclamation of the gospel is considered 'Ptolemaic'. This older picture envisages Christ or the church at the centre of the universe of religions with all others revolving around that centre. The inclusivist strategy of relating religions to Christ through implicit desire for salvation or some similar notion represents the attempt to develop 'epicycles' to account for observational anomalies, like the obvious saintliness of many non-Christians. Inclusivism is a theological equivalent to the kind of thinking sixteenth-century astronomers were engaged in as they valiantly tried to shore up the inadequate cosmology of the ancient world. Karl Rahner, with his inclusivist account of anonymous Christians, might be portrayed as a theological Tycho Brahe. In this context, Hick presents his own position as a revolutionary change in perspective: a theological equivalent to the work of Copernicus. The analogy is clever. It draws attention to the relative simplicity of Hick's work. It also casts traditional Christian positions into the role of stubborn Luddites desperately trying to preserve doctrines from a bygone age in the face of counter-evidence.

Of course, the Copernican revolution was not to stop with Christians. Hick also indicated the need for orthodox believers in all religious traditions to undergo a similar revolution in self-understanding. However, at this stage, Hick was still writing and speaking to a largely Christian audience. The implications for Christians is that we should recognize that the centre of our worship is God, not the church or Jesus of Nazareth. God is at the centre of our faith. Therefore, the significance of Jesus or the church is found in their functional value in helping us come to God. We need a tradition to provide the vocabulary, symbols and shared experience in order to come to God. But that vocabulary and symbolism are not at the centre of our faith. Prior to the global age of inter-religious co-operation we probably did not need to question the exclusiveness of our saving message. However, with globalization comes an awareness that other religions also provide access to God. They have their own vocabulary and symbolism but share with us common worship of a divine being. Ptolemaic theologians will try to explain the good people of other faiths by appealing to complex epicycles, such as 'anonymous' Christianity or the universal work of the Holy Spirit, but Hick had found a simpler explanation. Once Christ is no longer seen as unique or exclusive then one can redraw the relationship between Christianity and other faiths.

Before we move on it is worth pausing to weigh up the value of this analogy. It has great rhetorical force in commending Hick's position. It also indicates other aspects of how Hick saw his own position developing and its implications for western theology. We shall investigate Hick's Christology in more detail, as this is clearly key to the development of his thought but first we can probe some of the implications of the analogy a little further.

The analogy can distort the issues at stake. Julius Lipner pointed out that according to the analogy there are only two positions: the *absolutist* (Ptolemaic) or the *pluralist* (Copernican).[29] This analogy forces us to choose between something out of date and prescientific and something else that is contemporary and enlightened. This is a false dilemma.

The analogy with the Copernican revolution fails at this point because the historical debate concerned two alternatives: either the earth at the centre with complex explanations of planetary motion, or the sun at the centre without the same need for those complex explanations. The choice lay between two competing 'exclusivisms'. Either the sun or the earth lay at the centre of orbital motion. The analogy breaks down when applied to religious pluralism. Here the choice is between myriad centres of faith, and the problem is why Hick should consider the choice of 'God' as the centre of faiths escapes the charge of being any less Ptolemaic than any other centre.

Why should a 'God' at the centre be less absolutist than Jesus, Allah, Nirvana or Brahman being the centre? Hick describes this revolution in theology as the result of having to 'stand back in thought from the arena of competing systems, surveying the scene as a whole, to see something that is hidden from the Ptolemaic believer.'[30]

What Hick supposes to be hidden from the Ptolemaic believer is the fact that most people tend to follow the religion of their parents and of their culture. Hick claims that if one is able to 'stand back' from personal commitments and loyalties, then one is able to survey all the relevant factors as a whole and see the basic distinction. The distinction is between the Ptolemaic positions of all mainstream religions and the Copernican shift of perspective in which all those religions can be interpreted. This is not a simple either/or choice between one model and another, as in the astronomical analogy, but between loyalty to a religious perspective and being able to distance oneself from any religious loyalty. At this point the analogy has broken down.

The problem can be pushed further. If the theologies of the most devout people are, in some sense, Ptolemaic or pre-Copernican, then how can Hick maintain that his own perspective is not Ptolemaic? He is continuing to claim another exclusive centre – this time the 'God' worshipped by Christ. So it may be claimed that Hick's Copernican revolution is not really a call to leave exclusivisms behind, but a call to adopt a new one, this time with God at the centre. This problem would only become more evident as Hick's work progressed, and we shall survey this development in the following chapters. However, we can pause to notice how awkward Hick's choice of the noun 'God' becomes.

The title of the book in which Hick's argument was first published, *God and the Universe of Faiths*, proves a misnomer in the light of his developed position. If 'God' were at the centre of the universe of faiths then that might satisfy the theistic traditions of Christianity, Judaism and Islam: but what would it have to say to the agnostic traditions of Hinduism and Buddhism, and to the atheistic traditions of Zen Buddhism and Shinto?[31] In the development of Hick's work we will see how the revolution had only just begun; the centre of faith would be something other than God.

The sense in which the Copernican revolution was only the start is as true for astronomy as it would be for theology. The change in cosmological perspective did not end with the heliocentric view. The sun was at the centre of our own solar system, but the entire universe, including the celestial firmament with its zodiacal constellations, did not really revolve around the sun. Faint fuzzy blobs did not turn out to be patches of gas within our solar system but the light from distant galaxies with their own vast collection of suns. The centre of the universe would have to shift elsewhere. Our relatively unimportant main sequence white dwarf star was only the centre of a very minor collection of celestial bodies. Indeed, in later astronomical developments talk of a central pivot seemed less helpful in relation to the movement of the galaxies. Modern cosmologists would say that the universe has no centre; 'Since space is curved, it is somewhat like the two-dimensional space on a balloon and just like there is no centre to its expansion there is no centre to the expansion of the Universe.'[32] This development of the Copernican revolution is also evident in Hick's theological work. Later speculation led him to shift the religious centre away from God to the 'Real'.[33] It is this process that can now be traced through the further stages of Hick's career to its end. The Copernican revolution set Hick on a trajectory away from God being at the centre of faith and we need to consider carefully what ends up taking that space.

By 1973 Hick was in print claiming that Christians should not regard their religion as the one, true way to God but as one of many active options available in the world today. This also implied that Christian theology was not the only source of religious truth. All the religions had answers to the ultimate questions of life and death. These must all be worth listening to. For that reason, Hick's work after this time develops his thought in the context of comparative theology rather than uniquely Christian theology. The publication of *Death and Eternal Life* would be a masterful first example of what pluralist theology would look like. The Copernican revolution had given Hick the impetus to rethink how theology was done and only because of this shift could he produce a theology of the afterlife that gained something from multiple religious traditions.

3

The World Religions

Living in Birmingham brought John Hick into close relationships with people of many different faiths. Hick's interest in pluralism was not simply an abstract theological concern, it was also fuelled by dangerous racial tensions within his local community. He was a foundational member of an inter-religious group called All Faiths for One Race. Originally created in order to protest the visit of an all-white cricket team from apartheid South Africa in 1970, the organization sought to harness the energy of those from any religion who would unite against racism and division. As a prominent speaker and writer, Hick contributed significantly to their engagement with society. In doing so, he faced death threats and intimidation. He also found himself drawn to the cultures and personalities of these neighbouring faiths.

John Hick had travelled far in his thinking by the mid-1970s and developed a significant reputation in both theology and philosophy. He had solid credentials to embark on a radical reframing of Christian theology within the context of the world religions.

The Identity of Jesus Christ

One of Hick's first published articles, in 1948, was a critique of the Christology of D.M. Baillie. Hick criticized Baillie for failing to provide a Christology that fully reflected the historic position of the church represented by the creeds. During the 1950s Hick continued to consider himself a mainstream Christian regarding his basic commitment to orthodox Christology. Even when he came to publicly express doubt regarding the virgin birth he did not consider this to undermine his view of Christ as God incarnate.

Christology was brought into question as a corollary of Hick's increasingly pluralist view of the world religions. His encounter with men and women of other faiths made the orthodox view less tenable. If Jesus were truly the unique incarnation of God on earth, then other religions, at best, are relegated to being temporary movements awaiting fulfilment in Christ. At worst, they are human perversions blinding people to the truth of Christ as God's sole means of salvation. The Copernican revolution in theology demanded a revision of Christology.

A new view of Jesus is found in *God and the Universe of Faiths*, but at this point Hick's position still entailed a high view of Jesus as the incarnation of divine love. While not a Chalcedonian form of orthodoxy, it was still a position that maintained a unique role for Jesus. Hick entirely abandoned the orthodox view of Christ soon after this. The infamous 1977 publication, *The Myth of God Incarnate*, represented a watershed moment in Hick's rejection of orthodoxy.

Hick edited this collection of essays which all cast doubt on the possibility that Jesus was God incarnate in any literal sense. The consensus of the contributors seemed to be that Jesus did not understand himself to be God. The source of the orthodox doctrine lay more in misunderstood Near Eastern mythology and Greek philosophy than in the Bible. The shared preface to the book begins with an observation from the poet T.S. Eliot that 'Christianity is always adapting itself into something which can be believed'.[1] This statement justifies reformulating Christian doctrine in the light of contemporary knowledge. Hick and his collaborators were not seeking to maintain a faith already given[2] but to develop a faith fit for a modern world.

Hick's problem with the doctrine of the incarnation was that it attempted to describe the identity of Jesus in ontological terms. In other words, the doctrine was trying to say something objective about him. It did this through using the Greek expression, *ousia* (substance). By describing Jesus as *homoousian* (of one substance), the

Nicene Creed had affirmed a literal identification of Jesus with God. Fellow contributor Michael Goulder declared, 'The substance idea was a part of the world view of the later Roman Empire, and involves contradictions which cannot be resolved.'[3] The philosophical baggage of substance language created more problems than it solved in seeking to understand the identity of Christ.

Hick raised philosophical objections to the use of substance language. How could it be possible for one, historical, particular, limited, fallible human to also be the one, eternal, infinite, perfect, divine being? For example, if Jesus was limited in knowledge (as the gospels suggest in Matt. 24:36; Mark 5:30) then, Hick reasoned, he cannot be the same individual as the all-knowing God. Or, if one affirms that Christ was really the omniscient God then he cannot be identified with the limited human of the gospels who necessarily lacked knowledge. According to Hick, affirming the identity of God and Christ as of one substance is like affirming the existence of a square circle. It is a contradiction in terms. As a philosophical or factual statement it is meaningless. However, it may still be useful language serving some other purpose, as Hick would seek to show.

Hick had prepared the ground for his new Christology in *God and the Universe of Faiths*. He had already dismissed the traditional view as a 'static' concept of the identity of Jesus. Instead, he proposed a 'dynamic' concept. The incarnation is not a fact about Jesus but a description of an activity that both Jesus and God were engaged in.

Jesus incarnated the love of God in his actions towards other people. His will was so perfectly matched to that of God that it was possible to say that whatever Jesus willed, God willed. For this reason, the disciples felt as if in the very presence of God.

This statement of incarnation is a long way from an orthodox Christology. It is a description of what Jesus did, not of who he was. In that sense, anyone could incarnate the love of God. The difference between Jesus and other human beings was a matter of degree, not kind. Most humans have flickering moments when their will might match the divine will, whereas Jesus reached a state of absolute identification with the will of God.

However, even this subjective view of incarnation still posed a problem for the Christian engagement with other religions. After all, could not similar claims be made about the leaders of other faiths? Hick's Christology had to be revised further to take into account the presence of the divine in all the world religions. The revision was not difficult to make. If Jesus incarnated the divine will then why could we not see something like that taking place in the Buddha, Muhammad and Guru Nanak? There was no longer any reason to maintain a uniqueness to the status of Jesus.

The obvious objections to Hick's revised Christology are found in Scripture and tradition. There are Scriptures, 'I am the way, and the truth and the life. No one comes to the Father except through me' (John 14:6) or 'Salvation is found in no one else, for there is no other name under heaven given to mankind by which we must be saved' (Acts 4:12). There are statements of the church fathers, such as Ignatius in *c.* AD 100, 'There is one Physician, who is possessed both of flesh and spirit; both made and not made; God existing in flesh; true life in death; both of Mary and of God; first possible and then impossible, – even Jesus Christ our Lord.'[4] The Catholic creeds continue in the same vein, such as the early Apostles' Creed: 'I believe in God, the Father Almighty, Creator of heaven and earth; and in Jesus Christ His only Son, our Lord.' Christians were straining to find language to affirm the uniqueness of Christ. Even if they were wrong, how could Hick argue that his understanding of the Christian tradition was correct?

Hick's response was to propose that the language of incarnation and divinity applied to Jesus in earliest times has been misunderstood in later church history. It was originally intended as 'mythological' language. Hick urges Christians to strip away what he considers later developments in order to see the historical figure behind the myths. By 'myth', Hick does not mean that the language is entirely false. He means that it is an exaggerated, poetic way of describing the person of Jesus. Behind such mythology, Hick describes the real Jesus as 'intensely and overwhelmingly conscious of the reality of God. He was a man of God, living in the unseen presence of God. He was so powerfully God-conscious that his life vibrated, as it were, to the divine life; and as a result his hands could heal the sick.'[5]

Hick's new Christology dispensed entirely with the unique status of Jesus as God incarnate. Jesus was a man imbued with an overwhelming sense of God. We may find the same sense of the divine in religious leaders and founders from all periods. These saintly figures may have had various levels of experience of the divine but any difference between them was a matter of degree, not a matter of kind. Christian tradition chose to use the mythological language of incarnation to describe the experience of Christ's followers. It was a mistake of later theology to interpret this mythological language as if it were factual. Hick's Christology could use the same vocabulary but with a profound difference of meaning. By doing so, Hick sought to defuse the problematic Christian confession of the uniqueness of Christ.

A feature of his work from here on is that Hick wrote on theological themes from a global religious perspective. Rather than writing about an issue in terms of a Christian theological framework, Hick would gather insights from all the major world religions and, having subjected them to philosophical analysis, offer tentative claims regarding metaphysical reality.

The Afterlife

In 1976 Hick published *Death and Eternal Life*. As we have seen, this work does not develop a particularly Christian theology of the future but sets out to produce a religious theology, not dependent on a single tradition. He explores ideas about death with reference to existentialist philosophy, parapsychology, humanism and some of the major world religions. Research for his work included the extensive trips to India and Sri Lanka.

Hick would often draw on the data provided by parapsychology and accounts of near-death experiences to help bolster his idea that the universe has a religious dimension and that personal identity will continue, in some form, beyond the grave.[6]

Hick is a 'critical realist' regarding religious language. This means that while he accepts that some religious language is poetic or expressive of our feelings, there remains a core of literal truth in religious speech. This includes the claim that existence continues beyond death. Rejecting the concept of hell or eternal punishment, an implication of his Ireneaen theodicy, Hick is optimistic that the future existence beyond death will, eventually, lead to absolute and universal bliss. The resurrection of the body is the mythological picture given for this in Christian thought.

The world-views of eastern religions shed further light on a possible conception of the afterlife. Hick argues that the concept of reincarnation is compatible with the Christian doctrine of resurrection. These traditions at least share the common conviction that life continues after death. They disagree over whether this life should be conceived as a continuation of existence in this physical reality or a transformation into another state or new order of reality. This disagreement is not simply between those who hold a Judeo-Christian concept of resurrection and those who hold a Hindu concept of reincarnation. Even within those varied traditions the vision of the afterlife can be understood in quite contrary ways. The simple, shared conviction is that personal identity continues beyond the grave though the pictures given in religious traditions are diverse. Are those pictures contradictory? Hick thinks not. He proposes that the self may progress through many further worlds in which he or she will have further opportunities to achieve the goal of moral and spiritual perfection; 'a series of lives, each bounded by something analogous to birth and death, lived in other worlds in spaces other than that in which we now are'.[7] If it is the case that there are future lives to come then there may have been many lives already lived in the past. This abstract account could be compatible with both reincarnation and resurrection doctrines. Those historic doctrines are compatible, if mythological, ways of describing this literal process.

The argument of *Death and Eternal Life* requires that there be an ultimate, transcendent significance to the 'self'. In fact, neither the term 'God' nor 'self' translates easily into eastern terms. Many traditions of

Hinduism and Buddhism deny that there really is a true self. The very concept of our individual identity is part of the problem. It causes the ignorance from which we need liberation. According to these traditions, the ultimate state is not a matter of individuals enjoying the company of a God from whom they are distinct. The ultimate state is the dissolution of individual identity. The self is absorbed into the ultimate divine reality, much as a drop of water might be absorbed into an ocean. At this stage in his work, Hick sides with one tradition of Hindu thought against another. He wishes to maintain personal identity as something which continues through future lives. However, the Christian teaching on selflessness inspires him to think that there may be some truth to the idea that future perfection implies the extinction of the self. Reflecting upon Christian mystic writing he posits, 'We are to become so transparent to the divine life that we no longer live as separate self-enclosed individuals.'[8] Perhaps there is a sense in which even the extinction of the self in Nirvana could carry a grain of truth when understood along these lines? Hick thinks so.

Hick's interest in the afterlife was a constant thread. We have noted how as a child he had experienced clairvoyant attempts to contact the dead at séances. His experiences left him unconvinced. However, various studies of parapsychology, extra-sensory perception and near-death experiences were more persuasive. Hick would add his own personal experiences at various times to the list of evidences for an afterlife. In 1985 Hick's youngest son, Michael, died in a tragic accident at the age of twenty-four: 'Some weeks later, back in Claremont, I had a brief vivid waking vision of Mike standing beside me and then going away through an open door, this having a positive rather than a negative feeling.'[9]

Hick remained convinced of some form of life beyond the grave throughout his later work. It becomes a unifying theme in his treatment of the world religions. Whatever else they may disagree upon there is a shared cosmic optimism about our eternal destiny.

Hick had returned to America in 1982 and taught for ten years at Claremont Graduate School. He held the position of Danforth Professor of the Philosophy of Religion. During this time he continued to

travel extensively and engage with the world religions. He retained his
URC credentials as a minister but his tone was increasingly sceptical
of mainstream ecclesiology. He describes a visit to Turkey and the remains of the church where the Nicene Creed had been agreed. Along
with other conference participants, Hick stood on the ruins and re-
cited the creed though, he adds, doing so 'in inverted commas!'[10]

The Case for Pluralism

Most of Hick's printed output after this time concerned the pluralist
hypothesis. He refined it further and answered charges of his critics,
culminating in probably his most significant single volume, *An Interpretation of Religion*. Much of the content was originally delivered as
a series of the distinguished Gifford Lectures at Edinburgh University
in 1986–7. This lecture series has been given for over a century and
includes notable contributors William James, Karl Barth and Alvin
Plantinga. While the lectures themselves can be a discrete affair,[11]
they are of great influence and continued to establish Hick's reputation as a foremost philosopher of religion.

An Interpretation of Religion was published in 1989 and formed a
comprehensive and formidable statement of religious pluralism as a
philosophical position. Hick sought to harmonize insights from his
previous work in order to present a coherent case for his interpretation of religion as the common human response to the divine.

'Interpretation' is a key word for Hick. Not only did this volume
provide an interpretation of religion, it also presented the case that religion is itself a way of interpreting reality. Hick clarified his thought
on epistemology but drew on the same essential insights that he had
made in his doctoral thesis on faith and knowledge.

Following *God and the Universe of Faiths*, Hick continued to argue that all the major world religions were culturally conditioned
responses to a divine reality. However, we have already noted that
to suggest God is the centre of faiths is to privilege the monotheistic faiths. How can Hick's new map for the universe of faiths

accommodate non-theistic or polytheistic faiths? In the 1989 volume Hick dispensed with God as anything more than another culturally conditioned image. Behind the universe of faiths lies a divine reality more accurately described as the Ultimate Real (sometimes, simply, Ultimate Reality) or He/She/It. This transcendent being could be compatible with both theistic and non-theistic faiths. The entire package of religious traditions, scriptures, rituals and doctrines can all be relativized as human constructs that tell us more about the human condition than about the divine reality.

Hick can develop his thought in this way because he could build on the epistemology he had already developed. Using Jastrow's famous picture of the duck-rabbit, Hick points out how a pattern of lines on paper can be interpreted in two different ways: as a rabbit or as a duck. Borrowing the terminology, if not the philosophy, of Ludwig Wittgenstein (1889–1951), he describes this experience as 'seeing-as'.[12] We see the picture 'as' a duck or 'as' a rabbit, the picture in itself being ambiguous, open to either interpretation.

Hick went further than he had done in earlier work in emphasizing the organizing nature of the mind. Borrowing from the work of Kant, Hick postulated that the Ultimate Reality, the 'noumenon', was beyond any possible human experience. The reality we experience is the 'phenomenon', or the way the 'noumenon' *appears* to us. This Kantian epistemology allowed Hick to make a radical distinction between the descriptions of God offered by the world religions and the Ultimate Reality behind those descriptions. Utterly conflicting truth claims need no longer be a problem. Religions are not offering descriptions of God, but only partial descriptions of the human experience of what lies beyond. Even the most different and apparently contradictory descriptions could ultimately be compatible given how unknowable the Real truly is. In keeping with this epistemology, it would not make sense to speak of 'God' and the 'universe and faiths', as 'God' is a word of description in the realm of phenomenon. A better expression now would be 'Ultimate Reality' and the 'Universe of Faiths'. Hick proposes the 'Real' or 'Ultimate Reality' as less loaded terms to refer to the Divine Being than terms such as God, Allah or Brahman.

This conclusion has enormous implications for our understanding of religion. Religions are human constructions that provide a context in which we can dimly experience the Ultimate Reality. They are not disclosures of that reality or repositories of divine truth. Given this framework, most of the major world religions can be recognized as of largely equal value in providing a context for this experience.

However, *An Interpretation of Religion* does continue to maintain some level of factual truth claiming in religious traditions. Hick identifies this core and explains how truth claims work through an epistemological position known as critical realism.

Critical Realism

Hick developed his thought during a period of theological change. During the 1960s there were radical theological movements that parted company even with the liberal, sceptical tradition. These new ideas included non-realist epistemology. In many ways, non-realism might have seemed attractive to Hick. Proponents argued that religious language has a functional or symbolic value but does not describe anything objective. While this sounds similar to some of his ideas Hick argued against such an epistemology.

A naive realist position would simply affirm that religious language is a direct, straightforward and literal description of objective, divine realities. So when a naive realist describes God as love they mean that God really is a personal being living in heaven and capable of loving relationships. A non-realist might also describe God as love. But they would not mean to say anything about an objective being, they may not even assume the existence of God. To non-realists 'God is love' means the same thing as 'Love is God'. It is a way of expressing our value system, not a way of describing objective reality.

Hick offers critical realism as a middle position. He does not believe that religious language gives a literal description of divine realities.

However, he maintains that his position is still realist because whatever else religious language may do, it still assumes that there really is a transcendent being behind our experience.

Hick draws upon the evidence of mystics who have lived in the light of their experience of the Ultimate Reality.[13] This evidence, he suggests, points to the possibility that there really is a fifth dimension, beyond space and time, which we call the metaphysical or supernatural. Religions are not merely poetic expressions of human experience but point to a reality beyond us. This is critical realism.

Hick retired from Claremont Graduate School in 1992 and returned to Birmingham. His subsequent writings, of which there were many, continued to clarify and explain the pluralist view. *The Metaphor of God Incarnate* (1993) distinguished between the experience of the first followers of Jesus and later doctrinal formulations. He provided more technical reasons for his revised Christology. *The Rainbow of Faiths* (1995) was an interesting attempt to present the case for pluralism through an imaginary dialogue between himself and two imaginary critics. One of his last books, *Between Faith and Doubt* (2010), also used this structure. Another substantial explanation of pluralism was published as *The Fifth Dimension* (1999). Perhaps the last significant text he published was *The New Frontier of Religion and Science* (2006), which provides a positive case for religious faith. The book presents evidence from neuroscience to show that not all religious experience is illusory. During this time Hick also completed his very readable autobiography (2002).

Hick died on 9 February 2012, still holding tenaciously to his pluralist interpretation of the world religions. He attended a Quaker meeting house and practised Buddhist meditation as part of his personal spirituality. Shortly before his death I had the opportunity to discuss Hick's thought on Premier Radio and the transcript appears as the Appendix to this volume. To the very end, Hick maintained his sharp mind and strong commitment to the pluralist explanation of the world religions.

4

Consistent Faith

The corpus of Hick's work, briefly surveyed here, spans sixty years. We have noted major shifts in his thinking and how this has been expressed in his writing. Hick moved from being an evangelical Christian, through being a mainstream liberal minister into becoming a pluralist, radical, theologian in the course of his academic career. Because he has produced so much material it is not surprising that there should be changes and modifications to his thought. I want to suggest, however, that Hick's Copernican revolution, even in its later modified forms, is essentially consistent with his early epistemology. Indeed, my thesis is that the seeds of his pluralism were already sown in his theory of knowledge, and I conclude that there has never been a radical change in Hick's theological framework. Certainly, various theological beliefs have undergone revision but these were only ever peripheral to his basic philosophical commitment. As we shall see, the claim that Hick's work can be treated in such a unified way has been the subject of debate.

Hick notes in his preface to the 1966 second edition of *Faith and Knowledge* that despite the revision he has made to his work, the book remains 'an exposition of the view of faith which seemed to me, and still seems to me, most adequate'.[1] In 1988 there was a reissue of the second edition in which Hick wrote a new preface. Here he continues to maintain that the work is foundational to everything else he has written and notes that his subsequent writings 'proceeded in a natural trajectory from the [earlier] epistemology'.[2]

The word 'trajectory' is a useful one and indicates the kind of continuity to be found in Hick's work. Of course, he admits that his theological position has changed substantially, but maintains that 'the theology, whether old or new, does not affect the basic epistemological argument'. This important statement reveals the distinction Hick is happy to make between his philosophy and his theology: his philosophy provides foundations that are stable and compatible with a number of different theological positions, while his theology becomes a kind of second-order discourse. His theology could shift without causing any major problem for his philosophical position.

Hick has always been, primarily, a philosopher of religion.[3] His philosophical position determines his theological position. This is significant, because sometimes the impression is given that philosophy is a neutral discipline. On the contrary, there are countless different philosophical positions and they have a significant bearing on metaphysical beliefs and values. It will be my claim that while Hick's theology has changed out of all recognition, his philosophical position has barely changed at all.

Continuity or Discontinuity

Gerard Loughlin has proved an insightful critic of Hick's work and has drawn attention to major incoherencies that have developed in the course of the years. In particular, he is critical of the notion that Hick's work can be treated as a unified whole. He goes so far as to make the strong criticism that Hick himself is deluded over the coherence of his literary output. Loughlin's claim is worth considering here as it seems to conflict with the attempt in this volume to deal with Hick's work as a unified project.

Macmillan reissued many of Hick's major works in 1988, each with a new preface. A similar set of reissues with new prefaces occurred in 2010. A preface is an obvious opportunity to provide a new introduction to a book, respond to critics or point out where the author's view may have changed since earlier printings.

The 1988 reissues occurred one year prior to the publication of *An Interpretation of Religion*. Consequently, an impression is given that the corpus of Hick's work forms a coherent whole. This impression is reinforced by the use of similar dustjackets and typefaces. The use of prefaces further bolsters this impression by allowing Hick to become, in Loughlin's words, 'the narrator of Hick's texts'.[4] By becoming a narrator of his own work he is able to harmonize his contradictory arguments into a single system. The role of the narrator is one who can explain away the significance of changes and smooth over the contradictions by pointing out the original intentions of mistaken ideas. Loughlin tries to demonstrate the underlying discontinuity of Hick's work. He does this by identifying three theological themes that have changed over time: eschatology, Christology and theodicy. By surveying how each of these areas have been modified we will be better placed to assess Loughlin's claim that Hick's work cannot be treated as a coherent whole.

Loughlin draws attention to Hick's use of eschatological verification, which developed in three stages. In 1957 his use of the term 'kingdom of God' serves to describe the post-mortem encounter with God. In his 1966 preface he identifies the person of Christ with the kingdom of God in order to make his Christian commitment clear, though moving to more personal language. It is not so much an encounter with a theological concept ('the kingdom of God') as an encounter with a personal being (the person of Christ). However, in later writings he severs the connection between Christ and the post-mortem encounter. From this point on, the afterlife becomes vague in Hick's writing and no longer verifies any particular religious claims. This kind of movement away from Christian content towards abstract terms prompts D'Costa to describe the version of eschatological verification that appears in *An Interpretation of Religion* as 'minimalist' because it dispenses with 'specific details of eschatological expectations'.[5]

Regarding Christology, Loughlin identifies two different accounts of Christ, both of which are evident even since Hick's Copernican revolution in theology. On the one hand there is a functional account of the incarnation in terms of *agape*. The love of God and the love of Christ are one. Functionally, Christ incarnates God's love by being identified with his will. However, on the other hand, Hick also provides a mythological reinterpretation of all incarnation language. Such language is a poetic way of expressing what the Christ story means to us. So there is both a functional Christology and a subjective version used interchangeably. Loughlin suggests that Hick tries to maintain these two accounts alongside each other even though, strictly speaking, the mythological description renders the functional account redundant. It is of no surprise that as Hick's work continues he dispenses altogether with a functional account of the incarnation.

Regarding *theodicy* there has been another striking change in Hick's position. Loughlin charts the change from a Christian theodicy, through a theistic theodicy, to a theodicy that does not require the existence of a personal God at all. In order to facilitate this shift, Hick reinterprets his earlier work on theodicy in the light of his ideas about mythological language. 'Hick is able to stand back sufficiently far from his own Irenaean theodicy to see that it is also a myth, just like Augustine's theodicy. He is able to apply to his theodicy the mytholographical analysis he had formerly applied only to his *agape* Christology.'[6]

As with his Christology, so with his theodicy, Hick's earlier Christian understanding of these concepts is emptied of substance in favour of them being seen as helpful myths by which we live. Loughlin notes that myth becomes a useful device in Hick's later writing, enabling him to reinterpret his earlier thought in a way that brings it into harmony with his later work.

The substance of Loughlin's criticism is that Hick fails to recognize how radical a revision he has made to his own work. In some way, each major text that Hick writes presents a major revision of what went before. Loughlin even claims that the revision is so great that each publication discards everything that went before. If this thesis is correct, then it is impossible to engage with Hick's work as a unified whole. Perhaps Loughlin is correct in one sense but not in another sense. Before I make this point there are two useful responses to Loughlin's charge that can be considered. The first is that given by Hick himself.

Hick disliked the tone and style of Loughlin's article, suggesting that it explained his own work as 'an extraordinary – even fantastic – literary conspiracy theory'.[7] Responding to the charges, Hick points out that his prefaces draw attention to both discontinuities and continuities in his own position. He denied any attempt to mask the changes and developments in his thinking. However, the question remains: how radical are those changes? Were they only developments of his thought or had he made a major shift?

With regard to epistemology, Hick rejects the notion that eschatological verification was ever crucial. He maintains that it is useful to establish the meaningfulness of religious language against the objections of the logical positivists. It was never intended, as Loughlin claims, to establish the truth of the Christian faith.

With regard to Christology, Hick argues that Loughlin is mistaken to regard his *agape* model of the incarnation as a departure from orthodoxy. According to Hick, this departure would not occur until later, 'somewhere in the late 1970s',[8] when the *agape* account had largely been abandoned. By the time he dropped the *agape* model he had begun to develop a pluralist view of the world religions. Well aware that the pluralist hypothesis was not compatible with the orthodox doctrine of the incarnation Hick knew he must abandon this belief. Therefore, he did not attempt to fuse the *agape* model with his new perspective on the world religions. Loughlin's attempt to identify inconsistency here simply ignored Hick's open admission that he no longer held to the uniqueness of Christ in any form. However, in this response, Hick barely deals with Loughlin's objections regarding his use of myth, conceding that it is a 'highly elastic concept'.[9] The elasticity of the term does create some confusion in Hick's work.

Hick freely admits a substantial revision to his theodicy. His theodicy, being an explanation of how a good God could permit suffering and evil, relies heavily on personal survival beyond death and future lives beyond this one. His revision draws upon his developing sense of the function of myth. In earlier writings, major elements of eschatological language were understood to be literal descriptions of what lies beyond the grave. But now, understanding that language to be mythological, Hick admits that 'it speaks in human terms of that which transcends the scope of our human capabilities'.[10] Hick maintains that this is a legitimate expansion of his work in the light of the world religions rather than an inconsistency. But Loughlin has clearly identified an important problem here. The reissue of *Evil and the God of Love* gives the impression that Hick's theodicy remains fundamentally unchanged. However, in the light of Hick's understanding of mythology he has placed these ideas in a very different framework. Language describing the afterlife and ultimate blessing is no longer intended to apply literally to what lies beyond the grave. This raises the awkward question of what exactly it does then describe and we will return to this point later.

Philip L. Barnes made useful observations on the exchange between Loughlin and Hick. Commenting on the issue of continuity and discontinuity in the corpus of Hick's work, he notes three senses in which the word 'development' may be used. It may mean, 'drawing out and making explicit what was originally implicit; rejecting what has gone before; or, finally, expanding one's position by the incorporation of new insights, arguments and ideas'.[11] Hick's theological position develops in all of these ways and yet none of them necessarily implies inconsistency. Barnes questions Loughlin's contention that there is a clear contrast between an early and a later Hick. Rather than discontinuity, Barnes argues for a continuity: 'Hick's theology should be interpreted as the increasingly systematic drawing out of his initial starting point rather than being divided into two different and opposing parts.'[12]

Barnes accepts Loughlin's point that eschatological verification has developed in Hick's work, but argues that this is not really central to his epistemology so its development is of little significance. Rather, the central theme in Hick's epistemology is that of 'experiencing-as'. Hick introduced the term in the Royal Institute of Philosophy Lecture series in 1967–8 but it described faith in a way entirely consistent with the much earlier first edition of *Faith and Knowledge*. In each statement of his epistemology there was a rejection of faith as a cognitive response to doctrinal claims in favour of faith as an interpretative category. The range of possible interpretations considered by Hick increases with his pluralist hypothesis. Where once faith had been synonymous with Christianity it may now apply to any of the major world religions. But such a range is already possible in Hick's early work because of his assumption that the universe is religiously ambiguous. From his earliest work in philosophy, Hick described faith in very subjective terms that would allow his epistemology to be easily translated into the categories of another religion. Thus even his most recent work maintains the same basic epistemology.

Barnes suggests that the main reason why Loughlin denies that Hick's work has continuity is because Loughlin thinks Christology is key. There is no doubt that Hick radically changed his mind regarding the identity of Christ and he freely admits this change. But is Christology really the key thread that holds Hick's work together? Loughlin's objections would find purchase if he were writing about the work of a systematic theologian. Given a substantial revision of the doctrine of the incarnation one would expect a systematic theologian to have revised most of the rest of their work in Christian theology. However, Barnes demonstrates that for Hick, Christology 'was not an integral part of his epistemology of Christian belief'.[13] Therefore, changes in Hick's understanding of Christ have no bearing on his epistemology. Hick's theory of religious knowledge has no intrinsic relationship to Christian theology in particular. This was as true of his doctoral research as of his final publications. The force of this point is that Hick should not be understood as a Christian theologian at any point in his academic career. Whatever his personal beliefs or creed may have been, structurally his work is not Christian. Much of the argument that follows in this book will seek to substantiate this claim.

Regarding consistency, we can identify a coherence to the body of Hick's work. It has remained consistent in the way Hick developed his philosophical understanding of religious knowledge. This is the real key to Hick's work.

Loughlin emphasizes discontinuity in Hick's position because he treats Hick as a Christian theologian. Of the three areas he considers, two are distinctively Christian areas: *Christology* and *theodicy*. However, even the third area, *epistemology*, is dealt with as a discussion of Hick's eschatology or view of the afterlife. Again, this is a Christian theological view of what happens after death. In other words, Loughlin highlights the radical discontinuity of Hick's theological position with regard to eschatology, the person of Jesus and the problem of evil. These changes in Hick's thought make it impossible to take his work seriously as a unified whole if understood as Christian theology. However, if one accepts with Barnes that Christian theology has only ever been marginal to his work, then such discontinuity loses significance. In terms of basic epistemology, Hick's position remains largely consistent. Nah is correct in his caution that 'Hick's philosophy of pluralism should not necessarily be seen as overly radical and discontinuous shifts so much as relatively continuous, if not awkward, developments within a single pluralistic paradigm'.[14] Hick deliberately avoids earthing his assumptions in any one particular religious tradition. The result is a work of philosophy that attempts to be theologically neutral. Hick's defenders would often make the case that his philosophical work cannot be judged by theological standards. This distinction is dubious. As far as it goes, one may say that theologically Hick underwent a revolution in thought, but philosophically he was quite consistent.

I will argue that such neutrality is impossible. Hick's work is theologically inconsistent on major areas of Christian doctrine. He would be the first to admit that. But his philosophy still makes theological assumptions about the nature of God, creation and salvation. The issue is not whether Hick is a theologian but what *theos* his work is a response to.

5

On Knowing God

We can now consider Hick's theory of religious knowledge in more detail, recognizing its significance for the whole of his work. It is important to emphasize that Hick considered himself an apologist for theism. From his earliest work it is evident that he wanted to make the case for belief in God and argue against the alternatives.[1]

Throughout his career, Hick maintained a case against atheistic naturalism. He was convinced of a supernatural, divine order to reality which could not be explained away. In this chapter we will return to Hick's first published book, *Faith and Knowledge*. As we have seen, this was written long before his adoption of a pluralist theology. Yet his theory of knowledge is able to accommodate his later theological revolution without revision. This is key. Hick was primed to be a pluralist from the very beginning of his academic work. Paul Helm predicted this direction. Responding to his early statement of epistemology, Helm noted that Hick's description of faith 'requires a different account of religion as well'.[2] Helm's observation proved astute. Taking the view of religious knowledge that Hick did would inevitably lead to a very different view of the world religions. This is the consistent component that directs Hick's developing theology. As his epistemology is the only stable element in his entire work, if he can be faulted at this point, then the grounds for his pluralist proposal may also be shown to be flawed.

Hick's overview of different theories of religious knowledge is useful and helps us to understand both his own position and why he rejects the alternatives. His outline of various positions on religious knowledge is another example of his great ability in simplifying and categorizing complex ideas.

Thomist-Catholic Faith

Hick rejects what he describes as the Thomist-Catholic propositional model of faith. This model would encompass many traditional Reformed and evangelical approaches to faith too. With reference to Thomas Aquinas, Hick describes this model as holding faith to be a relationship we have to ideas rather than to God. Those ideas are 'propositions' or verbal statements. This is a heavily intellectual approach to religion. Salvation, according to Hick's description of this model, requires that we 'believe explicitly such central articles as the Incarnation and the Trinity' insofar as one is able to understand their cognitive content.[3] We are saved by believing in certain truths. Therefore, the difference between faith and other forms of intellectual knowledge concerns the degree to which the evidence supports the beliefs. The reason why we call it faith, according to Hick, is that the religious believer has great personal certainty in the truth of propositions that are not self-evident to the sceptics.

The Thomist-Catholic tradition has held a high view of the capability of human reason to establish evidential grounds for holding a religious belief to be true. A good example of this is Thomas' 'five ways' to prove the existence of God. Even without special revelation, this view of doctrine tends to regard human reason as able to establish the main foundations of belief. However, there are no indubitable proofs. Commitment to a belief requires some kind of step beyond the evidence. Hick uses Newman's metaphor: 'The lamp of private judgement may be required to enable us to find our way; but once we have reached home we no longer need it.'[4] At this point, Hick is particularly focused on the Roman Catholic brand of this approach to doctrine. Faith does not finally rest with human reason or personal feelings but with the authority of the church. Reasons may be tentative and subject to change. But, like a ladder or lamp, this is no problem. Once they have served to bring us to our destination we may discard them. Like a faulty ladder, if our reasons prove weak or false, we may discard the ladder but still be glad that it brought us to our destination.

A Reformed version of this model, which Hick does not describe, would not endorse the church as the final authority but might appeal to the word of God as having this same function.[5] So even if our reasons for believing in the Bible as the word of God were later found wanting we might continue to believe in the Bible as having a self-authenticating authority.

Though having different forms, this approach to faith shares three common themes. It is *intellectualist*, identifying faith with a set of propositions. It is *fideist*, because reasons only serve a temporary purpose and faith is ultimately grounded in a self-authenticating source. Third, this approach is *voluntarist*, as faith is an uncompelled choice we make to believe things that go beyond the force of the evidence.

This model of faith also entails a matching concept of revelation. Faith and revelation are correlative terms: it is the human response (faith) to the divine disclosure (revelation). Therefore, the Thomistic-Catholic model describes revelation as a divine communication of truth in verbal form. This verbal revelation is preserved in the Bible and, according to some traditions, in later church councils. Faith amounts to trust in the truths of verbal revelation.

Hick's explanation of the Thomist-Catholic model really attempts to categorize under a single heading a vast range of Christian thought. Along a spectrum it would include traditional Catholicism, Barthianism and Reformed theology. The various views are held together by their commitment to a faith that could be expressed in doctrines and confessions of faith. It is of little surprise that in Hick's later work such an approach to faith would prove a barrier to the pluralist hypothesis. But it is important to notice that in his very first published work he had already outlined and rejected such a doctrinal understanding of faith.

Hick does not expressly state, at least in his early work, his exact objections to the Thomist-Catholic view. Rather than providing clear critical objections he notes that the 'notion of divinely revealed propositions has virtually disappeared from Protestant theology'.[6] Hick assumes that because the view has less support it is therefore less tenable. Perhaps in the 1950s it was possible to say this in British academic circles but the reality is that propositional revelation has continued to be defended and explained throughout the years. It cannot be so simply dismissed. But Hick refrains from engaging with it. The real reason why he gives it such short shrift is because it is not compatible with his view of what faith is. For Hick, faith is not a response to doctrines or beliefs. His alternative points to a more subjective description of revelation.

Faith as Interpretation

Hick's conception of revelation is not one of divinely spoken truths but of divine presence. Revelation is the felt presence of God. Consequently, faith is not primarily about particular beliefs, it is 'man's awareness of God'.[7] In this sense, faith is similar to any perceptual experience. We become conscious of things, other people and God either by direct experience or by inferring their existence from other experiences that we have. Faith is the particular experience of supernatural reality but it is not a unique kind of knowledge. We exercise a form of faith in all perception.

Hick describes the active role of the mind in experience as interpretation. We have to impose some kind of order on the sensory information that floods our mind. We see significance all around us. We are often aware of this process. For example, when we are trying to make out a blur on the horizon and then realize it is a house. Sometimes we cannot work out what a shape we are looking at is until someone tells us that we are looking at a picture of a face. Then it becomes clear. Much of the time we are not aware of this process. It is subconscious. But all the time there is a process of interpretation underway as our mind seeks to order reality and make sense of our experience.

At this stage in Hick's writing he only makes a passing reference to the key influence on his work. Hick is essentially describing a simple outline of Immanuel Kant's philosophy, 'In its most general form at least, we must accept the Kantian thesis that we can be aware only of that which enters into a certain framework of basic relations which is correlated with the structure of our own consciousness.'[8] Hick's indebtedness to Kant becomes ever clearer as his work progresses and so we must return to this later.

Hick's view of knowledge should not simply be categorized as subjective as if he were claiming that it is 'all in the mind'. His view is more complex than this. But it is ultimately impossible to distinguish the objective reality from our interpretation of that reality. We have no objective frame of reference from which to make that distinction.

This description can make Hick sound like a radical relativist, which he was not. He did hold to the 'critical realist' view of knowledge. There is a reality that exists independently of our perception. Hick's epistemology only means that we have no direct access to such an objective reality. Whether we are discussing knives and forks, or angels and demons, we are talking about a world as it appears to us through the interpretative work of our mind.

Objectivity is no more than the world as we assume it to be. There is no point at which we can describe the world apart from the functional involvement of our mind. While Hick continues to maintain his realist view of knowledge – there is a reality that is the source of our ideas – his epistemology strictly limits what we can truly claim to know. All knowledge is information that has already been shaped by our minds.

Hick defines interpretation carefully in order to include the entirety of knowledge. At one level we might think that interpretation is the intellectual activity of making sense of something, like the way we interpret a play or a piece of art. Hick calls this kind of interpretation 'explanation' and it is an important second-order intellectual activity that we do engage in. However, the kind of interpretation he is identifying he calls 'recognition'. This describes a more immediate act of the mind recognizing the significance of something when we sense it. Recognition includes the interpretation of sense experience as a bus, an animal or a friend. It is as much an act of interpretation as making sense of a Shakespeare play. The difference is that it is immediate and instinctive. This description of interpretation as recognition is a key used by Hick to understand all knowledge.

The Religious Interpretation of the Universe

Hick distinguishes levels of interpretation. The first step might be to interpret a red rectangle as a book. The second step might be to interpret the book as a bound document. The third step could be to interpret the meaning of the document as a narrative. Each step of interpretation involves increased complexity but builds on what went before. A higher step presupposes the previous but then super-imposes a new dimension of meaning.

Our interpretation of reality is also shaped by what Hick calls our *focal awareness*: we cannot possibly be aware of everything going on around us. Only certain things have significance for us at any given time and hold our focal awareness. This becomes apparent when something catches our attention and distracts us from what had been our focal awareness. Perhaps we are reading a book and not aware of music playing in the house until a familiar song catches our attention. Then our focal awareness shifts from the meaning of the book to the sounds of the music.

This theme of focal awareness is important because it highlights how little of our environment we are really attentive to. Our limited minds have to be selective. We focus on what concerns us or what we expect to find. To take in more we overload our minds and paralyse our actions. So even in being selective our minds are active in shaping our interpretation of reality.

Hick describes our situational awareness as threefold: *nature, man* and *God*. These three situations of awareness correspond to the three steps of interpretation. Our first, simple, step of interpretation in-volves our awareness of the natural world in which we live and need to survive. This must be close to instinctive or learned very early in our development such that we have little awareness of this as an intellectual process. The second step of interpretation concerns human and social relationships in which we find moral significance. This may still be exercised instinctively – as we find behaviour attractive or unattractive – but it clearly involves learning and reflection. The third step encompasses both previous levels, but moves beyond them to include openness to transcendent or divine reality.

The order of the three steps of interpretation is important. Each level of awareness presupposes and builds upon the previous levels. The sequence is significant because it gives priority to natural knowledge over religious knowledge. We only come to the religious interpretation of the universe after the prior interpretation of our natural environment. When we return to the theme of religious pluralism we will see how significant this ordering is. It provides a basis for Hick's claim that there is a common, prior vantage point from which the adherents of all the various religions may view their traditions and beliefs. While it may seem that religious knowledge is being privileged to a high position in the levels of interpretation, it could just as easily be pointed out that religious knowledge is being relegated to an appendix of thought.

Hick's description of religious faith is one part of a general epistemology. All knowledge involves interpretation. The levels of interpretation are to do with the complexity of the subject matter and the degree of variation in human responses.

At the level of natural knowledge most people would share a common view of what mushrooms kill and what weather may be predicted from cloud formations. There is little scope for pluralism in matters of natural knowledge.

The second step of interpretation is that of finding moral significance in the world: 'It is characteristic of mankind to live not only in terms of the natural significance of his world but also in the dimension of personality and responsibility.'[9] The second step of interpretation places the natural world in a framework where we feel responsibility. The world is not simply bricks and bodies but a moral reality in which people should be treated in particular ways. To see a person lying in the road bleeding from an injury may only be an interpretation at the level of natural significance. However, to respond to that person with empathy and feel the obligation to supply help is to take the second step of interpretation. We see the moral significance of our situation. Of course, there are people who lack this moral sensitivity. Some may respond differently to the situation but still consider themselves to be acting morally. Perhaps they are a soldier and the body is that of an enemy and they are in a dangerous situation. They ignore the victim and continue their mission. We would not call the soldier immoral. They are still exercising moral judgement but in a context that must weigh up other considerations. However, other people simply lack moral capacity. We consider them mentally ill if they really feel no empathy or responsibility in such circumstances.

An important difference between natural and moral interpretation is the extent to which the interpretation we make is voluntary. The natural level gives little room for variation. The ethical level allows scope for diverse responses. There is more room for variation of opinion and feelings. This difference is magnified when we take the third step of interpretation and consider religious faith.

The religious interpretation of the universe rests on those steps that preceded it. The religious significance of reality is mediated through the natural and ethical significance that we already respond to. Hick calls this third step a 'total interpretation' of reality.[10] It is the step in knowledge where we make sense of everything we know according to one unifying theme. At this stage in his thought, writing *Faith and Knowledge*, Hick works with an explicitly Christian position that we know will be heavily qualified as his work progresses. So at this early stage he describes the religious significance of the universe in theistic terms. Hick describes the religious believer taking the third step this way: 'His interpretative leap carries him into a world which exists through the will of a holy, righteous and loving Being who is the creator and sustainer of all that is.'[11]

The use of the word 'leap' here is illuminating. Each step of interpretation is an increasingly voluntary act. As the moral interpretation implies greater cognitive freedom (do you consider this an act of murder or self-defence?), so the religious interpretation will involve greater freedom still. It is not evidence that compels us to make the religious response, but a leap of faith. Climbing this epistemological staircase requires more freedom of choice and less compulsion. At the final step, religious faith, is an uncompelled act of human response to an awareness of the existence of a divine being. It is much more like a leap than a step.

The Hidden God

In Hick's later work this divine being would be described in ways compatible with any of the major world religions and eventually taken out of a theistic context. However, the basic epistemology would remain unchanged. Religious faith is the total interpretation of the physical world and the ethical demands on life in the light of the experience of a divine reality.

Why is the religious dimension of life not clearer? Why is the existence of God not more akin to the existence of a mountain or a goat? The essential theme is that of the personal and ethical character of God. God and people share the ability to be in moral relationship. The grounds of any loving relationship must be uncompelled. So for God and humanity to enter into personal relationship, faith must be uncoerced: 'If man is to be personal, God must be *deus absconditus*. He must, so to speak, stand back, hiding himself behind his creation, and, leaving us the freedom to recognise or fail to recognise his dealings with us.'[12]

Hick claims that the only alternative to this *deus absconditus* would be a manipulative God who would coerce men and women into faith. The natural world is coercive in the sense that there is little variation in our possible interpretations of nature. However, people respond to the divine dimension in a wide range of ways. The reason is that God 'desires, not a compelled obedience, but our uncoerced growth towards the humanity revealed in Christ'.[13] Hick provides a theological reason for the uncompelled nature of faith. It is because of God's desires and intentions. The purpose of God is also explained in very christocentric terms: to make us more like Christ. At this stage of Hick's work we can see a clear commitment to a Christian theological framework and yet a view of religious knowledge that will be very open to engaging with religious pluralism.

Hick uses Wittgenstein's work to coin his own term 'experiencing-as' to describe the way reality is shaped by the human response.[14] Various factors influence the way an event or person is experienced. Whatever those factors may be, some will experience reality as mediating the existence of a divine being. However, because the divine being has no interest in compelling such a response we cannot expect to find some single argument or piece of evidence that will clinch the argument for or against the existence of God.

This leads to the obvious and important question: how do we know that there is a God? Critics could easily suggest that experiencing reality as religious simply reveals the imaginative disposition of the believer and has no bearing on whether there is a God or not. Hick does have a response to this challenge. We will consider this response in terms of his early work but also make reference to much later writings where Hick continues to defend the reliability of religious faith. The interesting point is that the enlargement of his thought to encompass religious pluralism really has little bearing on his basic epistemology.

6

A Faith for All People

We have already seen Hick's commitment to a realist account of religious language. His proposed 'eschatological verification' was an attempt to establish that believers, whether right or wrong, were certainly intending to say something about that objective reality. But can one show that the claims of the religious believer not only intend to communicate objective truths but also can be demonstrated to be likely or plausible? At this early stage in his work, Hick was not concerned with pluralism as such but only with the debate between atheists and theists. Hick was very familiar with the various arguments for the existence of God but doubtful of their validity.

The Probability of God

Whatever evidence is used, arguments for the existence of God are usually presented in terms of probability. One common theistic argument is based on apparent design. The appearance of the universe suggests it is more likely the product of an intelligent designer than not. The claim is not that the apparent design of the universe proves the existence of God; only that it makes the existence of God more probable than not. An example of such a claim is found in the work of Richard Swinburne who describes rational belief as that which is 'rendered probable by [the] evidence'.[1] For a belief to be rational, according to Swinburne, it must have a probability closer to 1 than to 0 and/or a greater probability than its rivals. Given a number of factors, outlined by Swinburne, the probability of God existing is greater than the alternatives.

Hick always considered this approach dubious. His epistemology presents religious knowledge as a total interpretation of reality. It is not simply an interpretation of one bit of reality with which other bits can be compared. We do not have several universes which we might compare in order to establish whether this one is more likely the product of an intelligent designer. What we mean by the universe is the totality of all things, and Hick considers religious knowledge to be a total interpretation of the way the universe appears to us. There is nothing by which such a totality can be compared or measured by way of a probability argument. It is important to emphasize that Hick and Swinburne are using very different definitions of faith.

However, Hick's argument also works against the atheist case. Probability cannot be used against Christianity. It might be suggested that the scale of evil in the world weighs against the claim that the universe is the product of an intelligent designer. But this argument is equally faulty. We cannot compare the evils of this universe with the evils of another universe. Both theism and atheism are total interpretations of reality. The difficulty in deciding between them is not a lack of relevant information but a lack of any logical vantage point from which we could make the assessment. 'There is no objective measuring rod by which to compare the depths to which wickedness can sink with the heights to which goodness can rise, and so to balance the problem of evil, which challenges theism, against the problem of good, which challenges naturalism.'[2]

Neither the theist nor the atheist can settle their differences by appeal to objective arguments or evidence. Debates between such worldviews cannot proceed as if there were neutral ground but ultimately require the 'attempt to bring the other to see the universe as he himself sees it'.[3] For example, a theist might appeal to the evidential value of fulfilled prophecy or answered prayer. But the atheist may well dismiss this as a selective use of evidence. What about unanswered prayer or unfulfilled prophecy? The 'evidence' in these examples depends upon the voluntary choices of the believer in their interpretation of reality. The believer and the non-believer do not start with the force of the evidence but with an experiential awareness. Just as we might feel the moral urgency of a situation where we witnessed cruelty, so we might feel the religious significance of prayer. According to Hick what divides believer from non-believer is this area of epistemology. The consciousness of divine reality justifies the believer having faith. Similarly, though conversely, atheists may also be justified in their unbelief because they are not conscious of such a presence.

From Christian Faith to Religious Faith

Despite the radical developments in Hick's theology, we can clearly see that there is a basic consistency which runs through his work. Hick's account of faith provides an anchor for the substantial unity of his thought. The major revision that Hick makes to his work is to move from considering faith in specifically Christian terms to terms that are compatible with a plurality of religious traditions. He is able to make this shift with minimal effect on his view of faith. His epistemology was always open to this move towards the pluralist vision. In order to show this we can take note of the extent to which his early description of faith required Christian convictions. Having done this it will be obvious how easily he could dispense with those convictions in favour of a more general religious faith.

Hick defines faith as a human response to our environment which experiences the religious dimension. As a total interpretation of our surroundings it relates us to an objectively existing God: 'Enfolding and interpenetrating this interlocking mass of finite situations there is also, according to the insistent witness of theistic religion, the all-encompassing situation of being in the presence of God and within the sphere of an on-going divine purpose.'[4]

This description of faith is not only theistic but assumes a personal God with purposes of his own. Hick is also keen to stress his realist view of religious language. The God of faith is not simply 'the Divine' in some vague sense, but a personal being capable of purpose and presence. Hick emphasized this personal nature of God in his description of *deus absconditus*. God deliberately hides, as it were, to ensure our response is freely made.

Using the analogy of human relationships he contrasts the I–It relationship of natural knowledge with the I–Thou relationship of religious knowledge. True relationships with other people require that we no longer see them as an 'it' but as a 'thou' to whom we are responsible. The Divine Being is not an object for a discussion but a person to respond to. This description of theism is offered in an explicitly Christian framework.

Furthermore, this description of a relationship with God is rooted in an orthodox view of the incarnation. Hick affirms the assumption made in the study of the history of religions that religious development is evolutionary. In his early work the concept of a personal relationship with God lies at the height of this evolutionary development. The history of religion has been marked by 'gradual liberation' of individuals from the group mentality of primitive religion to a sense of the personal divine mind with whom we can have a loving, voluntary relationship.[5]

Hick points to the doctrine of the incarnation as the 'classic exemplification of this principle'.[6] Jesus Christ is the culmination of the gradual process in which God has revealed himself. 'In Christianity the catalyst of faith is the person of Jesus Christ. It is in the historical figure of Jesus Christ that, according to the Christian claim, God has in an unique and final way disclosed himself to men.'[7] At this stage Hick clearly maintains a christocentric description of faith. He is concerned with the historic figure of Jesus of Nazareth as the great exemplification of faith. He distinguishes two senses in which faith is related to Christ. There is faith *in* Christ, meaning the act of responding to Jesus of Nazareth as the Saviour. There is also faith *from* Christ meaning the act of interpreting the universe in the light of who Jesus is and what he claimed.

Hick also relates his epistemology to the doctrine of salvation. Classic Christianity has always maintained that, in some sense, we are saved by faith. Historic debates over the relationship between faith and works have sought to clarify this. Hick steps into these debates with his account of faith and knowledge.

While Christ's teaching on morality does include certain prescriptions for a holy life, nonetheless the purpose of morality is more than simple rule-keeping. Hick points out that Jesus levelled a critique against the religious establishment of the day, teaching that the 'kingdom is extended not merely by securing conformity of men's overt deeds' to the law 'but by changing people themselves'.[8] There is an integral connection between faith and works. Christian faith precipitates a radical transformation of life. Faith is not mere assent to a set of beliefs but a change of outlook. Hick's epistemology readily explains what is meant by saving faith. To experience the universe as the creation of the Divine Being is to be transformed in outlook and behaviour.

We have identified three features of Hick's early statement of his epistemology that are distinctively Christian. First, faith relates people to a personal God in an I–Thou relationship of love, presence and purpose. Second, faith is both exemplified by and made possible through Jesus Christ. Third, faith is revealed in a life transformed by the teachings of Christ.

Losing Christian Religion

However, the more general epistemology developed by Hick does not rely upon any of these distinctive Christian characteristics. They are the context in which Hick as a Christian pastor and professor sought to explain himself. As his pluralist theology developed he would be able to utilize the same epistemology to explain any religious tradition. At the outset of *Faith and Knowledge* Hick indicated that his Christian tradition had an illustrative role rather than a formative role in his epistemology: 'For this book is not a comprehensive treatment of the place of faith in the religions of the world, but only an essay on the epistemology of faith as it occurs in that form of religion which constitutes a live option for most of the participants in our Western stream of culture.'[9]

These opening remarks betray the priority of Hick's philosophy of knowledge over his theological convictions. He does not offer an epistemology that has been formed by biblical insights. Rather, he offers an epistemology that may be illustrated by biblical examples. The description of faith does not depend upon Christianity being true.

The relationship of the Christian faith to Hick's work is clearly illustrated by his use of Scripture. In a work of philosophy it is not necessarily a fault that a Christian author makes little or no reference to Scripture. Furthermore, a philosophical work may be shaped by the Christian world-view without citing Scripture. However, Hick does choose to use Scripture and, therefore, the way he does so is worth considering.

Hick quotes the Bible eighty-three times in *Faith and Knowledge*. Of these, eighty are found in the final part where he brings his theory to bear on Christian belief. Three quotations appear in the substantial body of the work where he seeks to develop his view of faith. This is not a criticism in itself, but it does reveal the relationship between theology and philosophy in his work. Hick is happy to cite Scripture as illustrative of the points he wishes to make. But his account of how we come to know God is based only on neutral, general categories of thought that will be acceptable to both the religious and non-religious.

What is particularly noticeable in this way of developing a theory of religious knowledge is how little time it has for claims of historical revelation. Other than the existence of Jesus, Hick has no real concern with supposed events in history. In fact, the real significance of Jesus is found in our response to him (whether historical or not) rather than in any specific historic issues surrounding his life. No adjustment would need to be made to the argument of the book even if all the gospel writers were shown to have been in error.

Hick's account of faith places the emphasis on immediate experience of the universe rather than a response to historic events. This is profoundly important, and may even been taken to indicate that from his first publication Hick was not describing Christian faith. Once again, Paul Helm shrewdly noted this in an early assessment of

Hick's epistemology: 'Though Hick's model of religious knowledge as cognition-in-experience *might* work for certain cases it is not appropriate as a model for religious belief as it operates in a historically-grounded religion such as Christianity.'[10] Hick's conception of the knowledge of God relies upon an experiential awareness of the divine rather than a response to historic revelation or miracles. So even at this stage in his work, Hick was not particularly concerned with matters that most Christians would consider of primary importance (1 Cor. 15:3–8). The historicity of the exodus, life of Christ and resurrection are only instances of ideas that prompt faith. They are not uniquely formative for faith.

Can We Be Sure of Our Faith?

Hick's much later, comprehensive explanation of the pluralist world-view, *An Interpretation of Religion*, clearly builds upon this epistemology. No great amendment needs to be made to the view of faith found in *Faith and Knowledge*. In fact, it is more accurate to say that Hick's later work simplifies his epistemology to his logical essence. The Christian superstructure is stripped away to reveal its foundations – a view of faith that is unconnected to any historical or traditional particulars.

Hick continued to maintain that the universe is religiously ambiguous. There is no historical or logical proof that can decide the issue of the existence of God. This ambiguity is not peculiar to religion but is part of the very structure of human knowledge. We are never able to get beyond or outside the way things appear to us. So our understanding of the universe is always shaped by the meaning we impose upon it. Therefore, the Christian believer is not able to claim that God exists but only that they experience the universe as the creation of a loving, personal deity.

There is one test of beliefs that we can employ. Belief inspires behaviour. Our interpretation of the universe will inspire appropriate behaviour. This is true at the level of our interpretation of natural significance. At this lower level, the physical world around us still depends upon our subjective interpretation. We cannot claim objective knowledge as if we were able to step outside our minds. However, this physical level of interpretation is subject to obvious physical testing. If the behaviour our beliefs inspire leads to successful living in the physical world we have good reason to trust our interpretation. Take the example of edible and inedible food. Beliefs about what mushrooms are edible and which are toxic is clearly something that will be tested in behaviour. We might be free to choose to believe all kinds of things about mushrooms and never be sure that our beliefs are correct. However, eating certain types of mushrooms will cause sickness or death. In this way, there is only a very narrow range of parameters regarding what might constitute a viable interpretation of the natural world. 'Thus at this level our cognitive freedom is minimal; the physical world compels us to interpret its signals correctly and to live in it in terms of its real meaning for beings such as ourselves.'[11]

Our interpretation of the universe cannot be the product of guesswork or imagination alone. Interpretations arise from experience and are tested by experience. Experience is the key factor in knowledge and Hick's epistemology relies upon the crucial role of present experience in shaping religion.

As we have seen, Hick introduced the term 'experiencing-as' into the second edition of *Faith and Knowledge*. It was a clarification of his thought rather than a revision. Hick modifies Wittgenstein's expression 'seeing-as', in order to apply the concept more broadly. What Wittgenstein had understood as a moment of experience, Hick applied as a more general description of experience. There is ambiguity in even the simplest natural situation, but we do not notice it because the subconscious processes of the mind actively deal with that ambiguity. This is as true of natural knowledge as it is of religious knowledge. The critic may try to give the impression that faith is a special case of belief. Usually, this impression is given in order to dismiss faith in God as a leap of faith, lacking evidence. Hick's epistemology emphasizes the role of faith in all knowledge. Faith is not a special case of belief. All knowledge must be based on experience, whether we call it religious faith or natural knowledge.

The difference between natural knowledge and religious knowledge is found in their degree of ambiguity. The universe compels certain natural beliefs. The universe does not compel religious faith. Therefore, for those who do have religious faith there are a range of different possible responses. Belief in the personal God of Christianity is only one of those possible responses. For Christians, Christ will be the object of their faith; other traditions have alternative foci. The world process is itself the object of Buddhist faith, open to reinterpretation as either the 'stream of life, death and rebirth' or 'in a radically different way it is Nirvana!'[12] Whatever the religious tradition, the same process is at work. An otherwise ambiguous reality, the universe as a whole, finds order and meaning through our personal interpretative faculties. A basic religious experience causes men and women to interpret the universe in those religious terms.

In Hick's early work, Christianity provided the primary illustrative material. In his later work he distances his argument from any particular tradition. His account of faith can be illustrated with reference to any religious tradition.

Freedom to Believe and Disbelieve

Religious traditions act as filters of reality. However different religious traditions may seem to be, they all have this basic function of helping us to interpret our experiences and live our lives in the light of a perceived supernatural dimension. Christianity is neither a unique nor a supreme example of such a filter.

Hick's epistemology ends up requiring the pluralist hypothesis. If we consider his three-step epistemology we can see that it points towards a diversity of religious interpretations. Each step of his epistemology assumed greater cognitive freedom. Only natural knowledge was compelled. Moral and aesthetic knowledge respond to more ambiguous aspects of reality. While there is remarkable consistency over what is perceived as beautiful or moral there is clearly still opportunity for greater diversity. This diversification increases at the level of religious reality. It follows that the diversity of the world religions is exactly what Hick's epistemology could be taken to predict.

In his early work, Hick gave a theological reason for this cognitive freedom. True personal relationships must not be compelled if they are to remain personal. Because God desires that men and women exercise their free will in choosing to love him, Hick describes God as 'hiding himself behind his creation'.[13] In his earlier work, this could be understood as part of his libertarian understanding of free will. God compels no one to believe. If God were to provide incontrovertible proof of his existence then this would amount to manipulation and coercion.

However, this line of reasoning is too dependent on the Christian tradition for Hick's later work. It assumes a loving, personal deity who has purposes in permitting uncompelled responses. In later work Hick broadens the religious ambiguity of the universe to include non-theistic traditions. He struggles to find ways to express the idea of cognitive freedom without assuming a personal divine being because 'It's easiest to make the point in theistic terms'.[14] His summary of the religious perspective on cognitive freedom in a final publication is that 'It is the teaching of each of the world faiths that the divine reality does not force itself upon us, but leaves space for an uncompelled response on our part'.[15]

According to Hick, arguments for and against the existence of God have only limited value in confirming the validity of religious experience. They prove nothing in public debate. The only compelling factor is the experience of the believer. Those who have it will believe, those who do not will refuse to believe, 'For any hint of transcendence meets a blank wall in a mind which automatically interprets everything in naturalistic terms.'[16]

Hick concedes that it is perfectly rational for the atheist to claim that 'the feeling of an unseen presence could all be hallucinatory in character'.[17] However, as an argument against religious experience it has little consequence because the reverse is also true. The feeling of the universe as devoid of supernatural significance could also be hallucinatory. The approaches of Freud and Durkheim to religion

attempted to explain religious development without making reference to any supernatural reality. However, each is a case of reductionism that depends 'upon a prior naturalistic conviction'.[18] In a mirror
image of the believer's experience, the naturalist already has a sense
of conviction about the way things are that determines his or her
interpretation of the evidence. Hick concludes that these arguments
over the existence of God or the supernatural cannot negate the basic
ambiguity of the universe. Most people may have convictions that
they find personally compelling, but no one can claim to know the
absolute truth about the religious significance of the universe. The
universe is open to interpretation because it does not compel a religious interpretation. 'It seems, then, that the universe maintains its
inscrutable ambiguity. In some respects it invites, whilst in others it
repels a religious response. It permits both a religious and a naturalistic faith, but haunted in each case by a contrary possibility that can
never be exorcised.'[19]

This fundamental ambiguity means that there can be no absolute
certainty that the universe has any religious significance at all. Perhaps
it is no more than a closed causal system of physical processes. The
choice between theism and atheism is primarily driven by personal
experience. This ambiguity provides the basis for Hick's approach to
the world religions. Indeed, Hick's epistemology leads us to expect
religious pluralism. If we cannot be sure if the universe has religious
significance how much less certain should we be of any particular
religious interpretation? A plurality of religious interpretations is inevitable given the ambiguity of the universe.

This description of faith might lead us to simply describe Hick as
an agnostic. Certainly, the impression is given that matters of faith
should be held lightly, given our radical uncertainty. But this is not
quite fair. To understand why, we need to consider a distinction that
Hick draws between his work as a philosopher and his life as a believer.

7

Sceptical Faith

Christianity and Commitment

Hick was an active practitioner in religious life. He engaged directly in interfaith groups' concerns with issues of social justice and racism. He served as an ordained minister, preached sermons and practised various forms of prayer and meditation. In 2009 he became a member of the Religious Society of Friends (Quakers). Was Hick any longer a Christian in any recognizable sense? That question is outside the scope of this book but at this point it is more appropriate to consider whether Hick was an agnostic. His epistemology certainly suggests such a description.

There is a distinction between Hick's philosophical description of faith and what he describes as the experience of faith. Philosophically, the universe is religiously ambiguous. However, our experience of the universe as either religiously significant or not can be overwhelming. That is why religious convictions can be so strong. The universe just seems to be that way.

We need to be able to reflect on our faith at two levels. There is the direct, lived experience which for many will lead to their identification with a particular religion. Then there is a distinct, second-order reflection on that experience which Hick suggests should lead to his pluralist interpretation of religion. Hick claims that he has no desire that religious people should give up their personal confidence in the religion to which they belong. In fact, it is only possible to make sense of the religious feelings within a particular tradition. 'For whilst the objective ambiguity of our environment consists in the fact that it is capable of being interpreted in a variety of ways, its consciously experienced and actively lived-in character consists in its actually being interpreted as meaningful in a particular way which, whilst it operates, excludes other possible ways.'[1]

Hick's pluralist proposal requires that we understand our faith in two different ways simultaneously. Philosophically, we must accept that the universe is religiously ambiguous while emotionally or experientially we remain convinced that the universe is religiously unambiguous. This distinction explains how Hick could continue to maintain that he was both a practising Christian minister and a proponent of religious pluralism. As a Christian believer he could make use of theological and liturgical traditions to shape his experience. As a pluralist philosopher he could suspend those commitments and consider the phenomena of religion in strictly philosophical terms. Is such doublethink really possible? Hick remembers visiting the church where the Council of Nicea had met with a group who wished to publicly recite the Nicene Creed. Some did this in 'Greek, some in Latin, some in English, and some (including me) in inverted commas!'[2] Hick became a master of theology in inverted commas. Can a Christian have both a personal, experiential commitment while also holding a philosophical position that suspends such commitment? Hick believed so, and this must be attributed to the primary place given to philosophical description.

In Hick's thought, philosophy is the primary discipline. Philosophy determines and clarifies theological reflection. The pluralist hypothesis, being a philosophical position, is offered as an all-inclusive interpretation of particular patterns of religious belief and behaviour. It cannot be prevented from extending its interpretative range to explain the devotional life of believers. Philosophical conclusions arbitrate over the truth value of theological ideas or personal experiences.

For this reason, Hick comments that every religious tradition should re-evaluate itself in the light of the pluralist proposal, 'It is for the adherents of each of the great traditions to look critically at their own dogmas in the light of their new experience within a religiously plural world.'[3] No religious tradition is left untouched. The Buddhist, Muslim and Christian may continue their personal cultural practices but they must reinterpret the meaning of their faith in the light of Hick's philosophical insights. Thus for Christians it is their commitment to the uniqueness or superiority of Christ that must be reformed in the light of pluralism.[4]

A good example of this is found in the theological thought of Raimon Panikkar. Attempting to relate his convictions regarding Christ to his empathy for other religions he writes, 'Christ is the only mediator, but he is not the monopoly of christians and, in fact, he is present and effective in any authentic religion, whatever the form or the name. Christ is the symbol, which christians call by this name, of the ever-transcending but equally ever-humanly immanent Mystery.'[5] Panikkar's reinterpretation of Christ transforms him from a unique person to a universal symbol. Likewise, Hick reformulates theology in the light of a very different perspective.

Philosophy determines theology. Hick's resolution of the tension between personal religious convictions and the religious ambiguity of the universe is to place those convictions in a new context. Religious commitments must be suspended in favour of a more basic admission that religious pluralism is true and that our traditions have only relative value in helping us respond to an ambiguous reality. This suspension of commitment has led to Hick's position being usefully labelled 'transcendental agnosticism'.[6]

Is Hick agnostic? He always professed not to be. His defenders point out that he remained a practising Christian, albeit of a very liberal wing, to the end of his life. Hick himself claimed to believe that there is a transcendent Ultimate Reality that is the real ground of human religious experience. However, all these protestations do not really negate the primary role of his epistemology. Hick's view of religious knowledge is that we can have no absolute certainty regarding religious reality. We can be very confident in our experience. We cannot be confident in the reality to which we think that experience points.

We can identify the kind of agnosticism that best describes Hick's position by considering a philosophical tradition called scepticism.

This philosophical school of thought has had a long tradition in western culture and its similarities to Hick's approach to religion are instructive.

The School of Scepticism

Terence Penelhum surveys the tradition of scepticism from its origins in ancient Greek philosophy, taking 'Pyrrhonian' scepticism as the classical example. This school sought to demonstrate that there simply is no clinching argument in favour of any dogmatic convictions. In particular, the certainty with which rival Greek schools of Epicureans and Stoics held to their doctrines was not justified. According to the sceptics, such certitude is not possible because of the 'incapacity of human reason'.[7] The chief purpose of the sceptic movement was to help people recognize the limitations of human reason. Beliefs are the product of probabilities and none can be held with dogmatic certainty.

However, the sceptics did not simply leave their followers in a state of intellectual doubt. The Greek sceptics presented their ideas as a practical philosophy. Penelhum describes the sceptic as a philosopher who, while doubting everything, nonetheless lived in conformity to cultural norms, though 'in an undogmatic, or uncommitted, or belief-less way'.[8] The sceptics had a practical view of needing to live within the conventions of Greek society while simultaneously holding an intellectual position that doubted such conventions. There are habits of life that help one to live as if a range of presuppositions were true, even though – at a theoretical level and in philosophical discussion – one must admit that such certainty really has no foundation at all.

Hick did not acknowledge a direct connection between his pluralist thesis and the methodology of the sceptics but a comparison of those methods demonstrates how similar their approaches are. Penelhum describes the method of the classical sceptics of ancient Greece in these terms:

The Sceptic will assemble all those arguments that Dogmatists have used to show that it not only appears that *p*, but really is, and then will assemble all the arguments that contrary-minded Dogmatists have used to show that even if it appears that *p*, it is not; this assemblage will bring upon him an incapacity to judge either that *p*, or that not-*p*. This will not make it cease to appear to him that *p* . . . but it will enable him to live with his fellows who insist that *p* by conforming in his actions to their beliefs without affirming them.[9]

Hick and the sceptics both develop a world-view based on methodological doubt whereby no particular proposition can be held to be entirely certain. This is because of Hick's distinction between reality as it is really is and reality as it appears to us. The practice of setting arguments for *p* and for not-*p* against each other is a simple way of undermining confidence in absolute truth. Exactly such an approach is found in Hick's description of arguments for and against theism and naturalism.[10] The data is ambiguous. We cannot be confident whether theism or atheism is true. We cannot be confident that one religious tradition is more reliable in its description of divinity than another. There are strengths and weaknesses in all the options. Therefore, we must suspend judgement on ultimate reality.

How then should we live? Hick shares with the sceptics a common approach to life. While suspending judgement on the validity of any given world-view, from day to day one must live in the light of a particular world-view. For practical reasons, the chosen world-view is highly likely to be that of parents or peer group. It is a practical decision to live as if a particular religious tradition were true.

Obviously, the sceptical insight that the universe is ambiguous and that we can be certain of nothing cannot leave that particular tradition unchanged. While the sceptics might have chosen to live with the same cultural conventions as their dogmatic Greek neighbours, they clearly held to those conventions much more lightly. The sceptics would hold the beliefs of their peers or culture but 'disinfected' of 'those specious underpinnings of belief and valuation that have given it meaning'.[11]

The sceptics had come to realize that there was no way of knowing what was certain or true. But nor was such knowledge necessary to a contented life. Penelhum uses the term 'quietude' to describe the kind of conformity to tradition practised by the sceptic. The sceptics doubted the truth of their tradition but peaceably conformed to it. Given that we can never know ultimate reality, why bother disputing what that ultimate reality might be?

Hick makes a similar claim regarding the way we should hold our religious commitments, given the religious ambiguity of the universe. In the wake of his Copernican revolution, Hick continued to claim to be a Christian and follow Christian practices, but only because they help one to live in an appropriate way, not because Christianity gives some direct knowledge of the world beyond appearances. For a pluralist, creedal confessions may be professed but only as poetic or liturgical expressions of commitment to a certain way of life. We recite creeds in inverted commas. Like the sceptic, Hick presses for a kind of 'quietude' in religious life where believers should be encouraged to live in conformity with the tradition of their culture without believing that this tradition gives direct insight into the nature of ultimate reality.

Coercion and Tolerance

A significant motive for Hick's development of his philosophical position was the need to resolve interfaith tensions. Hick came to these disputes and rivalries with an epistemology that already defused their significance. In his earliest work there were theological reasons for Hick's belief that a personal God permitted great cognitive freedom. If God wanted a genuine relationship with the human race then he would not coerce them to believe. No historical proofs, logical arguments or claimed miracles could provide absolute evidence. Only in the light of prior commitments would the experience of miracles be taken as proof by the believer. Hick already had an epistemology of religious faith that relativized religion. God would permit religious diversity because he would compel no one to believe.

Penelhum pointed out that Hick's approach to coercion is mistaken. Hick confuses 'having the truth made clear to one with being shattered into submission'.[12] Having the truth made clear to one (for example, through reason, revelation or miracles) removes any grounds for reasonable doubt, but does not restrict human freedom. Any human subject is free to reject those evidences. It may be true that such behaviour is irrational, but this is irrelevant because even acting irrationally would still be an exercise in cognitive freedom. Whether belief is free or not is a separate issue from whether we find the evidence compelling or not. Paul Helm also argues against Hick's use of freedom in this regard: 'Another alternative is to believe in God, and to obey God because it is thought that there are good grounds for believing in and obeying him. And if someone has good grounds (as he thinks) this need not imply that this obedience is compelled either in the sense that it is heteronomous or that it is accompanied by feelings of compulsion or constraint.'[13]

Helm points out the crucial distinction between the negative sense of compulsion and the feeling someone may have that the grounds for believing in God are overwhelming. Even if we believe because of the weight of evidence we are still acting freely and remain responsible for our beliefs.

The Freedom of Christ

Can we be freely compelled to believe? Ironically, Hick provides a good example of such free but 'coerced' faith in his description of Christ. Despite the dramatic revisions in his Christology, a clear pattern emerges in his description of what kind of faith Jesus had. In his early work we read, 'For in whatever manner Jesus first impressed his disciples – whether as wonder-worker, as a teacher, or as a magnetic and numinous personality – the outstanding fact about him, which soon gripped them, was his sheer moral goodness and purity, his total lack of concern for himself and the absolute dedication of his life to his heavenly Father's purposes.'[14] In this description of Jesus, Hick uses the words 'sheer', 'total' and 'absolute' to stress the quality of his faith. This was a man consumed with the sense of God's existence and purpose. There is no suggestion that Jesus had come to make a reasonable choice in response to an otherwise ambiguous universe. Such a characterization of Christ continues in Hick's contribution to *The Myth of God Incarnate*. Here he describes Jesus as 'intensely and overwhelmingly conscious of the reality of God'.[15] Again, Hick is not describing someone exercising cognitive freedom, but someone 'overwhelmingly conscious'. In a last attempt to retain a broadly orthodox Christology, Hick sought to explain the oneness of God and Christ as a metaphor for the identification of the will of Jesus with divine reality. He describes the relationship between God and Christ as 'analogous to that in which the radiating energy of the sun "causes" the falling of its rays upon the earth's surface'.[16] Again, the emphasis is upon the overwhelming sense of God in the life of Jesus. It does not seem that Jesus was freely responding to an ambiguous situation.

By the time Hick wrote *An Interpretation of Religion* he no longer needed to try to defend any form of orthodox Christology. However, he still maintained a high view of the intensity of the religious experience of Jesus. Placing him alongside a number of other significant holy people in various religious traditions, Hick notes that for Jesus 'it was entirely rational to believe that God is real; and indeed that it would have been irrational on his part not to'.[17] The faith of Jesus, which should inspire our own, was not a freely given response to an ambiguous universe. In the much later work, *The Metaphor of God Incarnate*, we find a very strong description of the coercive nature of his religious experience: 'From the point of view of the psychology of religion we can say that only an extremely intense God-consciousness could have sustained Jesus' firm prophetic assurance and charismatic power. The heavenly Father was utterly real to him – as real as the men and women with whom he interacted every day or the Galilean hills among which they lived.'[18]

This description of the faith of Jesus raises some interesting problems for understanding Hick's epistemology. According to this description, the reality of God was no different to Jesus than the reality of the hills. We noted that a primary distinction between natural knowledge and religious knowledge is that more religious matters are less compelled and permit greater variation. In *Faith and Knowledge* Hick provided a moral justification for this distinction – God did not want to overrule our freedom to choose.[19] This implies that the response of Jesus, along with other 'great saints', does not have the moral quality of religious faith. It was more akin to natural interpretation. Elsewhere, Hick even describes the faith of Jesus as 'involuntary'.[20]

Hick's treatment of faith and certainty are inconsistent. This is demonstrated in his descriptions of the faith of Jesus. He commends the faith of Jesus as the exemplary model for Christians and yet the faith of Jesus is the product of compulsion. Jesus, were he the only figure in history to have had a faith like this, would still be the example that disproves Hick's own account of uncompelled faith. Furthermore, Jesus is not unique according to Hick but only one of a number of holy people who shared this kind of faith. This 'great cloud of witnesses' demonstrate that there is nothing inconsistent about free moral agents having religious faith even though compelled to do so by reason, revelation or miracles. Compulsion in these examples does not imply being violently forced to believe. This is Penelhum's point that Hick confuses being shattered into submission with seeing the truth clearly. There is no incompatibility between compulsion and freedom: we are responsible for our choices and beliefs even if we are compelled to believe them.

Reasons to Believe

Hick provided some very thoughtful explanations of various arguments for and against theism. Throughout his life he retained a strong interest in the evidential value of near-death experiences. However, Hick maintained that faith is justified only through personal, compelling religious experience. In his contribution to *Arguments for the Existence of God* Hick observed that religious beliefs do not normally arise from speculative rational arguments or logical proofs: 'The claims of religion are claims made by individuals and communities on the basis of their experience.'[21] Therefore, it is somewhat beside the point to test the rationality of a person's belief on the basis of proofs or logical reasons. Rather, the appropriate test would be whether the experience of a believer is strong enough for them to be justified in what they believe.

Clearly, most people do not claim the kind of vivid, unrelenting religious experience attributed to Jesus. Therefore, how can ordinary believers be justified in basing their religious outlook on experience which is probably much more fleeting and ambiguous?

Hick uses a parity argument in response to this by showing that religious experience is analogous to sense experience. Classical sceptics had denied that sense experience could provide a basis for certainty. How could we ever really show with absolute assurance that our experience of the physical world provided a true picture of what the physical world is? Whether it was Plato's metaphor of the cave, or Descartes' suggestion that the world we experience might be the product of a deceiving demon, thinkers had always wrestled with this most basic question. The sceptics had denied that we could find certainty but instead proposed living life on the assumption that our experience was reliable.

Hick follows the work of the later Scottish sceptic, David Hume,[22] in conceding that there can be no theoretical guarantees that our sense experience is reliable. Hick agrees with Hume's claim that belief in an objective world of space and time was not the product of philosophical reasoning but an example of what they both call a natural belief. Hick and Hume both appeal to natural beliefs in order to overcome otherwise sceptical conclusions about the reliability of our experience. The solution to this scepticism is to admit the limitations of our theoretical knowledge and accept the cultural norms or common sense of our culture as natural beliefs.

Hick highlights two features of sense experience that encourage us to trust it. The first is its involuntary nature – it is so compelling that we feel unable to resist it. The second is the practical advantage it gives us, living on the assumption that sense experience is reliable.

If we live on the basis that our sense experience is reliable then we are able to 'act successfully' in the world.[23] Taken together, these two features provide ample reason for people to trust their basic experience of the natural world even without any convincing, logical arguments.

Religious experience is, for many, of a sufficiently compelling quality that it would seem reasonable to trust its reliability. It may possibly even be so compelling that it would seem insane not to trust it. For such rare individuals (such as Jesus or the Buddha), 'he is no more inclined to doubt its veridical character than to doubt the evidence of his senses'.[24] But what of those whose experience is not so strong?

Justified Ordinary Belief

In *An Interpretation of Religion* Hick uses the principle of credulity in his account of religious knowledge. The principle is that, given no obvious countervailing considerations, one should trust that how one perceives things is the way they really are. Countervailing considerations might include the amount of alcohol recently consumed, the effects of drugs, or the brevity of the experience. While these are difficult to quantify, such factors at least bring our experience into question. However, if such countervailing considerations are not present, then, according to the principle of credulity, not to trust our basic perceptions would be insane.

The principle of credulity readily applies to the great religious leaders or saints who seem to have had an overwhelming experience of transcendent reality. Does it also apply to ordinary believers? Hick acknowledges that anyone who does not have compelling religious experience 'cannot have the same justification for belief as those who do'.[25] Hick considers two different kinds of ordinary believer. There are those who have no religious experience of any significance. For them, their faith probably depends upon the faith that they are impressed by in the lives of others. The faith of saints expressed in their moral and spiritual fruit could generate a kind of secondary, or dependent, religious experience.

The second kind of believer are those who do have a religious experience but it is much less intense, no more than a 'remote echo' of the kind of experience described by the great saints.[26] These remote echoes may come in the form of moments of heightened awareness but they are sporadic and less compelling. Even though such ordinary belief is less solidly grounded they provide enough reason for belief.

According to Hick, faith is always justified by some form of experience. In effect there are three levels of experience that can justify belief. The first is being impressed by the claims of someone else who has a religious experience. The second is to have personally had momentary but significant peak experiences. These experiences would tend to be taken as confirmation of the more profound experiences that others have had. The third, strongest, level is that of the great saints or religious founders themselves whose religious experience is continuous with their experience of the natural world. While each level varies in the extent to which it provides grounds for reasonable belief, nonetheless each level provides enough reason to justify belief. Hick rests his case for the rationality of faith on the personal experience of the believer. Whatever the intensity, faith is justified by experience.

There are two particular features of Hick's account of justification which make his epistemology amendable both to his earlier orthodox Christian phase and his later pluralist vision.

First, Hick's description of experience is *individualist*. A religion as a whole is not the subject of justification. It is the personal, or private, faith of the believer. Therefore, one can marginalize the significance of a religion; what matters is the intensity of the personal experience of the believer. This description can readily incorporate the Buddhist, Muslim or Christian. The intensity of their personal experience is what counts, not the credibility of the confessions and claims of their religious tradition.

Second, Hick's description of experience has *minimal content*. It is largely an account of a quality of experience rather than an account of the content of experience. His use of such expressions as the 'divine presence' or 'limitless goodness' to identify the content of religious experience is deliberately vague. So little can be expressly said regarding the content of religious experience that Hick is easily able to extend his epistemology from Christianity to incorporate any of the major world religions.

I would contend that the view Hick expressed in his first published volume inevitably led to his pluralist vision of the world religions. The Christian faith certainly provided the context for his formation as a theologian and philosopher. However, that Christian faith was never more than illustrative of his fundamental convictions about the nature of religious belief.

I now want to explore further the origins of Hick's approach to religion and demonstrate that religious pluralism, as defined by Hick, is simply the fruit of the Enlightenment approach to religion. The success of his proposal is really the success of a revolution in modern thought that happened three centuries ago. It only appears to be a dramatic new proposal when it is contrasted with Christian orthodoxy.

When we unpack the implications of Hick's epistemology we can see that it is the inevitable consequence of Enlightenment thought. In order to make this case we will outline the theological work of Immanuel Kant. Interestingly, it was Kant who set himself the task of responding to the sceptical challenge of Hume and providing justification for practical religion even in the absence of proof. Hick was pursuing the same aim. He also concedes Hume's sceptical point and tries to find a way forward from it using a strategy much like that of Kant. Kant's epistemology, though elaborated by him at far greater length and complexity, is essentially of a piece with that of Hick's. Once we have shown how Hick fits into the intellectual development of the early Enlightenment we will be much better placed to assess the pluralist proposal and make a response.

8

Immanuel Kant and Religious Knowledge

It is hard to overestimate the influence of the German philosopher, Immanuel Kant, on western thought. Born in 1724, he describes himself being shaken by the philosophical scepticism of David Hume. In the light of Hume's radical suggestions, Kant came to believe that much of philosophy and theology was far too speculative. Instead, he argued that all knowledge is shaped by pre-theoretical concepts of the mind. However, beyond his work in epistemology Kant made important contributions to astronomy, ethics and the philosophy of mind. A key figure in the Enlightenment, Kant developed his own theology in the light of a new age of reason.

Kant's philosophy has always exercised a degree of influence on Hick's thought. This influence became more explicit over the course of his lifetime's work. Very little of Kant's primary sources are cited by Hick but that makes the significant overlap even more striking. Hick himself claimed only to be using Kant's insights in epistemology but the more we compare their work the more we see that they both shared the same view of religion. Hick distanced himself from this claim, partly because he was not a scholar of Kant, 'I have only borrowed from Kant his basic noumenal/phenomenal distinction, and am well aware that his own epistemology of religion is very different from that which I am recommending.'[1] However, as we outline more broadly Kant's treatment of religion the similarities become very clear. This probably is simply a reflection on the fundamental nature of their epistemology. Given the view of faith and knowledge held by both Kant and Hick, it is inevitable that they share a common view of the nature and limitation of religion.

Kant's Abiding Influence

In his early work, Hick rejected Kant's claim that God and immortality were only postulates of reason. Kant held to a very intellectualist view of faith. Hick preferred to establish these beliefs on the basis of experience. He distanced himself from the intellectualism of Kant: 'For the purpose of our inquiry, the main comment to be made upon this Kantian theory is that it leaves no room for any acquaintance with or experience of the divine, such as religious persons claim.'[2] Rather than a postulate of reason, a very intellectual way of expressing it, God is a felt presence. Hick gave far more credence to experiential forms of religion than Kant ever did. However, in a later work Hick did appeal to Kant's explanation of morality as a way of justifying faith: 'To recognise moral claims as taking precedence over all other interests is, implicitly, to believe in a reality of some kind, other than the natural world, that is superior to oneself and entitled to one's obedience.'[3]

Hick shares Kant's conviction that the existence of God is indirectly justified by moral belief. Morality assumes a transcendent, objective reality that is not simply part of the natural order. This is the second stage in Hick's epistemology. The moral interpretation of reality moves beyond the natural stage and, along with aesthetic belief, paves the way for belief in supernatural reality.

Hick argued that this use of Kant's treatment of morality is one with which Kant himself would not have been unhappy. He believed that Kant's own thinking was developing in this direction and would have eventually brought him to a position not unlike Hick's own: 'in the later very fragmentary *Opus Postumum* Kant moved toward a different view according to which the experience of the moral law, instead of being treated as the basis for a theistic postulation, is thought of as in some manner mediating the divine presence and will'.[4] To place the emphasis on religious experience rather than on an intellectual presupposition would certainly have moved Kant's thought more in line with Hick's approach to religion. In practice, there is little evidence that Kant had such sympathy for religious experience. But it does remain the case that Kant and Hick share a conviction that moral awareness is a signpost to a greater dimension.

Hick affirms what Kant calls the 'categorical imperative' and described it as a high point in the German philosopher's work. Hick claims that in the imperative Kant has given a philosophical expression to Christ's golden rule, to do to others what we would wish done to us.[5] Kant used the 'categorical imperative' as a way of describing the self-justification of ethics – they do not need to be justified with reference to anything else. Hick describes this approach to moral reasoning as compatible with both Christianity and Buddhism. Kant's 'man of duty' who does things with no thought of personal reward is equivalent to the *arhat* of eastern thought.

Hick describes Kant's ethics as 'a useful stepping-stone to the more positive and mysterious things that are said about nirvana in the pali canon'.[6] The reference to the Pali canon is to the standard collection of Theravadan Buddhist scriptures in the Pali language. At first blush it seems so alien to the world of the New Testament with which Christians are familiar. Hick finds Kant to be helpful on this point because the categorical imperative is a way of describing ethical obligations that are neutral and not dependent on any particular religious tradition. True moral behaviour gives no thought to consequences and is done unconditionally, and this theoretical exposition of the core of moral belief requires no particular religious framework.

It is no surprise then, that Hick finds helpful parallels for his epistemology in the work of Kant. In particular, Kant's thought helps Hick to elaborate what he means by knowledge as interpretation. Hick has always stressed the role of interpretation in knowledge. His earliest work defined faith as an interpretative key in religious experience. However, his early statements of this theory did not explain why those interpretations stubbornly remain so diverse. In contrast, across the world today there is substantial agreement on the basic fruitfulness of the scientific method. In comparison, religious diversity appears embarrassing. Why should religious belief vary so wildly around the world? Why is there no apparent progress in belief? In this early work, Hick explained this with his stress on cognitive freedom. However, that explanation only referred to the choice between a naturalistic and a theistic interpretation. We could freely choose to interpret the world in the light of the existence of God or as devoid of such a being. This early work did not explain why there should be such a range of different non-naturalistic interpretations. The world does not divide into Christians or atheists or even theists and atheists. In a world of religious diversity the supernatural options seem endless. To explain this pluralism, Hick finds the key in another aspect of Kant's epistemology.

The basic argument of Hick's later statement of religious knowledge relies upon the crucial distinction between 'the Real *an sich* [as it really is] and the Real as variously experienced-and-thought by different human communities'.[7] Human communities create the religious traditions. They do not perceive the Real as it is but only as that experience is conditioned by the cultural context in which it occurs. Therefore, the Real as perceived is not the same as the Real that is not perceived.

The theoretical framework for this claim is provided by 'one of Kant's most basic epistemological insights', which Hick expresses in general terms as: 'the mind actively interprets sensory information in terms of concepts, so that the environment as we consciously perceive and inhabit it is our familiar three-dimensional world of objects interacting in space'.[8]

There is an active component in human knowledge. The mind does not passively receive sensory information from which to construct our view of the world. The empiricist thinker, John Locke, famously expressed a more passive view by describing the mind as 'white paper void of all characters' until written upon with ideas from experience.[9] According to Kant, the paper already has a form and shape. But nor is our view of the world only the product of the mind. Kant's genius was in recognizing the contribution of both the active mind and sense data in the creation of what we call knowledge. The characteristics of dimensional experience – time, space, substance, causality and so on – are all categories of the mind through which otherwise chaotic sensory information is ordered and given meaning for us. Therefore, we can still claim that there is an objective reality called the natural world while also admitting that we have no direct access to that reality. Our descriptions of reality are already shaped by our mental machinery. We only know the world as it appears to us.

Hick is well aware that he is describing only one, relatively simple, aspect of Kant's thought. He freely admits that his own application of Kantian epistemology is not one of which the eighteenth-century philosopher himself would necessarily have approved. Indeed, Hick claims that Kant was only articulating a principle which has always had a place in western traditions of thought. In some form it is discernible in Thomas Aquinas and the Muslim theologian, Al Junaid.

However, it would be misleading to imply that Hick was only drawing upon Kant for illustrative material. He is adopting a very specific Kantian insight, the distinction 'between an entity as it is in itself and as it appears in perception'.[10] The distinction, characterized as *noumenon* and *phenomenon,* assumes a fundamental limit to human knowledge. There is no direct knowledge of the divine. This distinction is formative for both Hick and Kant in understanding theology, as we will see. The connections between Hick and Kant are much more than a mere illustrative parallel.

The Pluralist Modification of Kant's Thought

Hick is concerned to apply Kant's insight to the third step of interpretation, religious knowledge. This is the stage in his three-step epistemology where Hick identifies the greatest cognitive freedom. Kant's principle helps to explain why there should be such diversity among the world's religions.

Hick makes an analogous use of Kant's insight to describe the Ultimate Reality as the *noumenon* and the actual beliefs and traditions of the religions as *phenomenon*. This is not how Kant applied his insight. For Kant, God was a postulate of morality. Moral behaviour assumes a divine order to reality. Hick places the emphasis on religious experience:

> For Kant God is postulated, not experienced. In partial agreement but also partial disagreement with him, I want to say that the Real *an sich* is postulated by us as a pre-supposition, not of the moral life, but of religious experience and the religious life, whilst the gods, as also the mystically known Brahman, Sunyata and so on, are phenomenal manifestations of the Real occurring within the realm of religious experience.[11]

Hick affirms the existence of God in the same way that Kant affirms the noumenon: it is the ground of phenomena. The existence of the Real explains the way things appear. Just as Kant takes the appearance of reality as an indicator that there is such a thing as an objective reality behind those appearances, so Hick understands appearances as pointing to the existence of God.

Despite Hick's emphasis on religious experience, God remains a postulate in his thought. Whatever the divine reality is, it can never be directly experienced. It is an intellectual assumption that helps us make sense of our subjective experience.

This point is not always evident when Hick's work is read as a coherent whole because, in his earlier writing, he was more comfortable describing the experience of God.[12] But, when considered in the light of the Kantian epistemology, there really is no such thing as the experience of God. There are experiences, from which we may infer an objectively corresponding reality. But we are not experiencing that reality, 'When we speak of a moral God . . . we are speaking of the Real as humanly experienced: that is, as phenomenon.'[13] It is easy to miss just how significant this point is. To use Kant's language, the 'moral God' of faith is itself *phenomenon*, not *noumenon*. When we discuss God, we are discussing an experience, not an objective reality.

Hick describes images such as the 'Creator God' or 'Heavenly Father' as the persona of the Real. It is this persona that is the object of our experience, not the Real itself. Many sympathetic supporters of Hick's work fail to see how profound this distinction is. We need to give Hick's account of God a little more consideration here.

The Real is not something that men or women ever experience. It is something postulated as the necessary explanation for religious experience. Despite Hick's own claims, it seems clear that the nou-menal Reality is just as much (and as little) a postulate for Hick as it was for Kant. The only difference between them on this point is that Kant describes God as a postulate of morality rather than of religious experience. However, even this difference is not significant. As we have already seen in Hick's three-step epistemology, religious experience is essentially moralistic: it includes, while transcending, the second step of moral interpretation. Religious experience is a kind of deeper appreciation of moral experience, rather than something wholly different.

The central theme running through Hick's later theory of knowledge and Kant's epistemology is the absolute divide between the Real *an sich* and the Real as experienced. For Hick this theme is particularly useful as it explains both why there should be a diversity of religions (pluralism simply reflects diverse experiences and personalities) and why religious people should accept those differences (there being no way of settling them). In a moment we will see why this is deeply problematic but first we can take further Kant's own expression of the phenomenon–noumenon relationship and its implications as a theory for our knowledge of God.

9

The Receding Real

Kant and the Sceptics

At first glance, John Hick's debt to Immanuel Kant seems limited. Kant provides a philosophical insight, not dissimilar to a theme found among the world religions, which justifies the pluralist position. However, as Hick's work progresses his position on the nature of God and the value of the world religions becomes increasingly vague. There is less and less that can be said about 'God' and less of any real significance to be found in the world religions. I want to show that this is because of Hick's commitment to Kant's epistemology. His theory of knowledge is much more than just a secondary philosophical theory. The Kantian insight is not simply an interpretation of religion, it is the obliteration of religion.

Kant was part of mainstream German rationalist thinking until he came across the work of David Hume who, in Kant's famous words, 'interrupted my dogmatic slumber'.[1] We have already considered David Hume as a representative of the sceptic tradition in philosophy. His treatment of causation brought to surface a fundamental problem in epistemology.

A simple example of causality is the heat we feel when we sit by the flames of a fire. Hume describes the relationship between the two as an example of a basic problem in epistemology. 'Thus we remember to have seen that species of object we call *flame*, and to have felt that species of sensation we call *heat*. We likewise call to mind their constant conjunction in all past instances. Without any farther ceremony, we call the one *cause*, and the other *effect*, and infer the existence of the one from that of the other.'[2]

Hume is like the child in the story of the emperor's new clothes. Everyone assumed the emperor was wearing fine new clothes because they were told that is what they should see. It took the honest boy in the crowd to point out that the emperor had no clothes. David Hume points out that there is no experimental evidence for the thing we call 'causation'. All that we can ever demonstrate is the constant conjunction of events and the natural habit of relating them to one another through the concept of cause and effect. Things happen at the same time. We might be able to provide explanations for why we think one thing causes another but that key little linking word, 'cause', can never itself be proven.

Hume applied this kind of analysis to many areas of thought and exposed the weakness of empiricism. Many of our most treasured beliefs are not based upon sensory evidence or experience, as empiricists thought, but rather on simple habits of the mind. Exactly what Hume wanted to make of this startling conclusion has been the subject of much debate. Mainstream interpretation of his work would label him a sceptic. Bertrand Russell accuses Hume of a kind of scepticism that represented the 'bankruptcy of eighteenth-century reasonableness',[3] and Hume certainly used rhetoric that provides ammunition for this kind of response. For example, Hume claimed that 'sceptical doubt arises naturally from a profound and intense reflection on those subjects, it always increases, the farther we carry our reflections' such that 'Carelessness and in-attention alone can afford us any remedy'.[4] The more we think, along Hume's lines, the more sceptical we become and the only solution is to not worry too much about it.

Natural Instinctive Knowledge

Norman Kemp Smith, another influence on Hick, broke the long tradition of interpreting Hume as a sceptic and, instead, emphasized the place of natural instinctive belief in forming knowledge.[5] It was while at Edinburgh University (1941–2) that Hick studied under

Kemp Smith and so we need to pause and consider this formative influence. Hick describes himself as 'deeply influenced by Kemp Smith',[6] though this influence is rarely directly cited in Hick's work. There is a single citation in *Faith and Knowledge* which suggests Hick's epistemology follows the same line of thought as his Edinburgh teacher. In *An Interpretation of Religion*[7] Hick makes a passing reference to the value of Kemp Smith's interpretation of Hume. It is intriguing that this insight will be another constant in Hick's work from his wartime studies at Edinburgh throughout his published career.

Kemp Smith saw in Hume not a call to classical scepticism but an admission that much of our knowledge is based on tradition and instinct. If this is correct, then the implications for religious faith are enormous, as Hick's career would demonstrate.

Hume's scepticism is to be understood as a methodological ploy to demonstrate the significance of commonsense habits of the mind. The significance of such instinctive natural beliefs is lost in the schools of empiricist and rationalist philosophy. Hume's rhetoric, often quite humorous, plays on the failure of philosophy to be able to provide a theoretical ground for our beliefs. There is more than one way of responding to Hume's challenge. However, the most sophisticated response must be that of Kant.

Kant understood the sceptical challenge posed by Hume's work and set himself the task of establishing new foundations for knowledge. Following Hume, Kant accepted the a priori status of many beliefs (such as causation). We already believe in causation before we begin to identify examples of cause and effect. So what theory could justify this acceptance that key beliefs are held a priori?

Hume had really set the problem for which Kant saw himself providing the solution. Kant contrasted his own work with that of Hume, who 'ran his ship ashore, for safety's sake, landing on scepticism, there to let it lie and rot; whereas my object is rather to give it a pilot, who, by means of safe astronomical principles . . . may steer the ship safely, whither he listeth'.[8]

In his response to Hume's apparent scepticism, Kant maintained that the mind was formed by a priori intuitions. For example, the notions or categories of space and time are intuitions. They are already present in the human mind when we experience things in space and time. Therefore, all reality already appears ordered by the mind in terms of location (space) and temporal sequence (time). Knowledge is simply impossible without the a priori contribution of these intuitions.

Kant drew up a list of the concepts of the human mind, which provide the framework in which all of our experience occurs. Kant's solution to Hume's scepticism was to affirm the subjective contribution of the human mind to knowledge, while also arguing for empirical realism. That realism was a basic presupposition of knowledge. The categories of the mind assume the existence of an objective reality. Thus, Kant must concede that there is a basic distinction between the way things really are and the way they appear to us. If we are to know anything at all, then certain a priori categories must be used which themselves assume an objective order of reality. There is no other path to knowledge. To know something is to use 'concepts which have their origin quite *a priori* in the pure understanding, and under which every perception must be first of all subsumed and then by their means changed into experience'.[9]

Religion and the Categories of the Mind

Hick makes analogous use of Kant's categories of the mind. Instead of using categories such as space and time, Hick considers the role of tradition and doctrine. These function in ways that are analogous to the categories of the mind because they provide the context for religious knowledge and experience. The analogy is far from perfect. After all, in contrast to the role of Kant's categories, doctrines or traditions may be adopted for a variety of reasons and be dropped or changed as time goes by. Unlike the categories, religious beliefs can be held with varying degrees of strength and conviction. Kant's categories are not like this because they are a priori and not dependent on experience. However, Kant's work still provides a useful picture for the way religion functions, at least according to Hick. But does this mean that Hick is simply borrowing a helpful illustration from Kant's work? I think the similarity of their work is much closer than this.

Kant and Hick share a commitment to a form of dualism at least in epistemology. There is a sharp divide between the world as it really is and the world as it appears to us in experience. The phenomenal world is ordered and comprehended by the active participation of the mind, while the noumenon is beyond direct comprehension. Phenomenon describes the world as it appears to us. Noumenon describes reality as it really is. We can never have access to noumenon and this suggests a form of epistemic dualism.

In his *Critique of Pure Reason* Kant sheds further light on the limits of human knowledge. Here he considers the possibility that there might be some sixth sense, perhaps a mystic sense of the noumenon. Such a sixth sense would provide direct knowledge by acquaintance. If this sense existed, then it would be a direct, unmediated experience of the noumenon as 'an object of a non-sensible intuition'.[10] Kant is really weighing up the possibility of direct experience which, if possible, would rule out such a dualism. In religious terms, it would allow for a direct experience of the divine reality.

However, Kant does rule out such a possibility. All objects are comprehended as part of sense experience. As experience is always shaped by the mind no direct acquaintance is possible. We have 'no intuition, indeed not even the concept of a possible intuition, through which objects outside of the field of sensibility could be given, and about which the understanding could be employed *assertorically*. The concept of a noumenon is therefore merely a *boundary concept*, in order to limit the pretension of sensibility, and therefore only of negative use.'[11]

It follows from this argument that the only things we can say about the noumenon are negative claims. We cannot say anything positive (what Kant calls *assertorically*) we can only say what the noumenon is not. In effect, the idea of the noumenon simply prevents anyone from taking the sceptical pathway to solipsism. The solipsist claims that there really is nothing beyond the figments of our imagination. Kant refuses to tread such a non-realist path in his epistemology. There is the noumenon. But we must remain agnostic about what that 'something' may be. Whatever noumena (plural) are, the understanding 'sets boundaries for itself, not cognizing these things through categories, hence merely thinking them under the name of an unknown something'.[12] As such a sentence betrays, it is not difficult to justify describing Kant as agnostic. Of course, what Kant means by 'noumenon' is not God, or even Hick's more abstract Real, but all of reality considered in itself apart from human experience. Nonetheless, Kant is agnostic regarding the nature of reality and this is a clear parallel to a form of theological agnosticism that develops in Hick's work.

Kant's epistemology offers two ways of describing reality. One reality is accessible and dependent on the active participation of the mind. The other reality is a conceptual hypothesis about which nothing can be said. The concept is a necessary assumption if we are to hold a realist epistmeology. We assume the noumenon in the experience of phenomenal reality. But this concept cannot be a subject for assertions.

Hick's pluralist thesis makes good use of this dualist view of truth. The noumenon is the postulate of the plural phenomena worshipped, adored or revered by the religious traditions. Such an analysis has great explanatory power. It can hold on to the existence of a divine being while also providing a simple way of explaining the great diversity of faiths. However, having established how close Hick's work is to that of Kant we can begin to see how significant objections to Kant's proposal then apply to the work of Hick.

A first concern is over the legitimacy of Hick's reading of Kant. This concern comes in various forms, and those well versed in Kant sometimes make the pretentious claim that Hick's use is too shallow. This seems to be the least interesting objection to Hick's use of Kant.

Terry F. Godlove makes a significant critique of Hick's use of Kant by pointing out that a pluralism of conceptual schemes was not something Kant envisaged and nor would it be compatible with Kant's epistemology.[13] Hick wants to use Kant's work to explain a diversity of conceptual frameworks, theist and non-theist. In contrast, Kant uses the fact that human beings share a largely common conceptual framework as part of the evidence that his epistemology is along the right lines. Godlove points out the universality of the Kantian categories – all people share them – and that this is demonstrated by the broad consensus in human experience.

It is true that this feature of Kant's work is passed over by Hick who wants to explain religious diversity, but it does not seem to be a fatal objection. Hick admits that he is modifying Kant's work for his own purposes. However, there is a second objection raised against Kant's own work which becomes even more problematic when Hick tries to use it in his case for pluralism.

The Grounds of Realism

Kant's epistemology has been subjected to much discussion and diverse interpretation. For the purpose of this book there is a crucial question asked of Kant's work which we can also ask of Hick. How can we really be sure that our language points towards something that is really 'there' and not just in the mind? Kant's answer will draw attention to the noumenon as a postulate for all knowledge. Nothing gets off the ground without our prior assumption that there is a noumenal reality to which we respond. For Hick, the Real does not have the same fundamental place – it is one thing among many things. Therefore, when we direct the problem at Hick's work it becomes even more pressing.

Critical realism makes the claim that there is an objective reality, discerned through the critical faculties of the mind. A fundamental problem is that the notion of objectivity itself cannot be known through experience and so must be a construction of the mind.

The implications of this point cannot be lightly avoided. There is nothing of any significance that we can say about the noumenon – not even that it exists. Kant describes the realm beyond appearances as 'empty (for us)',[14] as entirely abstract and unknowable. There is nothing that can be said about it.

Kant wants simultaneously to hold that there is something there and that we can say nothing about it. However, the thing-in-itself, when abstracted so completely from the possibilities of perceptual knowledge, loses all meaning and content. Its function then seems merely a sop to realism, which Kant needed in order to distance himself from the two extremes of solipsism and idealism.

But was it important for Kant to avoid such possible conclusions? Why not just abandon the notion of a real 'in-itself' altogether and turn instead to radical non-realism? In the area of philosophy there is an example of just such an approach in the work of Richard Rorty. In the area of theology one may add the example of Don Cupitt. Such thinkers demonstrate that such a position is at least possible. Hick remained a critic of Cupitt and is sensitive to the charge that he might be guilty of the same non-realist conclusions. Though Hick denies it, his dependence on the work of Kant certainly raises the suspicion that he is inevitably being drawn here.

Kant tried to resist non-realism, just as Hick would do in his own epistemology. However, the problem persists. George Schrader makes the insightful suggestion that Kant is inconsistent in his epistemology because of two rival forces at work in his thought. One force is the philosophical position that Kant develops through his major work, the three *Critiques*. The other force is Kant's precritical commitment to God and Christian pietism. According to Schrader this precritical outlook constantly bedevilled his philosophy.[15] It is more like a religious baggage that Kant must struggle to carry with him in his philosophical development. These two forces give rise to a basic inconsistency in Kant's work. In order to posit an objectively existing God he must apply the categories of pure reason beyond their proper boundaries so that they tell us something about the noumenon. 'One may posit the thing-in-itself as the cause of appearances which are known, but then one is guilty of extending the category of causality beyond the realm of appearances, a procedure which [Kant] had explicitly repudiated.'[16] The attempt to make any connection between God and the reality we experience founders on this fundamental problem.

It is absolutely inconsistent to claim that the noumenon is the cause of the phenomenal world if causality is only a category of the mind, and not something that belongs to the thing-in-itself. In what sense could the noumenon be said to 'cause' something if this category cannot be applied to things in themselves? Schrader argues that 'while Kant flatly declared that reality in itself is theoretically un-knowable, he could not escape trying to formulate meaningful theo-retical concepts of it'.[17] Hick faces the same fundamental difficulty as Kant. How can one ascribe features such as existence or personhood to the Ultimate Real? And how can one use the language of causation to connect anything we experience with the Real as its ground?

Nicholas Rescher attributes the inconsistency in Kant to a loose-ness in the way he formulates his ideas. Rescher distinguishes two ways in which Kant describes causation. On the one hand, there is '*authentic causality*, which is genuinely experientiable' and, on the other hand, '*generic grounding*, which is merely intelligible'.[18] Fol-lowing this distinction, Kant does not mean to imply that there is an authentic causal relationship between noumenon and phenomenon. Using Hick's vocabulary, the Real does not cause our experiences of the Real. Thus when Kant speaks of one 'affecting' the other he does not mean this in causal terms. Instead, it is a principle of 'Sufficient Reason' that 'controls what we must think to be case, rather than what we can claim to know regarding nature'.[19] Kant has undermined the objectivity of causation but must retain it for his epistemology to remain realist in any sense. Having denied that the category of cause can apply to the noumenon, he appropriates an alternative term, 'af-fecting'. Such verbal sleight of hand tries to magically hold on to causation but under another name.

The price of denying a causal connection between noumenon and phenomenon is a radical dualism, and the dualism implicit in Kantian thought leads inexorably to agnosticism but perhaps even to atheism. We cannot really say anything about reality itself, only about our experience of reality. These problems haunt the development of Hick's religious epistemology.

William L. Rowe applies these problems in Kant's work to Hick's distinction between the Real as noumenon and religious beliefs as phenomena. He asks what remaining ontological status can be claimed for phenomenal descriptions of the deity. Do they describe something that really exists? His answer points ahead to a conclusion Hick himself would resist: 'Although Hick does not commit himself,

I suspect that he thinks of them as analogous to "veridical hallucinations" – no such entities really exist, but the "appearances" are occasions of a salvation/liberation process in which human beings are transformed from self-centred to reality-centred beings.'[20] If Hick did commit himself to such a conclusion then his position would be no different from that of an atheist.

To be consistent with Kant's thought, phenomena cannot be described as 'real' because they are only ever constructions of the mind. They are formed in response to an unknown (and unknowable) reality. Thus Rowe seems entitled to describe Hick's phenomena as non-existent. Hick, following this consistent conclusion, ought really to deny the actual *existence* of God, Christ, Allah, Brahman, and so on. All he may consistently do is to postulate a Real about which nothing can be said. It is postulated as a useful way of explaining our 'veridical hallucinations' that make us believe in God.

To push the problem further, following Schrader, it must also be emphasized that there can be no causal connection between the Real and the appearances perceived by the categories of the understanding. Causation is a category of the mind and not something that we can ascribe to the noumenon. This conclusion is absolute non-realism. We can learn nothing about the noumenon from phenomenal appearances. The category of causation is not open to us. The Real cannot be meaningfully described as 'existing' or 'causing', because we have no epistemic grounds to apply such terms beyond phenomena. Hick's choice of a Kantian epistemology involves an implicit rejection of religious realism.[21] George Michalson directs his critical objection at the work of Kant, but it can readily be seen how it also applies to Hick:

[A] sudden reversion to the idea that God is the ground of the highest original good hardly mitigates the speculative difficulties he has introduced with these considerations. Certainly Kant cannot assume the relation between the world and God that animates the cosmological proof, even apart from his criticism of the proof itself. For he has himself eliminated the role of causality in this relation through his transcendental turn.[22]

Kant's use of the word 'ground', given the impossibility of causation, has only rhetorical force in the presentation of his ideas. This same problem besets Hick's work. Given an absolute rift between the categories of the mind and Ultimate Reality there is a profound problem in claiming to know anything whatsoever about the Real.

The Vanishing Point

If Kant's distinction between noumena and phenomena was difficult enough for his own great mind to sustain, it certainly runs into problems as Hick seeks to incorporate it into his pluralist view of the religions.

If the Real is truly and strictly beyond the categories provided by religion and culture, then nothing can be said of it and, as a result, it can only be a 'nothing' of which not even existence can be predicated. Furthermore, not only are the objects of religious devotion to be distinguished from the Real in-itself, but there is also no way of making any connection between those objects and the Real.

Hick often uses the expression 'manifestations of the Real' to describe the connection between the Real and phenomena but, owing to his underlying epistemology, the word 'manifestation' is emptied of meaning. Normally manifestation would imply a causal connection between the source of the manifestation and the resulting event or appearance. But causality is a category of the mind and not to be applied to the source of any such manifestation. This problem is particularly acute given Hick's dismissal of the possibility of revelation. Revelation is a form of manifestation of something otherwise hidden. The reasons why Hick rules out the possibility of revelation necessarily rule out the possibility of manifestation.

Hick responds to such criticisms by maintaining that while our concepts or doctrines do not apply to the Real, we may 'make certain purely formal statements about the postulated Real'.[23] Hick wishes to distinguish between formal and substantive claims about God, and must do this in order to sustain the pluralist hypothesis.

As Christopher Insole has argued, the distinction is incoherent.[24] Formal claims about God are dependent upon substantive claims. Without any substantial knowledge of God, we have no basis for any formal, logical claims about God.

Despite this problem, Hick claims to identify two formal statements that provide important information about the Real. Following Anselm, Hick affirms that the Real is 'that than which no greater can be conceived' and, following Kant, that the Real is 'the noumenal ground of the encountered gods and experienced absolutes witnessed to by the religious traditions'.[25] These formal statements look encouraging as a foundation on which to build a realist view of religious language. However, in the light of his Kantian epistemology it is not easy to see what meaning such statements really have. What does Hick mean by a 'ground' for the encountered gods? Most likely, Hick means something like a causal connection that exists between the noumenal reality and the way gods appear to us. However, this suffers all the problems of applying causation beyond appearances to the thing-in-itself.

Hick's use of Anselm in this description is problematic. Anselm intended this as a formal description of God as part of his ontological argument for God's existence. However, for Hick the statement is used merely as a limiting concept: nothing greater than the Real can be conceived because the Real itself cannot be conceived. One could equally well postulate that the Real is 'that than which nothing less can be conceived' for all such a statement means. The word 'greater' has no significance for Hick's position, but simply pays lip-service to Anselm's classic argument for the existence of God. Anselm himself clearly did mean something substantive by his use of the word 'greater'. For example, in his response to Gaunilo he writes, 'For we attribute to the divine substance anything of which it can be conceived that it is better to be than not to be that thing. For example: it is better to be eternal, than not eternal; good, than not good; nay, goodness itself, than not goodness itself.'[26] Such clarity of description becomes difficult in the context of the pluralist hypothesis.

By 'greater' Anselm sought to describe God in his self-revelation as good, eternal, and as a God who exists. Such specific terms are simply not open to Hick for whom such language would represent an attempt to claim direct knowledge of the Real. Such knowledge is not possible. Therefore, Hick uses Anselm's language to point out only that the noumenon is beyond, or greater, than all conception. Such an empty notion shares absolutely nothing with Anselm's deeply theistic ontological argument. Anselm presents his case for God in the context of a devout prayer. The argument only works because there is already a definition of who God is, not simply a description of how God appears to us.[27] In this use of Anselm's words, Hick highlights how very different his conception of God really is.

There is an emptiness at the heart of Hick's concept of the Real that prompts Loughlin to point out that 'At the centre of Hick's universe of faiths there is "empty space"', which he likens to Roland Barthes' description of Tokyo,[28] a city which turns around a forbidden and empty space: 'The entire city revolves around a place that is both forbidden and indifferent, an abode masked by vegetation, protected by moats, inhabited by an emperor whom no one ever sees: literally, no one knows who does ever see him . . . it appears as an image that unfurls again and again in endless circles, around an empty core.'[29]

The God of Christian theism, evident in Hick's earlier work, recedes in the light of his later pluralist hypothesis to become the nebulous Real compatible with all religions. However, in the light of the Kantian epistemology we can see that this shift was inevitable. There never was a God to whom we respond, only a postulate of religious experience. Theology becomes not the study of God, but the study of human experience.

Hick makes eclectic use of his sources, and cannot be labelled as the follower of any one school of thought. Where helpful for his case, he draws upon Kant or Wittgenstein or Hume or Ayer in order to advance his work. With reference to Kant, Hick acknowledges his debt to a basic epistemological insight, but distances himself from other features of his philosophy. A closer inspection of Kant's theological concerns reveal many more parallels with the theology of Hick. Hick himself does not acknowledge these parallels, but I think it can be shown that his mature work was strikingly similar to the theology of

Kant. Why should this be so? Perhaps the reason is simple: a certain kind of epistemology, shared by Hick and Kant, will necessarily lead to a certain kind of theology. It is no accident that Kant provides an interpretation of religion that is surprisingly similar to the later developed work of Hick. Their philosophical position drives them towards similar conclusions. We will see this in the following chapter as we survey Kant's explanation of religion.

10

Reasonable Religion

Religion within the Limits of Reason

Kant is best known as a philosopher and, given the influence of the three works known as the *Critiques*, he is more often studied by students of philosophy than theology. Yet Kant himself wrote very directly on the application of his ideas to theological themes. *Religion Within the Limits of Reason Alone* was published in 1793 and its turbulent birth has led to some confusion over its purpose. Often it is understood as a work primarily concerned with ethics. Kant's influence endures because he argued that morality could be understood and pursued outside any particular religious framework. With the decline of Christian adherence in the West and the rise of secularism, some might think Kant's ideas would be eagerly pursued. However, this way of reading Kant marginalizes the importance of his work as theology.

Kant's first attempts to publish *Religion* were opposed by the censors. Written work on biblical texts required official approval. He managed to get *Religion* published only by avoiding theological censors and having it approved by the university philosophy department. This brought it into print but still brought him into conflict with the theological censors of his time. A royal decree was issued prohibiting him from writing on religion and the Lutheran church banned this work. The church clearly recognized a threat from Kant's treatment of the Bible.[1] Even if one considers Kant's book to be an explanation of morality we cannot avoid seeing it as obviously a theological discussion of morals. 'Morality thus leads ineluctably to religion, through which it extends itself to the idea of a powerful moral Lawgiver, out-side of mankind, for Whose will that is the final end (of creation) which at the same time can and ought to be man's final end.'[2]

Kant passed the book through the philosophy department for ap-proval but knew very well that it was a religious work. Ethics leads to religion. From reflection on ethical theory, Kant was inevitably led to consider more generally the function of religion. For him, religion provided a motivation and vision for moral life. Morality alone does not provide this motivation. We can outline Kant's description of reli-gion in terms of four themes. Interestingly, each of these four themes finds a parallel in John Hick's interpretation of religion.[3]

Theme 1: Freedom of the Will

Kant begins his consideration of morality with an account of the ori-gins of evil and the nature of the freedom of the will. His writing on religion is deeply concerned with theodicy. In keeping with his phil-osophy, he argues that the origins of evil lie with the exercise of free will: 'Man *himself* must make or have made himself into whatever, in a moral sense, whether good or evil, he is or is to become. Either con-dition must be an effect of his free choice; for otherwise he could not be held responsible for it and could be *morally* neither good nor evil.'[4]

Created morally neutral, human beings have a freedom of will that entails responsibility for choosing either to do good or to do evil. Kant assumes a libertarian view of freedom, quite opposed to the Augustinian or Calvinist emphasis on the bondage of the will to sin. This classic and Reformed view of the bondage of the will assumed the inability of a person to choose the good without divine inter-vention. Therefore, salvation and damnation are primarily divine de-crees rather than the result of human choices. Paul writes in Romans, 'Therefore God has mercy on whom he wants to have mercy, and he hardens whom he wants to harden' (Rom. 9:18). Commenting on this verse, John Calvin would write that Paul 'teaches that salvation is prepared for those only on whom the Lord is pleased to bestow mercy – that ruin and death await all whom he has not chosen'.[5] Kant cites the same verse but declares that such a teaching, 'taken according to the letter, is the *salto mortale* of human reason'.[6]

According to Kant, the Calvinist system takes a fatal leap (*salto mortale*) into determinism which makes moral thinking impossible. In contrast he emphasizes libertarian free will. Because our choices to do the good are utterly free and uncompelled we are to be praised or even rewarded for such good actions.

Kant has been noted for reintroducing a strong sense of moral evil in his philosophy. 'At a time when leading Enlightenment thinkers were united in attacking ignorance as the source of evil, embodied especially in outmoded traditions and superstitions, the aging Kant clearly argues that evil arises out of the will.'[7] Human beings are not inherently good creatures who, through right education, will inevitably choose the good. However, nor are they necessarily evil, born in original sin and affected by total depravity. Human beings are a mixture of good and evil but always retaining an ability to choose what is right.

Kant describes 'a seed of goodness' which remains in human nature of 'entire purity'.[8] There is no need for special grace or redemptive acts for men and women to choose the good. The seed of goodness is part of human nature and we have the means to do what is right. Kant makes a simple but influential point against Calvinist alternatives: 'For when the moral law commands that we *ought* now to be better men, it follows inevitably that we must *be able* to be better men.'[9] Moral commands imply practical ability. Where do those commands come from? Kant detaches moral commands from the need for a divine being to give those commands as this would also compromise his strong view of libertarian freedom. As Mark Johnson writes:

[Kant] argues that morality cannot be based on God's will as the source of divine moral law, for that would be to reduce freedom to a sham freedom to obey an 'other'. Yet he argues that morality *can* be based on universal law which we rationally give to ourselves . . . we are free just insofar as we are autonomous, that is, just to the extent that we give moral laws *to ourselves* of our rationality and freedom.[10]

Salvation is, then, the free pursuit of moral laws that we have autonomously chosen. What then of the historic Christian understanding of salvation as an act of God on our behalf? Kant does use the language of faith in the atonement which sounds orthodox but, as we will see in a moment, Kant understands 'atonement' as a symbol rather than a literal event.

In contrast to the historic Christian position, Kant wants to explain faith in terms of an active moral life rather than trust in the validity of certain beliefs. Like Hick, Kant defines faith in terms of an attitude to life rather than a trust in doctrinal statements: 'Where shall we start, i.e. with a faith in what God has done on our behalf, or with what we are to do to become worthy of God's assistance (whatever this may be)? In answering this question we cannot hesitate in deciding for the second alternative.'[11]

Saving faith is our commitment to being morally upright and choosing what is good. Religion, in any specific form, is secondary to this. Belief in the atonement might be useful, but it does not take precedence over commitment to the moral imperatives of pure reason. Kant's explanation of Christianity hints at some room for God to be active, but it is far from clear what this activity might be or whether it is, in any important sense, necessary.

Kant's emphasis on human freedom and cognitive choice lays the foundation for his reinterpretation of Christianity. How radical this reinterpretation is can be seen clearly with the benefit of hindsight. In surveying the subsequent history of theology we can see how new philosophical developments would shape Christian thought. Indeed, historic Christian confessions would be emptied of their meaning in the light of these philosophical developments. As Michalson writes in his survey of Kant's theology, 'With his aggressive account of autonomous rationality, Kant has cut off the head of the traditionally religious body, yet the corpse continues to twitch and move, as though life is still in it when it is not.'[12] Though Kant's theology sounds Christian, and maintains Christian vocabulary, the lifeblood of theology, the historic content of confessions and creeds, has been drained away.

Theme 2: Christology

The essence of religion, for Kant, is the moral law or imperative. In the light of this moral imperative he interprets the significance of the historical particulars of Christianity. Kant dissects doctrines to find universal themes that do not rely on contingent historical events. His evaluation of the meaning of the incarnation of Christ is not dissimilar to that offered by Hick.

The incarnation is taken to be the personification of goodness. Jesus Christ is understood as an example, or archetype, of what all people are to be. However, the historical Jesus has only a contingent relationship to this archetype: 'We need therefore, no empirical example to make the idea of a person morally well-pleasing to God our archetype; this idea as an archetype is already present in our reason.'[13]

The historical Jesus is no more than a representation of the archetype which already exists in each one of us and is accessible through the exercise of pure reason. In principle we need no knowledge of the historical Jesus or the gospel accounts in order to know what kind of people God calls us to be. Charlotte Allen notes that for Kant the future offered a time when 'Jesus would become obsolete'.[14] At the time Kant was writing on religion, the liberal approach to the historicity of the Scriptures was well under way. Indeed, Kant chided those whose following of Jesus depended on his metaphysical identity. We should recognize the authority of the archetype regardless of the historicity of the gospel accounts of Jesus. What does it matter if the miracles were literal, or Jesus rose bodily from the dead, or those accounts were historically inaccurate? Kant describes the value of the person and work of Christ in terms devoid of any reference to supernatural events. In fact, his significance is even devoid of historical events. The Christ of faith was becoming detached from the Jesus of history.

The central work of Christ lies in his bringing a message of encouragement to freely choose the good, a message not dissimilar to that of Kant. Concerning the resurrection and ascension Kant has little patience. He describes these as later additions to the gospel accounts valuable only as symbolic ways of describing the hope of eternal life.

Kant embarks on a process of interpreting the miracles as symbols in a way that prefigures Hick's interpretation of doctrine as mythological. The atonement is subjected to just such an interpretation. The moral requirement of men and women to die to selfishness 'is pictured as a death endured once for all by the representative of mankind'.[15] This analysis permits Kant to continue to use the language of incarnation, atonement and resurrection but all reinterpreted as pictorial language. This language is designed to convey truths otherwise accessible through pure reason. Kant is engaged in an early form of demythologization. Each classic theory of the atonement is subjected to such an analysis so that Kant removes the importance of a historic Christ in favour of a principle of human reason. As Benner notes; 'while one might be tempted to look to Christ as the archetype, Kant argues instead that this archetype must ultimately be found within the individual's reason.'[16] Christ has no atoning significance other than as a useful symbol for a principle already accessible to human reason.

Though this treatment of miracles has a heavy influence on his Christology, Kant cannot simply be described as anti-supernaturalist in his interpretation of Jesus. He does not claim that miracles are an impossibility, as a materialist philosopher might, but that like any other historical events these can never be treated as necessary for religious faith. The truth or falsity of Christianity stands or falls with the self-authenticating status of its moral claims: 'If a moral religion . . . is to be established, all *miracles* which history connects with its inauguration must themselves in the end render superfluous the belief in miracles in general.'[17] The validity of a moral command cannot be found in contingent events of history but is already engraved on the human heart. Miracles are ultimately irrelevant to the moral essence of religion. This treatment of religion as a philosophical-ethical teaching paves the way for Kant, as it will do for Hick centuries later, to a concept of a universal religion.

Theme 3: The World Religions

Kant is committed to the idea that moral religion must have universal applicability. Every man and woman must be capable of following moral religion regardless of geographical context, intellectual ability or access to any church. This seems an entirely fair assumption, and one that will also guide Hick's theology. Therefore, there can be no significant religious knowledge that is tied to particular historical events, personalities or traditions. All that is necessary for true religion may be discerned through the exercise of pure reason.

Joseph Runzo points out that this universal validity of religion is based upon Kant's assumption 'that any rational being who possesses the appropriate conceptual resources will arrive at the same, fully epistemically justified conclusions'.[18] The difference between moral (universal) religion and particular world religions is that only pure moral religion 'can be believed in and shared by everyone', while 'An historical faith, grounded solely on facts, can extend its influence no further than tidings of it can reach, subject to circumstances of time and place and dependent upon the capacity [of people] to judge the credibility of such tidings.'[19] To restrict religion to its historical form prevents access to those outside the knowledge of those events. It is also to confuse the core of religion – ethical transformation – with the external trappings in which it appears. The moral law necessary for this transformation is available through reason and does not require revelation. A universal, moral religion is accessible through reason and requires no knowledge of particular historical events.

It is worth making a note at this point of Kant's own terminology, which differs from contemporary usage. He describes as 'faiths' the particular religions of Judaism, Islam and Christianity along with denominations like Lutheranism. Underlying these faiths he identifies the '*one* (true) *religion*'.[20] So 'faiths' are particular examples of the universal religion. Contemporary scholar of comparative religion, Wilfred Cantwell Smith, uses the same terminology but in the opposite way. He argues that faith is a general category present throughout the world, whereas religions are historical manifestations of that one faith.[21] Hick follows Smith's more successful use of terminology but is essentially making the same distinction as Kant had made. Hick identifies faith as the universal dimension of religious experience underlying the diverse, specific religions of the world.

According to Kant's view of freedom and ethics, no one living in isolation from the traditions of Christianity can be any worse off in relation to God. The moral transformation that is the essence of faith is accessible to every person: 'They who seek to become well-pleasing to Him not by praising Him (or his envoy, as a being of divine origin) according to revealed concepts which not every man can have, but by a good course of life, regarding which everyone knows His will – these are they who offer Him the true veneration which He desires.'[22]

The concept of special revelation is, at best, redundant in Kant's theology. The value of particular faiths lies in the extent to which they encourage moral behaviour. He respects the Bible, not because it is a revelation through historical places and people but because it seems to offer the best moral teaching. This positive assessment has to be seriously qualified by the fact that Kant has little interest in the historical, literal meaning of the Bible but only its meaning when interpreted in the light of his philosophy. He claims 'an exposition of the revelation which has come into our possession is required, that is, a thorough-going interpretation of it in a sense agreeing with the universal practical rules of a religion of pure reason'.[23] The Bible, or special revelation, has value only when interpreted in a way that fits with the findings of pure reason. It is quite clear that the only teaching being elevated to such exalted status is Kant's own.

Kant even concedes that the interpretation may be 'forced' and completely depart from the literal interpretation of the text. As long as the resulting interpretation is in agreement with moral reason, it is valid. Kant is unapologetic for this approach, pointing out that Jews, Christians, Hindus and Muslims have all engaged in such reinterpretation to reconcile darker passages of their scriptures with the moral commands of pure reason.[24]

Doctrines, scriptures and historical events all serve a purpose in bringing men and women to an understanding of moral religion.

However, once one grasps the moral demand of pure religion, all such things may be dispensed with. Universal religion is compatible with any and every faith though it supersedes or transcends them. It is not so much that all religions lead to God as that all religions offer a potential path to the true, moral philosophy. One further feature of Kant's work demonstrates how well this position fits with religious pluralism.

Theme 4: The History of Religion

Kant's account of Judaism is deeply flawed. His description shares features with the general anti-Semitism of his time, which would lead, in the century that followed, to the most intense persecution of the Jews the world had ever seen.[25] Obviously, Hick would not share any of this sentiment and was vocal in his support for the Jewish people against racism and persecution. However, leaving aside the problematic way Kant describes the Jews we can still identify a common approach to the history of religion.

Kant takes an evolutionary approach to religion, drawing a distinction between primitive, this-worldly faith, and developed, transcendent faith. For Kant, Judaism is an example of the former faith. 'Judaism is really not a religion at all but merely a union of a number of people who, since they belonged to a particular stock, formed themselves into a commonwealth under purely political laws . . . it was *intended* to be merely an earthly state.'[26]

Kant dismisses Judaism for being merely a collection of political laws. As a faith it fails to direct anyone to transcendent significance and its concern with morality is directed only at public observance, not inward change. He assumes, wildly inaccurately, that Judaism has never held to a belief in an afterlife and that this makes it impossible for Judaism to hold any notion of ultimate reward or blessing. Such an interpretation makes Judaism incompatible with Kant's view of real religion.

A further example of Kant's abhorrence towards Judaism lies in his treatment of the doctrine of election. In some sense Israel was considered a nation elected, chosen by God.[27] Kant merely repeats the anti-Semitism of his time by declaring that this doctrine expressed Jewish 'enmity toward all other peoples and which, therefore, evoked the enmity of all'.[28] Essentially, Judaism was an example of primitive religion, only dimly expressing any sense of true moral religion. The function of such primitive religion was primarily one of maintaining sociopolitical order and stability among people in the face of chaos and disorder.

Addressing the development of religion after Judaism, Kant follows what we have already described as an evolutionary model. Kant acknowledges that Christianity arose from Judaism, but affirms that it brought an entirely new principle of morality. Christianity, along with other major religions, is now in a process of continuing evolution. The particular world religions are all in this process of change as they move towards the one, true, moral religion. Kant believes that the prophets speak of a hope that eventually pure moral religion will entirely replace the mythological forms in which that religion is currently found. Through evolutionary development 'in the end religion will gradually be freed from all empirical determining grounds and from all statutes which rest on history'.[29] Doctrines are myths that serve an interim purpose of helping men and women towards a higher good in their lives. But such particular teachings are only of provisional use and, unless discarded, will obstruct the realization of the true, universal religion.

This historical approach to religion leads Kant to make a prediction for the future. There will be a gradual abandonment of historic faiths until 'at last the pure religion of reason will rule over all, "so that God may be all in all"'.[30] This thought is best expressed in Kant's vision of an ethical commonwealth as the goal of human improvement. At Kant's own time in history religions would be a mixed blessing. On the one hand, they help cultivate a good life through their symbols and maxims. On the other hand, they can obstruct and distract from growth towards this common goal. The solution prefigures the pluralist hypothesis: recognize the truth of these philosophical conclusions while still encouraging a non-dogmatic use of religion as a lens through which one can nurture a moral life. In the meantime, what should we do with more primitive, dogmatic forms of religion? Kant declared that the 'euthanasia of Judaism is the pure moral religion'.[31] His apologists will defend Kant on the grounds that he intended this as a purely intellectual point rather than as a call to violence against a people.[32] Even so, his antipathy toward the historic form of the Jewish faith is a reminder of the potential intolerance that may be embedded in any liberal reinterpretation of religion. As we now return to Hick's pluralist hypothesis we can identify many features that naturally grow from the same soil as Kant's own thinking on religion.

11

Hick's Debt to Kant

We may summarize Kant's treatment of religion in terms of four themes. First, there is his libertarian view of free will. Second, his treatment of the incarnation and atonement as metaphors. Third, Kant identifies a moral essence in the world religions. Fourth, he presents an evolutionary view of religion as it has developed from the primitive to the sophisticated. We can outline Hick's pluralist proposal under these four headings and see how they compare.

Hick on Freedom and Morality

Hick's epistemology demands a libertarian view of free will. We have described his theory of knowledge in terms of three steps from natural interpretation, through moral interpretation, to religious interpretation. As we follow these steps the interpretation is increasingly voluntary. The religious interpretation of the universe is a total interpretation that follows the awareness of moral significance. Like Kant before him, Hick accepts that one may successfully interpret the moral significance of the universe without taking the further step of interpreting the universe in the categories of a particular religious tradition.

This picture of religious knowledge uncouples the connection between religion and morality. It follows that morality can be defined in very neutral terms, compatible with both theist and atheist beliefs. Moral claims precede and are independent of any religious claims we may feel. Hick identifies the essence of morality as the demand to treat others as having the same value as oneself. He claims that this is the teaching embedded in Christ's teaching in the Sermon on the Mount, in various scriptures of the world traditions, and is 'a translation of Kant's concepts of a rational person as an end and of right action as action which our rationality, acknowledging a universal impartiality transcending individual desires and aversions, can see to be required'.[1]

Hick shares Kant's perspective that morality is based upon universal truths anyone could arrive at through the exercise of reason. Furthermore, the pursuit of these virtues does not require any special work of God's divine help. As we have seen with Kant this leads to a simple form of salvation by works. To be saved is to seek to live a life that will be judged worthy. Hick joins Kant in what is in effect an endorsement of what church tradition considered to be Pelagianism. In the early church this was identified and rejected as a heretical form of Christian teaching. Pelagius, like Kant and Hick after him, was a critic of Augustine's notion of original sin. He attacked Augustine's formulation of the doctrine on the ground that it compromised human free will: 'Everything good and everything evil in respect of which we are either worthy of praise or of blame, is *done by us*, not *born with us*. We are not born in our full development, but with a capacity for good and evil.'[2] In contemporary religious thought there seems little controversial in such a statement but in the light of Christian theology Kant and Hick both take an alternative road to that of orthodoxy.

Pelagius made the same logical point that Kant would make centuries later: if one had no choice but to do evil, then one would not be responsible for it. Hick joins Kant in this Pelagian commitment to libertarian free will. All these thinkers share the perspective that morality can be distinguished from religion, such that any human being both knows the good and is able to choose the good. Knowledge of anything particular to the Christian faith is not necessary to the good life.

At best, Kant's description of salvation implies a kind of divine assistance in human moral improvement. As Michalson describes Kant's doctrine of salvation, 'We have here something like a postulation of human/divine cooperation in the recovery from radical evil, based on what amounts to a Pelagian appeal to divine assistance for those who do their moral best.'[3] However, given Kant's radical re-evaluation of the doctrine of God, it is hard to see what real additional element such a being could bring. Indeed, Kant's religion of reason provides a basis for morality entirely independent of historic faiths. Religions bring an excess baggage of ritual and doctrine, superfluous to ethics. Strip away those religious accretions but expose the primary ethical concern that lies at their heart.

Kant's vision of the future is that 'in the end religion will gradually be freed from all empirical determining grounds' including historical events or personalities.[4] Hick makes just the same distinction: 'In principle, then, and to a considerable extent in practice, we can separate out basic moral values from both the magical-scientific and the metaphysical beliefs which have always entered into their application within particular cultures.'[5]

Salvation is possible for all human beings regardless of their historical context because all are free to choose the good. This moral religion is universally accessible. It is not hard to see how Kant and Hick would have shared a similar optimism for the future development of religion along pluralist lines given this shared moral interpretation of the essence of religion. The future lies in the marginalization of specific religious ideas or metaphysical claims and prioritization of a common moral code.

Hick on Christian Doctrine

Hick and Kant share in the wider liberal theological tradition of demythologization. They share the conviction that supernatural concepts or descriptions can be translated into terms compatible with a naturalist world-view. The great, distinctive doctrines of Christianity are representational or symbolic uses of language. In his contribution to *The Myth of God Incarnate*, Hick offered a demythologized account of the incarnation. As we have seen, this involved a rejection of the literal interpretation as logically incoherent. The real Jesus was simply a man with a powerful, indeed overwhelming, experience of divine reality.

The metaphor Son of God or God the Son is a linguistic device which 'offers a way of declaring his significance to the world; and it expresses a disciple's commitment to Jesus as his personal Lord'.[6] This 'linguistic device' was used by the early followers of Jesus as a poetic means of describing their commitment to what Jesus meant to them. Such poetry became crude, literalistic doctrine in the later church, and Hick offers his own interpretation as a corrective. He claims to have recovered the real meaning of the language of incarnation.

In *The Metaphor of God Incarnate* the atonement is also subjected to this treatment and considered to be a pictorial rather than literal use of language. Hick rejects the doctrine of original sin, for which atonement is required, at least as a literal doctrine. Considered in pictorial terms it is 'a mythological way of referring to the fact of universal human imperfection'.[7] He weighs up various models of the atonement, such as the Christus Victor or ransom theory, and curtly dismisses them as 'embarrassing' and 'extinct'.

Hick also rejected belief in the historic fall of humankind for both philosophical and historical reasons. Historically, he considered the fall totally unbelievable in the light of modern geology and anthropology. To retain the language of the fall is to use mythological language: 'We can say that the earliest humans were, metaphorically speaking, already "fallen" in the sense of being morally and spiritually imperfect.'[8] The metaphysical reality of atonement is also abandoned in favour of a mythological interpretation of the doctrine. Hick portrays much of church history as having been a struggle to escape a literal view of the atonement. In *The Rainbow of Faiths* he claims that a gathering consensus now interprets the doctrine as pictorial language:

> And so the death of Jesus has become for many Christians today the manifestation of a self-giving love which is an earthly reflection of the divine love, rather than an astonishing transaction to enable God to forgive sinners. But this represents a transformation of Christian understanding that would, until within about the last century, have seemed utterly heretical and, at one time, deserving the direst penalties.[9]

Hick's view of religious language as metaphor or myth causes him constantly to seek a literal core of meaning. For him, to use the language of atonement is simply to make use of a story that describes someone giving themselves, even to death, in their love for others. This seems a strange interpretation given the apparent futility of Christ's death. Jesus did not die fighting oppressors, sabotaging Roman instruments of war, or leading a protest in the streets. He died on a technical charge of blasphemy, abandoned by his followers without offering any inspiring, Socrates-like speech. In what sense Jesus gave himself for others when he died, if not as a literal atonement, Hick does not say.

Hick distinguishes the death of Jesus from the stories we tell about his death. His historic death is of no metaphysical significance. It is our stories about him with which we are concerned. Hick's interpretation of doctrine uncouples our stories about Jesus from the historicity of his life and death. In fact, this is his approach to all doctrine. He engages with an apparently universal metaphor which has only a contingent relationship to a historic event. Hick provides no analysis of what historic basis underlies those stories and why they should matter so much to us today.

A clear pattern emerges in Hick's interpretation of the incarnation and atonement. His argument is that if taken literally such doctrines simply create too many logical and historical problems. The presence of such logical difficulties prompts us to interpret them as myths or metaphors rather than literal truths. This process allows him to harmonize any religious claims with his pluralist hypothesis.

Kant pursued a similar hermeneutics. He distinguishes between knowledge gained from history and knowledge universally accessible to reason. Particular, historical knowledge is not universally accessible and, consequently for Kant, cannot be universally necessary: 'We have noted that a Church dispenses with the most important mark of truth, namely a rightful claim to universality, when it bases itself upon a revealed faith. For such a faith, being historical . . . can never be universally communicated so as to produce conviction.'[10]

Kant assumes that for a religion to claim universal validity it must have content that is universally accessible. Claims based on historical events or particular revelation do not have this universal accessibility. Therefore, Christianity must not identify such historical or prophetic particulars as essential. Instead, Kant embarks on a reductive interpretation of key Christian beliefs. Once those doctrinal claims are shorn of their specific historical content they may be able to lay claim to universal validity. So let us consider Kant's Christology and compare it with that offered by Hick.

We have noted that Kant described Christ as the archetype of moral perfection. As an archetype, Jesus represents a moral quality to which every man or woman already has access. The doctrine of Christ, as expressed in orthodox theology, is merely a helpful exposition of this truth. Such a doctrinal formulation should never be considered essential. People may grasp the truth without knowing or affirming the literal teaching in which this truth is packaged. Kant's Christology has little to do with metaphysical truths about a historic person. Jesus was a pattern of a universal moral principle already accessible to all. The doctrines of the atonement or the Trinity are also treated to this analysis. The value of such doctrines does not lie in their correspondence to literal reality, but in the way they encourage moral improvement.

Hick interprets Christian doctrine in much the same way as Kant had done before him. He describes the doctrine of the Trinity not as a literal revelation of the nature of God, but as informing us that there are at least 'three ways in which the one God is humanly thought and experienced'.[11] Taken this way, the Trinity is an illustration of the pluralist hypothesis: God is experienced and described in a plurality of forms. Christian tradition has expressed that plurality in a threefold form, but it might have been two or four or more. Of course, Hick has not really described the doctrine of the Trinity at all. At best, he is providing a kind of modalist understanding of how one God might appear in different modes at different times but this was never accepted as an adequate formulation of the Trinity.

Kant interprets the doctrine of the Trinity as teaching us that 'God wills to be served under three specifically different moral aspects'.[12] This reflects Kant's concern with making the case that religious doctrines motivate moral behaviour. Again, it has little to do with historic formulations of the Trinity and more to do with a proposal that fits with his moral concerns.

Hick finds in the doctrine of the Trinity an implicit statement of the pluralist hypothesis. Kant finds in the doctrine an implicit statement of his own moral philosophy. Both reduce this profound doctrine to a symbolic picture of their own philosophical ideas. They also ignore the function of the Trinity in orthodox history. Obviously the term itself was not found in the Bible but developed in Christian history as a way of marking the boundaries of orthodoxy. As Richard Burridge puts it, 'The doctrine of the Trinity does not define the nature of God (for who can describe him?), so much as set limits for orthodoxy.'[13] Kant and Hick would both make reference to the doctrine for exactly the opposite purpose of its original intention.

Kant and Hick treat Christian doctrine as largely incoherent by the standards of reason. As metaphors, doctrines remain helpful in encouraging moral behaviour; but if one wants to understand the real meaning of religion, then one must strip away such verbal embellishments and discover the underlying, universal truth. They both hold lightly to the historical particulars of Christianity.

Search for a Universal Religion

In order to sustain his assumption that true religion must be universally accessible Kant maintains that the core of faith lies in moral rules. He distinguishes between a moral, or ideal, religion and the historic faiths which are its concrete expressions. If we wish to extend the value of religion beyond such historic boundaries we need to identify this moral religion: '*Pure religious faith* alone can found a universal church; for only [such] rational faith can be believed in and shared by everyone.'[14] Historic faiths, dependent as they are on particular scriptures or events, cannot be shared by everyone.

Hick pursues a similar line of thought. He also distinguishes between the essence of religion and its particular forms. An example of this is found in his treatment of conflicting truth claims. Christians claim that Jesus of Nazareth was executed by crucifixion, truly died and rose again (1 Cor. 15:3–8). Islam directly contradicts this claim with its own tradition that Jesus did not die on the cross but only a likeness of Christ (Qur'an 4:157–8). Such contradictions concern historical events and defining beliefs. Their presence prevents any simple attempt to reconcile the teachings of such faiths.

While such disputes might, in principle, be settled by historical research, on the whole they concern matters Hick considers difficult to settle by scholarship. Normal historical methods could certainly weigh down on one side or other of this dispute, but Hick considers any conclusion about matters of history to be the subject of some ambiguity. We do not have direct access to the events of the past and must rely on limited evidence and interpretation. At best we are weighing up probabilities.

In any case, Hick suggests that a growing number of people, himself included, 'no longer regard such questions as being of the essence of their faith'.[15] If one does not join this apparent groundswell of opinion and prefers to maintain that some historical event, such as the incarnation, is in some way essential to faith then, Hick concedes, the pluralist project would hold no appeal. 'But it remains true that for many other believers [historical claims] *are* of the essence of their faith, so that no amount of evidence could ever change their conviction, and that for such persons the pluralist vision may well at present be inaccessible.'[16]

Such an attachment to historic events is found in all the major world religions. The pluralist account will meet with this objection from every quarter. Nonetheless, Hick and Kant share a view of the essence of religion as moral teachings. In particular, the 'Golden Rule' of Christ is to be found in some form among all the religions.[17] Matters of dispute are framed as secondary issues. Hick provides a mythological interpretation of them in order to sideline their significance. Such an approach to religion suits the purpose of finding a universal faith. However, it deliberately relativizes historical claims. Kant did this two hundred years ago, Hick pursued the same strategy for the contemporary world.

Rethinking the History of Religion

There is another interesting parallel in the way Hick and Kant explain religious history. Hick outlines the history of religion in two stages. The first stage is that of the *pre-axial* religion. These are the very ancient, often pre-literate religions that still exist today in some parts of the world. Pre-axial religions are excluded from Hick's pluralist account as they do not share the broader vision of the great world religions that arose after a flowering of religious consciousness called the *axial age*.

There are two key themes in pre-axial religion. First, they have a *psychological* function in helping people make sense of life and death. Second, they have a *sociological* function, which Hick describes as 'preserving the unity of the tribe or people within a common world-view and at the same time validating the community's claims upon the loyalty of its members'.[18] My tribe, right or wrong.

Pre-axial religions are not concerned with grand metaphysical themes of life after death or the nature of a transcendent being. Life beyond the grave, though assumed possible, was described in dark, shadowy terms. It was an existence more to be feared than envied. It is interesting that such faiths exist on the fringes of the pluralist hypothesis. They still represent responses to the divine but they are failed or skewed responses. In more recent work, Hick did indicate their value as wisdom that still requires some preservation: 'The gift of primal religion to the modern world is a reminder of our unity with the whole of nature and our continuity and kinship with all life.'[19] However, evidence of cruelty, human sacrifice or immoral rituals would all indicate that they should be excluded from the central pluralist claim. They are not paths to salvation.

Kant describes Judaism in remarkably similar terms to Hick's treatment of pre-axial religion. Hick would place Judaism in the later axial period and certainly did not share Kant's anti-Semitic rhetoric. But Kant's rejection of Judaism shares striking affinities with the grounds for Hick's rejection of pre-axial religion.

Kant denies that Judaism is really a religion at all. Early, or pure, Judaism was merely a political organization. It was only concerned with outward ritual, social cohesion and tribal security. It guarded racial purity against forces of chaos that would dilute or corrupt its tribal identity. According to Kant, Judaism did not offer worship to a transcendent, moral being. The Jewish God is 'merely an earthly regent making absolutely no claims upon, and no appeals to, conscience'.[20] This was a common assumption about early Judaism at the time of Kant. The Higher Critical movement in Germany assessed the antiquity of the Hebrew Scriptures in these terms. Earlier traditions of Scripture were those which portrayed God in very simple, earthly terms as a super king called Jehovah who would walk in the garden. Later traditions of Scripture developed a more philosophical sense of El being the transcendent creator God not to be identified with any human or animal form. These claims of Higher Criticism were far from proven[21] but they provided the context for Kant's dismissal of Judaism as a primitive, idolatrous religion.

Kant also denied that Judaism had any significant concept of life after death. Again, this claim is frequently repeated but a flawed assumption. Hick would disown the accuracy of Kant's portrayal of Judaism but he certainly applies similar terms to pre-axial religion. Primitive religions are characterized in the same way that Kant caricatures Judaism.

Kant provides an evolutionary description of religious development. Long before Darwin's famous biological theory of natural selection, the evolutionary theme was common currency in scholarship. It was already an assumption that everything evolves from simpler forms to more complex whether through natural laws or human involvement. Hick describes an evolutionary path of religion through an axial age using the framework provided by Karl Jaspers.[22] The axial age represents a period between 800 and 200 BC in which human consciousness moves from the pre-axial primitive faiths to the religions of the modern world. Jaspers uses the term axial in the sense of 'pivotal' and represents the period of change from an old order of consciousness to a new age. This was the period of the Old Testament writings, the Greek philosophers and the Buddha.

The new stage in human history is marked by optimism in matters of religion. Hick underlines that during this age all the major religious options were formed, and each shares a common assumption that moral transformation of the individual is both possible and desirable, 'Thus all these post-axial faiths are soteriologically oriented.'[23] The common essence of post-axial faiths is the golden rule of moral duty to one's neighbour as if acting towards oneself. According to Kant, Christianity marks a complete break with Judaism at this point. Its defining feature is that it 'was to comprise a religion valid for the world'[24] and not just for a tribal group. It is as if Kant places the axial age a little later than Hick to present Judaism as pre-axial and modern liberalism as the fruit of that pivotal period of change.

Hick and Kant both share a view of human consciousness developing over time towards a moral religion. Kant describes it as a religion of pure reason, whereas we might say Hick describes a religion of pure experience. Either way, the supreme religion will be the one cleansed of its historic particulars and revealed in universal, moral themes. Kant declares: 'The one true religion comprises nothing but laws, that is, those practical principles of whose unconditioned necessity we can become aware, and which we therefore recognise as revealed through pure reason (not empirically).'[25]

A religion revealed through empirical means would make historical events essential. Matters of history, dogma and ritual may constitute the concrete form in which we find a religion, but for both Hick and Kant, these are non-essentials. The increasing extent to which religious people realize that this is true is part of the ongoing evolution of religion towards a purer form.

It is worth emphasizing how intolerant this statement of pluralism turns out to be. Hick and Kant both share a commitment to a pure, moral religion. The history of specific religions must be read in the light of this. Those earlier religions will generally be not as truthful and helpful as later developments. Their description of religious history only privileges their own vantage point and judges past religions in the light of what they consider a common essence among the faiths.

Conclusion

There are striking similarities between Kant and Hick's approach to religion, going far beyond Hick's acknowledged debt to a Kantian epistemology. Ultimately, Kant thought that religion affirmed two important theological facts: the existence of God and continued personal existence after death in which one would gain the ultimate reward for right behaviour. The difference between these two thinkers is that for Kant these were postulates of reason whereas for Hick they are postulates of experience. However, even this difference is muted when one recognizes that for Hick religious experience is simply a more profound type of moral experience.

How conscious is Hick of his debt to Kant? As we have seen, Hick makes little reference to Kant's wider work in his own writing. While many commentators describe Hick as Kantian, few press the similarities as far as we have done here. For example, Paul Eddy describes Hick's mature work as a neo-Kantian proposal but adds the following qualification: 'The term "neo-Kantian" is used throughout this essay in a very general sense; it implies no connection to the German philosophical movement of the late nineteenth and early twentieth centuries.'[26] Because Hick distances himself from any attempt to identify his work more generally with that of Kant it is not surprising that other commentators feel the need to make this distinction. However, we have identified a much closer connection than these remarks would suggest.

Hick is thoroughly Kantian in his interpretation of religion. How then can we explain the lack of direct engagement with Kant's writing on religion? The answer lies in the fact that Hick belongs to a more general movement of which Kant was, in many ways, the founding figure. They both share a commitment to the Enlightenment project. Hick arrives at a similar conclusion to Kant because he belongs to the same tradition of enquiry. Regardless of the extent to which Hick acknowledges this or gives specific reference to Kant, the fact is that he is driven to the pluralist hypothesis because its seeds were already planted in early Enlightenment thought.

Religious pluralism is the natural development of the Enlightenment worldview. With its approach to epistemology, commitment to materialism and an evolutionary account of history it is inevitable that this world-view would lead Hick to the pluralist hypothesis. Kant and Hick might be considered bookends of the Enlightenment treatment of religion. Kant stands at its introduction and Hick marks its conclusion.

12

The Enlightenment Tradition

In this book we have traced the sources for Hick's thought on religion. While he was shaped by his own experience of other faiths and concern with anti-Semitism in Birmingham there were already philosophical ideas that compelled him to reinterpret Christianity. The seeds for his pluralist philosophy were already taking root in his early work. Why should this matter in our understanding of Hick? Because his work represents, in the thought of a single theologian, the way Christian theological thought has developed over the past two centuries. By understanding the driving forces behind the development of Hick's theology we can also see the motivation for wider shifts in contemporary theology.

We have traced two intellectual sources for Hick's thought. The first was the tradition of scepticism, and the second the philosophy of Kant. These two sources are in fact both parts of a single tradition in western thought. Kant himself saw his work as a response to the scepticism of David Hume who had, famously, awoken him from his 'dogmatic slumbers'. So Hume's scepticism, and Kant's Enlightenment response are really two parts of one western approach to religion.

Hick, as he himself protested, may not have been consciously appropriating so much of Kant's work on religion. Certainly in his philosophy of knowledge, Hick distanced himself from many aspects of Kant's work. But the striking similarities lead us to conclude that Kant's theological thought naturally leads to something like Hick's ethical pluralism. The reason why their thought is so similar is that they are both part of the major cultural movement of the West that we call modernism or Enlightenment thought. Once we place Hick's philosophy of religion in this intellectual and cultural context we will be in a better position to demonstrate why its central claims should not be seen as compatible with orthodox Christianity. It is almost as if Hick's own personal theological journey away from evangelicalism toward pluralism is a microcosm of the theological shift in western culture over the past three hundred years.

Breaking with Tradition

The Modern Age is often described as beginning with the work of the French thinker, Rene Descartes.[1] His philosophical method turned away from the authority of tradition or revelation in favour of the authority of the thinking self. This methodological shift cannot be underplayed. There is no doubt that Descartes provided intellectual ideas that lay the ground for decisive change in the intellectual atmosphere of Western Europe. However, Descartes' own work remained part of the late medieval world-view rather than truly breaking with the past. After all, his method still relied heavily on a proof for the existence of God as a foundation for philosophy and in many respects he remained a traditional Roman Catholic of the period. The real shift was yet to come.[2]

Kant does make a decisive break with the past. He calls others to join him in a new era of intellectual thought: 'Enlightenment is man's release from his self-incurred tutelage. Tutelage is man's inability to make use of his understanding without direction from another. Self-incurred is this tutelage when its cause lies not in lack of reason but in lack of resolution and courage to use it without direction from another. *Sapere aude!* "Have courage to use your own reason" – that is the motto of enlightenment.'[3]

In this call to enlightenment Kant makes clear two key features that will mark the movement. First, it is a complete break with the past. By 'tutelage' Kant means any institution that imposes truth, meaning or morality from above. Tutelage relies upon an authoritarian tradition. While it could be despotic in form, this need not be the case. Indeed, Kant saw it as a more general threat to the general national spirit. As the eighteenth century drew to a close in Prussia, tutelage was 'self-incurred' because people were lazy – they wanted it that way. Just as a child spoilt by its parents grows lazy, so the population had come to enjoy not having to think for themselves. Enlightenment would be the intellectual act of breaking rank with imposed, or self-imposed, authority and developing an independence of mind. It would be humanity's coming of age. Whether Protestant or Catholic in form, the traditions of Christianity were part of the problem. They contributed to the shackles from which Kant urged people to break free. The Reformation had only replaced one religious authority (the church) with another (the Bible).[4]

The second key theme is summed up in the call '*Sapere aude!*' (Dare to know!). The way to knowledge and understanding is not through blind obedience to a tradition, but through the autonomous use of reason. Descartes had begun to walk this path but remained within a traditional Catholic religious fold. Kant describes his own summons as a call to 'go alone' in contrast to the slavish obedience of the masses who he compares to 'domestic cattle' – dumb, placid and essentially conformist.[5]

The person who rises to the challenge of the Enlightenment breaks with this commitment to tradition. They leave behind the mass of humanity, herded along in their communities, believing only what they are told. The new climate of the Enlightenment was to provide a context for free, uncoerced enquiry.

The most obvious traditions with which Kant took issue were religions. There are also traditions of art, philosophy and science, but Kant does not perceive them to be such a threat to Enlightenment. They were already developing independently of the medieval and Reformation world-view. Nor did they yet form comprehensive world-views in which satisfying answers to ultimate questions might be found. The homogenous nature of a religious tradition is the real threat to enlightenment thought. 'I have placed the main point of enlightenment . . . chiefly in matters of religion because our rulers have no interest in playing the guardian with respect to the arts and science and also because religious incompetence is not only the most harmful but also the most degrading of all.'[6]

Religion seemed to have special protection in the post-Reformation world, a protection not afforded art or science. The natural sciences were the subjects of free public debate and open to revision and re-formulation wherever necessary. Since the disastrous treatment of Galileo and Copernicus the church was careful to permit academic freedom in the natural sciences. In contrast, religion was not sub-jected to such criticism and revision. In fact, religion saw a virtue in being uncontested, not open to revision and holding an authori-tarian position within culture. As we have seen, Kant could only get his major theological work published through a philosophy depart-ment and not through a theology department. Even then he came under scrutiny and censure by ecclesiastical authorities. Perhaps his personal experience sharpened his antipathy toward religious authoritarianism.

Kant heralded, perhaps even set in motion, a shift in western cul-ture as significant as the Reformation. The age of enlightenment had begun with a reappraisal of religion. Given its fundamental role in both epistemology and the organization of society it had to be reli-gion that was re-evaluated if thought and civilization were to advance any further.

One particular forum for this intellectual reappraisal of religion is found in what became known as the Gifford Lectures. Lord Adam Gifford (1820–87) left in his will instructions and finances to support a series of lectures in natural theology at the Scottish universities. His will specified that the lectures would treat religion 'as a strictly natural science' in which it would be 'considered just as astronomy or chemis-try is'.[7] As a matter of fact, natural theology as Gifford conceived of it, was already on the wane by the time the lectures were instituted. This explains the remarkable diversity of later theologians who would give these prestigious lectures. The list would come to include such diverse names as William James (1901–02), J.G. Frazer (1923–5), Karl Barth (1936–8), Paul Tillich (1953–4), Rudolph Bultmann (1954–5), Richard Swinburne (1982–4), Richard Dawkins (1988) and Alister McGrath (2009).[8] Nonetheless, the original purpose of the endowment reflects the general attitude of the Enlightenment era to religion.

Alasdair MacIntyre, a critic of natural theology, describes the world-view of Lord Gifford and his contemporaries as dominated by the 'guiding presupposition of thought that substantive rationality is unitary, that there is a single, if perhaps complex, conception of what the standards and achievements of rationality are, one by which every educated person can without too much difficulty be brought to agree in acknowledging'.[9] The age of enlightenment encouraged great optimism. It ushered in the technological advances of the Industrial Revolution, scientific discovery and medical advances. Just as progress was being made in astronomy and biology, why should there not also be dramatic progress in our understanding of religion and morality?

The intention of the Gifford Lectures was to establish a firm, rational footing from which to describe and evaluate the world religions. Natural theology was prized, while revealed theology was dismissed. Miracles and revelation inevitably privilege the claims of one religion over another. Reason alone provides an arbiter for all the conflicting claims of the world religions.

It was quite fitting that the content of John Hick's *An Interpretation of Religion* was originally given as the Edinburgh Gifford Lectures of 1986–7. Regarding their published form, Paul Badham comments, 'Lord Gifford would have been delighted by this book. It is hard to think of any previous Gifford Lectures which more precisely fulfilled the terms of the will.'[10] Gifford had belonged to the opening movement of modernism with its commitment to treating religion according to the scientific principles of the Enlightenment. Human reason and a commitment to empirical methods of enquiry were to settle all differences, and Hick's methodology fits well with this vision of enquiry.

Objectivity and Neutrality

Alasdair MacIntyre, himself a contributor to the Gifford Lectures (the year following those given by Hick), provides a useful assessment of the essential presuppositions informing the Enlightenment approach to religion. He illustrates his central claim with the development of the *Encyclopaedia Britannica*.

The ninth edition laid bare grand claims of the editors and contributors to this encyclopaedia. Given a basic standard of rationality, the editors were optimistic that information from religion, politics, ethics, the arts and the sciences could be described in purely objective terms. Bias, commitments, preferences and values could be set to one side in the aim of producing an objective catalogue of knowledge. The ideal of the encyclopaedists was to present objective 'knowledge rather than opinion'.[11] Their hope was that in the wake of the Enlightenment age the 'Encyclopaedia would have displaced the Bible as the canonical book . . . of the culture'.[12]

In one sense, cultures have always sought to unify knowledge. The world of the Middle Ages in northwest Europe had tried to harmonize thinking within a common theological world-view. But this new drive towards a comprehensive, unifying conception of knowledge was undertaken in terms quite different from those of the medieval scholastics or post-Reformation Puritans. Such religious thinkers had held to a more doctrinally oriented approach to unifying knowledge. Theology was the queen of the sciences. A biblical world-view provided a context in which to make sense of the disparate data of life. Far from being a handicap to knowledge, the Christian faith provided a perspective from which to make sense of life. The editors of the encyclopaedia resisted such a religious perspective, and staked their claim on a neutral approach to research.

Philosophers of the Enlightenment, of which Kant is a founding example, argued for a method that would purify reason of its bias and prejudice. MacIntyre describes this Enlightenment project in this useful summary: 'It was a central aspiration of the Enlightenment, an aspiration the formulation of which was itself a great achievement, to provide for debate in the public realm standards and methods of rational justification by which alternative courses of action in every sphere of life could be adjudged just or unjust, rational or irrational, enlightened or unenlightened.'[13]

This aspiration lay behind the development of religious studies as a discipline. Rather than theology, with its commitment to a particular religious tradition, religious studies claim to provide a neutral vantage point from which to compare and contrast the claims of various traditions.

If such a neutral approach to religion is possible then two tools are required. First, there must be a universal language with which all religions can be described and compared. Second, there must be a universal standard of reason with which religions can be assessed. It is exactly such a neutral framework that Kant had tried to provide. His epistemology sought to describe how, behind the unique details of cultures and world-views, human beings share a basic structure to their minds. There is a form of pure reason, independent of our particular faith or perspective. Laying aside our religious affiliation, we find a striking number of common beliefs about reality. These common beliefs are so fundamental they cannot be laid aside as without them we can know nothing at all. Given a neutral basis for knowledge we can have greater optimism that we can discover universal truths that do not depend on revealed religion.

This optimism in matters of science and reason is easily identified through the nineteenth century. An objective approach to economics (Karl Marx), psychology (Ludwig Feuerbach), biology (Charles Darwin) and religious studies (William James) seemed to point in a common direction. The validity of human reason and the perception that much of religion was superstitious came to dominate the academic climate.

However, through the two world wars of the twentieth century this optimism was wounded and what is sometimes called a postmodern reaction arose. Intellectuals, particularly on the continent, more freely questioned the grand claims of a previous generation. The doubters of the previous century, such as Friedrich Nietzsche, had been dismissed as eccentrics. Now those doubts became mainstream. The modernist claims to pure reason, objectivity or neutrality were under review.

Some critics identify Hick as a postmodernist, but I think this is mistaken. The mistake may be explained by the fact that postmodernism itself is a confused and incoherent notion. Robert Cook identified Hick as postmodern in a robust assessment of his work[14] to which Hick responded with surprise that he should be charged a postmodernist.[15] Cook's point was that Hick could be categorized as postmodern in his rejection of any one religion having a true meta-narrative. All religions must be regarded equally with suspicion. Hick's defence is that he is normally accused of supplying just such a meta-narrative with his pluralist hypothesis, exactly what the postmoderns reject. Hick obviously fits the atmosphere of postmodernism while holding an intellectual position that remains thoroughly modernist. Hick could sound relativist in his treatment of religion while being as committed to an absolute perspective as any religious believer. This led Don Carson to comment on the exchange with Cook that there are two types of pluralist, 'There are religious pluralists, like Hick, who spin a theory that becomes a criterion, a position, a place on which to stand; and there are others who argue that there is no such place, none at all.'[16] Some pluralists might deny that there is any position from which to judge the world religions. Hick is not one of those. In fact, such a position would be incoherent – making an objective, universal claim that no such objective, universal claims can be made. Such postmodernism would not fit well with Hick's analytical philosophy.

However, it would also be worth emphasizing that postmodernism is really an extension of modernism itself. It extends Descartes' questioning of all certainties and knowledge to its furthest reach. Questioning the certainty of all knowledge includes doubting critical thought itself. 'I think therefore I am' is no indubitable starting point for knowledge, it is itself subject to doubt.[17] Even the most radical postmodern thought is the logical legacy of modernism. Without Rene Descartes there might be no Michel Foucault. In a similar vein, Hick's modernist philosophy fits well in a postmodern culture.

In Kant's great call to 'Dare to Know!' he urged the break with all past traditions of enquiry. Free the mind from the shackles of tradition. However, as MacIntyre observes, Kant's own legacy was not the abandonment of tradition but the privileging of a rival tradition. This new tradition placed the emphasis on a universal descriptive language and a rational system. It is in this tradition that Hick belongs. His work represents the inevitable interpretation of religion in the light of the values of modernism.

MacIntyre, as a moral philosopher, emphasizes the problem that accompanies liberal ethics. No ethical consensus emerged with liberalism. There was no scientific basis for morality, despite attempts like utilitarianism to try. Instead, liberalism encouraged the freedom of the individual to choose their own conception of the good and live accordingly. Individuals should have the freedom to choose their own moral rules as long as their practice would not prevent others from holding to their own conception of the good.[18] We may apply the same attitude to Hick's treatment of religion. Despite the insights of the psychology and sociology of religion, there is no consensus on religious truth. Better then to encourage a liberal climate in which one might choose whichever religion seems most attractive. As long as we do not restrict anyone else's religious tastes we have freedom to choose our own. However, this conclusion then raises an obvious question: to what extent does pluralism only relativize the value of the world religions in favour of giving a particular, liberal epistemology absolute status?

13

The Myth of Religious Pluralism

Traditions of Enquiry

The Enlightenment period presumed that there was common morality or rationality about which all would eventually come to agreement. Postmodernity brought that into question. On what basis do we make our common moral or rational claims? Of course this provocative question was already being asked at the time of Kant.

Regarding moral claims, Friedrich Nietzsche, the vociferous critic of Kant, saw the weakness in the new Enlightenment era. 'When one gives up Christian belief one thereby deprives oneself of the *right* to Christian morality . . . Christianity is a system, a consistently thought out and *complete* view of things. If one breaks out of it a fundamental idea, the belief in God, one thereby breaks the whole thing to pieces: one has nothing of any consequence left in one's hands.[1]

What clearer criticism of the Enlightenment project than this from one of Christianity's critics? Departing the perspective of the Christian world-view does not automatically entitle one to preserve Christian morality. For this reason, Nietzsche labels Kant a crafty or '*cunning*' Christian.[2] Kant sought to maintain the skeleton frame of Christian ethics, long after the body had decomposed. Perhaps Nietzsche's response to Hick would have been similar; the pluralist represents a 'crafty' Christian wishing to base an ethical imperative on an illusory universal foundation.

Alasdair MacIntyre uses the term 'tradition' to identify the shared community in which we resolve our moral disputes. Such a tradition provides concepts of justice, political institutions and a vocabulary for intellectual enquiry. Such traditions are not optional tribes to which we might choose to belong if we prefer not to go it alone. We already belong to a tribe. 'There is no standing ground, no place for enquiry, no way to engage in the practices of advancing, evaluating, accepting, and rejecting reasoned argument apart from that which is provided by some particular tradition or other.'[3]

Traditions provide principles of reason, examples of moral behaviour and precedents for new ideas. The attempt to identify a universal category of reason or morality is hopeless. MacIntyre seeks to show this with his analysis of the work of those who collaborated in the production of the encyclopaedias of knowledge during the Enlightenment period. They thought that they were working with a common system of reason and language in order to systematize all knowledge. In fact they were simply promoting their own Enlightenment tradition of thought above all other traditions. In religious matters this is surely clear in the reductionist approach of Kant to religion. His religion within the limits of reason is an analysis of Christianity in which every unique or particular element is stripped away. Any teaching dependent on the possibility of divine intervention or supernatural miracle is either abandoned or reinterpreted in a way that will fit with a naturalist world-view. What else is this but the abandonment of orthodox Christianity in favour of orthodox rationalism? The authority of apostles or popes has been exchanged for that of David Hume and the cultured despisers of religion.

Of course, ethics is far from the only area in which this observation can be made. What is the view from nowhere? Certainly, the natural sciences have not provided it. Thomas Kuhn drew attention to the role of culture and world-view in scientific discovery and progress. Major new discoveries may involve a break with the previous paradigm. The paradigm provides a plausibility structure for what a scientist is looking for, and what they are likely to find. Such a paradigm shift may simply be inaccessible to a scientist unwilling to see things differently. As a historian of science, Kuhn could point to various examples from astronomy (Copernicus), biology (Darwin) or cosmology (Hubble) where resistance was not simply rational objection. How does science progress? It is not always linear, sometimes it requires a gestalt switch, which Kuhn describes in religious terms: 'Conversions will occur a few at a time until, after the last holdouts have died, the whole profession will again be practicing under a single, but now different paradigm.'[4] With the perspective of the history of science it becomes clear that knowledge involves a tradition of enquiry that helps us see things the way that we do.

In some respects, Kuhn and MacIntyre, along with many postmodernists, sound like relativists and this charge is often made. It is an unfair charge, at least when directed at Kuhn or MacIntrye. MacIntyre argues, contra Enlightenment thought, that we must recognize genuine pluralism in matters of reason and morality but not concede that the truth itself is plural. For the Christian to concede that a Buddhist is shaped by a quite different tradition of ethics and reason need not imply that they consider Christian beliefs to be less *true* for a Buddhist. It is only to imply that trying to demonstrate that truth will be difficult. There are no neutral rules that will arbitrate between the value or truth of Buddhism and Christianity. But there are reasons why one might choose one over the other, or even convert from one to another. After all, this happens all the time.[5]

MacIntyre's concept of a tradition of enquiry is useful because it reminds us that no one can escape being part of a way of thinking, reasoning and evaluating behaviour that has a history. Kuhn's concept of plausibility structures is particularly important here. What is found plausible or implausible has much to do with the community in which we feel that we belong. What we find laughable or take seriously will depend greatly on such traditions of enquiry or scientific paradigms. The role of a paradigm is crudely displayed in Richard Dawkins' observations on religion: 'The nineteenth century is the last time when it was possible for an educated person to admit to believing in miracles like the virgin birth without embarrassment. When pressed, many educated Christians are too loyal to deny the virgin birth and the resurrection. But it embarrasses them because their rational minds know that it is absurd, so they would much rather not be asked.'[6]

The statement itself is absurd and without warrant, but the value of it lies in what it reveals about the mindset of Richard Dawkins. Whether a belief is embarrassing or not simply reflects the majority world-view of our contemporaries. Dawkins may simply need to get out more often.

MacIntyre highlights the fact that liberal modernism is itself a tradition of enquiry. It has no right to claim a neutral status as an arbiter of truth. Theologically, this tradition developed after Kant in the work of Friedrich Schleiermacher. It is not difficult to see how John Hick's philosophical project finds its natural home in this particular tradition of enquiry.

While Kant is a founding figure for modernist philosophy, Schleiermacher is the founding figure for its liberal theology. With deep roots in Christian pietism, he sought to establish a basis for Christianity in the midst of the new sceptical and increasingly secular age. Schleiermacher considered himself an apologist for Christianity as well as an innovator in theology. His twist on Kant's theology laid the ground for modern liberalism in its approach to the doctrines of God, humanity and Christ as well as promoting the new 'higher criticism' of the Bible.

The Father of Modern Theology

We have seen the close affinities between the work of Hick and Kant. Perhaps unsurprisingly, we can identify many more parallels with the work of Schleiermacher. In particular, Schleiermacher's emphasis on religious experience shares much with Hick's epistemology. There is no surprise then, that an essential continuity can be traced through the rise of modernism and the theology of Kant, Schleiermacher and Hick.[7] There is really one emerging theology of religions from this Enlightenment tradition.

Kant's condensed form of the Christian faith was strong on moralism but weak on the felt experience of God. In contrast, Schleiermacher responded to the rationalism of the age with an account of Christianity in which the essence of faith is found in religious *Gefühl* (feeling). The German word 'does not connote a sensation, as its English rendering would suggest, but a deep sense or awareness'.[8] Schleiermacher tried to show that it was a mistake to equate religion with ethics, as Kant had done, and miss this crucial dimension of religious feeling or awareness.

Schleiermacher notes that all our experience of other people is marked by the experience of 'dependence', a general quality of human feeling. However, there is also a higher state of such experience: the feeling of absolute dependence. He describes this feeling of absolute dependence as 'not an accidental element, or a thing which varies from person to person, but is a universal element of life; and the recognition of this fact entirely takes the place, for the system of doctrine, of all the so-called proofs of the existence of God.'[9]

Like Kant's categories, the feeling of absolute dependence is universal and self-evident. We cannot get behind that feeling to test its truth value. Nor does such a feeling belong in some exclusive sense to the Christian tradition. Rudolf Otto, an early scholar of comparative religion, would later follow a similar path and use religious experience as the key theme in his interpretation of a universal sense of a religious dimension.[10]

Although Christianity remained Schleiermacher's natural home, he subjected its doctrines to substantial revision. He understood the significance of Jesus to be found in the degree to which the feeling of absolute dependence was incarnated in his life. Jesus had the highest, or most intense form, of that experience. Therefore, the difference between Jesus and the rest of humanity was more a matter of degree than kind. We find in his historic example a more intense form of a basic feeling we all share. This approach to the essence of Christianity removes any unique or normative status and leaves it only as one example of a universal human experience.

Kant and Schleiermacher both abandoned a doctrine of historic or special revelation in their respective revisions of orthodox theology. One can see how a strong view of religious authority naturally arises from belief in special revelation. This would be anathema to both

Kant and Schleiermacher. If God has revealed himself then the means of that revelation, whether prophet or scripture, must be granted a unique authority. Throwing off the shackles of tradition leads those in the wake of the Enlightenment to place authority elsewhere, and so a concept of special revelation would always be a stumbling block.

Kant and Schleiermacher both heralded a Copernican revolution in their turn from external authority to subjective forms of authority. For Kant this would be found in his thought on the moral imperative, while for Schleiermacher this would lead him to an investigation into the role of religious experience.

Schleiermacher is what George Lindbeck describes as an 'experiential-expressivist' theologian.[11] Such theology emphasizes a basic unity of religious experience behind diverse religious phenomena. Such experience is expressed in councils, creeds and holy writings but they are not the same as the experience itself. Doctrines should not be treated as objective, or realist, descriptions of the world but as expressions of a felt experience. This experiential-expressivist approach to doctrine came to dominate in the liberal theological tradition of the twentieth century.

Experiential-Expressivism

The success of experiential-expressivism is explained by its ability to deal with religious pluralism and to relativize possible objections from the natural sciences or the psychology of religion. Doctrines that might be dismissed because of new scientific discoveries or changes in the moral outlook of a population can be retained as still expressing a genuine experience even though they may not be literally true. Regarding pluralism, doctrines which are divisive when considered literally can be harmonized when taken as expressions of subjective experience. A theology of religious pluralism will naturally take this approach, as Lindbeck observes: 'The rationale suggested, though not necessitated, by an experiential-expressive approach is that the various religions are diverse symbolisations of one and the same core experience of the Ultimate, and that therefore they must respect each other, learn from each other, and reciprocally enrich each other.'[12]

Religious creeds are symbolic ways of expressing a more basic shared experience. Lindbeck's account of experiential-expressivism suggests that Hick's type of religious pluralism inevitably arises from the liberal modernist framework born out of the Enlightenment. It is true that Schleiermacher, and a later example of an expressivist like Karl Rahner, maintained some sense in which Christianity was superior to or the fulfilment of non-Christian religions. In that sense Schleiermacher and Rahner remain theological inclusivists. However, such inclusivism is unsustainable. There is an inexorable draw from such a position towards some form of philosophical pluralism, as Lindbeck points out: 'When religions are thought of as expressively rather than propositionally true, this possibility of complementarity and mutual enrichment is increased, but it also becomes hard to attach any definite meaning to the notion of "unsurpassably true".'[13]

Traditions may be distinguished from each other by their outward form, but the underlying experiences that they express are much the same. Once we accept a common, comparable core we might still retain an assumption that some traditions are better than others but this is quite a slippery notion. Such value judgements are very subjective and probably reflect the prejudices of the judge rather than reflecting anything known about an inner experience.

According to experiential-expressivism, religions are different symbolic expressions of similar underlying experience. Therefore, the knowledge of God varies among the religions by a matter of *degree*, not as a matter of *kind*. One religion may claim to offer more religious information or revelation than another religion, but this cannot be understood as knowledge of a different kind. Thus all that Schleiermacher and Rahner can claim is that Christianity has a higher intensity or better expression of that experience. Even that claim can only be provisional. Religious knowledge, being a matter of degree, not kind, is only provisional and open to growth, development and change. For an expressivist to claim that Christianity is 'unsurpassably' true looks like nothing more than prejudice. There is no theoretical reason why the experience of a Christian or the creeds of Christianity might not be surpassed by others.[14]

John Hick's religious pluralism is a good example of the development of the expressivist liberal tradition. He puts emphasis on a proposed common religious experience and relativizes the truth claims made by adherents of those traditions. He does so because he believes that his philosophical position provides a key vantage point from which to unlock the real meaning of religion.

Since the Enlightenment, the attempt has been made to stand back, as it were, from a specific tradition of enquiry in favour of a supposed unbiased point of view. From such a vantage point, Hick both surveys the world religions and offers the pluralist hypothesis, a theory apparently independent of any particular religious faith. But we have reason to question the existence of such a vantage point. Although it is true that the pluralist hypothesis does not depend on any one of the world religions – Christianity, Islam or Buddhism – it does not follow that the pluralist hypothesis has no religious allegiance. The tradition from which pluralism springs is the ethical religion of Kant. The fact that this is not identified as a formal religion alongside the great, global faiths is a matter of its relatively recent pedigree and limited adherence. It is a religious perspective, just as much as any of the ancient historic faiths. It is a tradition from which an attempt is made to relativize all other traditions.

This objection to Hick's work often meets with brusque dismissal. The reply is given that Hick is only offering a second-order 'interpretation' of religion and not a religion itself. Gillis distinguishes between Hick as a philosopher and Hick as a theologian; 'Determining clearly that his work on pluralism is philosophy of religion and not theology will go a long way toward clarifying much of the discussion on the validity of his pluralistic hypothesis.'[15] Hick was himself quick to use this strategy to try to nullify the objection. But can such a distinction between theology and philosophy really be sustained when the subjects under consideration are central Christian doctrines? Even Gillis concedes that the 'line between theology and philosophy of religion is sometimes a fine one'.[16]

In the case of Hick's religious pluralism, I would suggest it is so fine as to reach vanishing point. Cheetham also understands the issue and makes this defence:

> In this sense, Hick's pluralistic hypothesis leaves religions as they are; that is, his pluralism is an explanatory hypothesis rather than a reductionist exercise. To explain further, if he was proposing a new first-order discourse or religion – with a 'Real' to be worshipped – then we might want to know (like Job) what this Real was like; and such first-order claims would compete with other religions like any other conflicting religious truth claim.[17]

After all, was he not the one trying to respect the world religions in all their diversity? Surely the pluralist hypothesis can be accepted as a philosophical interpretation of one's own religious tradition without becoming a religion in its own right? No one needs to convert to religious pluralism. Or do they? Cheetham concedes that Hick's position really leads this way.[18] Hick's descriptions of the future include a developing religious pluralism among the religions of the world. For Christians, Hick hopes that this will lead to a 'universal church in which the pluralistic vision has become established'.[19]

There comes a point when a reinterpretation is so significant that it departs in any meaningful sense from the historic understanding. The reinterpretation is a new idea. This is exactly the case with religious pluralism. The reinterpretation of orthodoxy empties its confessional and doctrinal claims of any obvious meaning and provides a quite novel new understanding. In this sense, Hick clearly did go through a process of conversion from orthodox Christianity to the liberal pluralist perspective. He retained his commitment to certain traditional forms of religious practice, at least until much later in life, but his actual beliefs changed. What can this be other than a *metanoia* (a change of mind)? We can demonstrate this most clearly by considering Hick's approach to language and myth.

Language, Truth and Myth

Hick has emphasized certain literary forms in the course of his work without devoting much space to discussing exactly how he uses them. In particular, his use of the words 'myth' and 'metaphor' deserve some consideration as they are so significant to his work.

Hick wishes to avoid the non-realist epistemology of Don Cupitt. Religions assert facts. Religious people make claims about reality. However, much of religious tradition and teaching cannot be considered factual. This is partly as a result of scientific development and new discoveries, alongside the way that much religious language is about creating a certain kind of culture and style of worship. Hick believes that these factors demand that believers reinterpret their language regardless of how their predecessors understood their faith. However, the most compelling contemporary reason for Hick to urge this reinterpretation is a result of a new awareness of religious diversity. So Hick wishes to retain the element of realist, factual language in religious confessions of faith while reinterpreting what he considers their more crude or exclusivist claims. Hick's account of religious language distinguishes between factual religious language and language that has a quite different function.

While in his early work Hick establishes the basic fact-asserting nature of religion, his thought leaves 'ample scope for the non-factual language of myth, symbol and poetry to express the believer's awareness of the illimitable mysteries which surround that core of religious fact'.[20] Hick describes as 'mysteries' those many areas where there are gaps in our knowledge. These gaps are filled by myths and poetry. The relationship of these myths to literal language is one of adornment. They are imaginary, non-cognitive uses of language that adorn religious faith. However, not all religious language has this status. Hick maintained that even if we interpret all religious claims as mythical it would not follow that we had nothing left of any factual consequence. Therefore, the basic realist intent of certain religious claims was maintained by Hick as a bedrock of literal language use.

We have already seen in our comparison of Hick's work with that of Kant that this literal core amounts to nothing more than claims regarding the existence of the divine, the objectivity of morality and the continued existence of the soul beyond the grave. As we might expect, religious claims beyond that minimal core will be understood by Hick as examples of myth.

The line between myth and literal language moves in the course of Hick's work, though not the basic distinction itself. In his contribution to *The Myth of God Incarnate* Hick builds on the work of his fellow contributors to describe the mythological value of a high Christology. He declares that the claim that 'the historical Jesus of Nazareth was also God is as devoid of meaning as to say that this circle drawn with a pencil on paper is also a square'.[21] Any statement that is a contradiction in terms cannot be taken seriously as a literal claim. Instead, such language is to be considered mythological. Given the provocative use of the word 'myth' in the title of the book it is remarkable how little attention is given to its meaning among the contributors. Hick offers this simple definition: 'And I am using the term "myth" in the following sense: a myth is a story which is told but which is not literally true, or an idea or image which is applied to someone or something but which does not literally apply, but which invites a particular attitude in its hearers.'[22]

Hick does not use myth to mean an erroneous view or mistake. Myth has a positive value. Nor need myth always mean a story – Hick describes non-narrative concepts or ideas as myths. What defines a myth for him is that it is a statement that might appear to be a literal truth claim but is not. It is a use of language not designed to describe reality but to evoke the appropriate kind of behaviour among those who use it. Therefore, a myth cannot be tested by its literal correspondence to reality. It can only be tested by examining the kind of behaviour it inspires in believers.

Hick provides a more sustained treatment of the distinction between myth and literal language in *An Interpretation of Religion*. A literal belief is one of which its truth value 'consists in its conformity or lack of conformity to fact' whereas a myth 'tends to evoke an appropriate dispositional attitude', so requiring a quite different test for its truthfulness.[23] Hick does not identify myth in terms of it being a literary type (akin to legends or sagas) but in terms of its function in language use. This explains why he easily slips between metaphors and myths. Despite their significantly different use in literature, Hick regards them all as non-literal uses of language. His loose definition of myth allows him to roll together metaphors, allegories, parables and even some forms of historical narrative.

He gives an example of a myth by describing a devious committee meeting as 'the work of the devil'.[24] The fact that Hick can describe this as a myth, when it is clearly a metaphor, shows how loosely he uses these terms. The unfortunate result of such a sloppy approach to technical language is that it results in only two types of religious language use. There is literal-factual language use and non-literal mythological language. All religious statements must be squeezed into one or other of these forms of language. What if a particular use of language has many functions or is able to do more than one thing? Surely at some point someone assumed the literal existence of a 'personal devil' when the phrase was first used metaphorically? A metaphor only works because it connects to some characteristics, realities or events that are literally true. In other words, a metaphor does not stand alone but works on multiple levels and has a history of development. If we are not aware of these levels and do not know its history we are likely to completely misunderstand the intent of an author or speaker.

Sensitive to some of these criticisms, Hick did qualify his use of myth a little in later writing.[25] While continuing to maintain that all myth could be reduced to its literal meaning, he granted more significance to the loss that this entailed. Using the example of how the word 'ploughing' may be used metaphorically, he points out that 'We must note that ploughing may have partially different associations for different people, so that the statement may evoke a range of differing responses. This openness of the web of associations prevents metaphors from being definitively translated into literal terms, for we cannot limit their field of possible associations.'[26]

Here in this later work, Hick provides a more positive acknowledgement of the power of metaphor but as if he has begun to open a door only to close it again, he then cautions, 'It is a mistake to think – as many vaguely do – that myths can express deep truths that cannot be expressed in any other way.'[27] Ignoring for a moment the slippage between metaphor and myths as if they mean the same thing, Hick remains convinced that these literary forms are merely embellishments to the literal truth claims at the heart of religion. And by literal he assumes that it must be possible to state those beliefs without a trace of metaphor.

This treatment of language uses shares the same assumptions as those MacIntyre identified with the encyclopaedists. They assumed all literal truths must be testable by the standards of empirical science. All truth must be expressed in terms of a universal language of modernism. Anything that did not fit those categories is to be understood as non-literal language. Taking the example of the atonement, Hick continued to dismiss the literal truth of the various theories. Instead, he understood the atonement to be a myth intending to evoke the right response: we should live self-sacrificial lives. We should dispense with the past theories of substitutionary atonement or Christus Victor because 'those traditional atonement theories no longer perform any useful function'.[28] It is function that determines the value of myths and metaphors, not access to reality. Therefore, if the functional value of an atonement theory is lost then the metaphor itself should be abandoned. Hick can only evaluate religious doctrine in these functional terms because of his philosophy of religious language. It is not only a dualist view (either literal or mythical) but dreadfully reductionistic (either fact or fiction).

Language and Myth

Hick's dualist view of religious language is related to the dualism of Kant's epistemology. The radical distinction between phenomenon and noumenon rules out the possibility of any kind of hybrid language. But this is a clumsy approach to the diversity of religious language use.

Compare Hick's definitions to the relationship between myth and truth described by Marshall in his entry to the *New Dictionary of Theology* where he notes a much more complex relationship between our use of metaphors and our attempt to describe reality: 'To say that a story is a myth is not to pronounce on its historical truth or falsity . . . A myth may or may not employ historical materials.'[29] Hick defines myth in such a way that its truth value is settled a priori. As far as external reality or history are concerned, myths are not true; only the literal essence which can be clearly extracted and stated in non-mythological terms could be true. Gillis points out the poverty of this approach to doctrine: 'What is not obvious, or at least not to Hick, is that metaphor discloses or reveals truth, and that it does so precisely in its form as metaphor. It does not refer to or rely upon any other language structure to do so.'[30] Hick cannot conceive of the possibility of a metaphor being true unless it can be stated in terms acceptable to his own modernist world-view. But imagine what would be left if we could only hold statements that were devoid of any metaphor to be true. Not only is an entire realm of supernatural reality ruled out of court, but even more immediate experiences may be emptied of significance. What is love without metaphor?

There are two types of myth according to Hick. The first of these are expository myths, which attempt to express some basic truth about human existence in imaginative terms. They can be reduced to literal terms with loss only to their emotive impact. Hick is optimistic that we can extract all we need from such narratives. His example, the story of the fall in the Garden of Eden, is instructive. He describes it as an ornamental way of telling us 'the fact that ordinary human life is lived in alienation from God and hence from one's neighbours and from the natural environment'.[31] This example brings to light the poverty of Hick's definition. There are two ways in which this example demonstrates this.

First, there is the problem of his drastic selectivity in such a supposedly definitive interpretation of the Genesis story. The interpretation of Genesis has been far more complex in Christian history.[32] This reflects the interwoven nature of historical claims and Hebrew storytelling. This is not unique to biblical history, as Longman observes: 'All history is ideological; that is, it adopts a perspective through which it tells the story. It interprets events, and does not just record brute facts.'[33] Any history will be selective and perspectival. This can hardly be surprising when we read a story in a primeval setting well outside our own experience. But could it still be historical? There are many features in the text that suggest historicity.[34] The fact that such historical content is embedded in the perspective and limitations of the ancient authors' world-view no more undermines its claim to be historical than those same limitations which must affect a modern-day television documentary. Even if the authors were mistaken we cannot lightly dismiss evidence that they believed they were describing historical events. We may call this 'theological history' to highlight the theological perspective of the author but this does not negate its historical value. Hick rejects the historical value of the story because he operates with a limited view of language. The presence of a miracle would be enough to place a story in the realm of non-literal myth. Once he has made this judgement its truth value can only be found in its function. With this crude distinction, Hick ignores centuries of theological debate and bars any possibility of learning about our history and origins from the Genesis account.

Second, there is an underlying problem that Hick is guilty of in this example. On his own terms, he simply substitutes one myth for another. His 'non-mythical' account of the fall includes the concepts of 'ordinary' human life, 'alienation', supposed relationships to God and to the environment. Surely the concept of a relationship to the natural environment is parasitic on our notion of a relationship to other people? How is Hick's description considered to be literal? He relies on metaphor and analogy because there is no other way to address these ultimate, transcendent realities. If we do concede that this account continues to include metaphors then can we not strip those away too? The inevitable process of removing metaphorical content draws one ever closer to having nothing left to hold. Hick dismisses this objection. Metaphors do not go all the way down; 'If there were no non-metaphorical language it would be meaningless to say of any use of language that it is metaphorical.'[35] This response entirely misses the point. Of course, there are differences between metaphor and other forms of language use. There are also different types of metaphors (for example, extended metaphors, conceptual metaphors and submetaphors[36]). And there are different degrees of metaphorical significance. The real issue is whether metaphor can convey truth regarding what Hick calls external reality, such as history or metaphysics. We know that it does because the pluralist hypothesis itself must rely upon a wide range of metaphors.

The second type of myth described by Hick deals with ultimate mysteries by using analogies, rather than stories. To say 'God is wise' is an example of this second type of myth. It is a way of speaking directly about something of which we cannot speak. Hick is describing here the role of systematic theology or doctrine. Hick's Kantian epistemology makes such systematic statements of doctrine largely redundant. After all, our language strictly cannot describe the Real *an sich*, or God as God really is: 'Thus it cannot be said to be one or many, person or thing, substance or process, good or evil, purposive or non-purposive. None of the concrete descriptions that apply within the realm of human experience can apply literally to the unexperiencable [*sic*] ground of that realm.'[37]

At a stroke, Hick destroys the possibility of theology, or God talk. What is God if neither person nor thing? What is morality if God is neither good nor evil? None of the descriptive language that we use in the human realm can apply to God. Doctrine is mythological in that it does not apply directly to the supposed reality itself. It has only a functional purpose in affecting the attitude and behaviour of the believer.

However, as we have noted, Hick is clear that not all religious language is myth. This is particularly important given his commitment to cognitive critical realism. There must be some literal content to the mythological world of doctrine. As it had been for Kant before him, the literal contents of religion are a few simple truths – that some kind of God exists, that there is a life beyond the grave and that moral choices have eternal significance. The truthfulness of myths is only found in how they orient us to these core claims.

If religious language is mostly myth, then there is little significance in conflicting truth claims. Hick claims that most supposed contradictions are only apparent. There are some contradictory matters concerning historical events (did Jesus really die on the cross or only someone who looks like Jesus, as some Muslim traditions suggest?) or even metaphysical ideas (such as the possibility of reincarnation) but Hick believes these to be of secondary importance.

A third area of contradictory beliefs, the ways in which religions describe God, may seem contradictory but probably only reflect our limited perspectives on a greater reality. As myths and metaphors they only contradict one another if we take them literally (a mistake) or if they encourage contradictory behaviour. On this point, Hick and Kant share the conviction that apparent religious conflicts arise from misunderstanding their central myths and metaphors. The underlying moral teaching provides a basis for unity among diverse religions. But we must pause to consider this dismissive approach to myth and metaphor in religion. The quest for a literal core is a seriously misleading way of interpreting religion.

Truth and Metaphor

The word 'myth' has become so ingrained in the popular mind as a synonym for something that is untrue that it is probably beyond rescue. C.S. Lewis, a scholar of myth and literature, described his own early prejudice toward myths as 'lies breathed through silver'. He changed his mind, largely through the influence of J.R.R. Tolkien, who crystallized in his poem, 'Mythopeia', the constructive and truth-revealing role of mythology.[38]

He sees no stars who does not see them first
of living silver made that sudden burst
to flame like flowers beneath an ancient song.[39]

Far from being an embellishment of the truth, myth and metaphor are pathways to the truth. Nonetheless, to describe the Bible as containing myth is self-destructive in a culture that has increasingly lost complex literary distinctions. However, we must still salvage metaphor as an important term, not just for religion but for all forms of knowledge. Hick's treatment of metaphor is crudely simplistic and reductionist.

Hick shares in a classical approach to metaphor with roots in the work of Aristotle, who is understood to have described metaphor as 'one of the means of giving decorous "effect" to speech'.[40] Metaphor was simply treated as an expendable ornamentation to otherwise literal language use, and the purpose of that metaphor was largely for emotive effect.[41]

This ornamental approach to metaphor is obvious in Hick's work. What Hick calls the natural and the moral interpretations of our universe both rely on literal truths. However, the religious level of interpretation adds no new information.

Because of Hick's epistemology, religious knowledge does not provide us with extra facts but only a certain way of interpreting natural facts. Therefore, religious language can be expressed in moral or natural terms at a cost to its emotive value but with no loss to its literal sense. Hick occasionally gives examples of this reductionist approach by restating doctrines such as the Trinity, incarnation or atonement without what he considers the adornments of metaphor. To the believer, he does not seem to have stated the doctrines at all.

Janet Martin Soskice provides ample demonstration that such a reductionist approach to metaphor is flawed. Metaphors are essential in all forms of discourse, though perhaps particularly so in religion. Metaphors are irreducible because they always have a relationship to a wide range of related metaphors which cannot be simply expressed in non-metaphorical terms. For example, to claim that 'God is my Rock' is to relate God to a whole realm of ideas and cross-references within a network of biblical and extra-biblical imagery. Of course, these metaphors affect our actions and attitudes. Hick is quite correct to identify them, but can they not also be understood as reality-depicting?

If God is our father, then as children and heirs we come to him without fear; if God is our father, he will not give us stones when we ask for bread . . . How shall we come to God? Without fear, because he is our father. And the model is only action guiding in virtue of its claim to be reality depicting, namely, this is how it is with our relationship to God.[42]

Instead of a reductionist approach, Soskice argues that the metaphors form part of a model for understanding reality – to reduce metaphors to something else is to destroy that model altogether. She summarizes her own argument against reductionism, which is worth quoting in full:

We have said that criticisms of metaphor in religious language often conceal a more radical critique of the possibility of any talk of God, of any traditional theologizing at all. This is so because the traditional empiricist criticisms of 'non-literal' speech are . . . in the end, attacks on the possibility of any metaphysics. The plan of our counter-argument has been to show that models and metaphysical theory terms may, in both the scientific and religious cases, be reality depicting without pretending to be directly descriptive, and by doing so to support the Christian's right to make metaphysical claims.[43]

Soskice makes the important parallel between religious and scientific language. Metaphor is used in both science and religion to be intentionally reality-depicting. This is not because the practitioners want to evoke the right response but because reality requires us to stretch our language. It is not because our vocabulary is too weak but because reality is too great that we must employ metaphors.

It is naive to hold up scientific language as particularly literal or non-metaphorical. Ian Barbour has argued at length that metaphor is an essential, irreducible element in scientific discourse. He asserts that 'a metaphor cannot be replaced by a set of literal statements' because it is, by nature, 'open-ended'.[44] Metaphors must be open-ended because they are examples of stretching language in order to understand reality more satisfactorily. Light moves in waves, stars die and gravitational force attracts. Whether in science or religion, metaphors are essential if we wish to understand reality.

Hick's attempt to demythologize religion, and strip away its metaphors, betrays a reductionist view of the religious dimension. God becomes the insipid 'Ultimate Real'; repentance and faith become the turn from 'self-centredness to Reality-centeredness'. Whatever religious doctrine we consider, the process of demythologization does not simply remove literary adornments, it changes its meaning and empties it of descriptive content. For Hick, this is inevitable because he assumes religious language cannot describe a reality 'out there' but only the personal disposition of the believer.

The Pluralist Myth

The wider modernist movement, of which Hick is only a part, has subjected religion to a reductionist analysis. Religious pluralism seems a natural consequence of this process. But in its attempt to identify a common core of literal content, modernism actually destroys pluralism. The religious diversity of pluralism is nothing more than literary adornments expressed in a range of cultural forms. While one might admire such cultural richness and the rainbow of faiths, such admiration is built on the assumption that such diversity is only in matters that are optional and poetic. The real truth is One – a simple, philosophical core of limited facts about the supernatural dimension.

Hick's theological endeavour rests on replacing one source of authority with another. Instead of investing authority in revelation or in church tradition, Hick prefers the authority of the Enlightenment tradition of reason. Granting authority to this particular tradition need not imply an anti-supernatural bias[45] but all too often it does. Religion within the limits of reason alone seems an emaciated thing. Religious pluralism not only brings the modernist tradition of Kant to a logical conclusion but also to a bankrupt one. All the major faiths might be equally true, but only because they are equally erroneous.

14

The Unknown God of Pluralism

What lies at the centre of Hick's universe of faiths? What began as God and the universe of faiths transformed into the Ultimate Real and the universe of faiths. I think we have clearly seen that any substantial content rapidly recedes in the light of the pluralist interpretation of religion. The Real is a metaphor for our emotional response to the universe, not a description of reality itself. Therefore, the Real is not a God whom we worship but a cipher for the religious condition. At the centre of the universe of faiths is not God but our own experience.

Divine Revelation

Hick's Copernican revolution in theology is an extension of Kant's Copernican revolution in philosophy. This revolution, sometimes referred to as the 'turn to the self', not only places the human knower as the starting point for philosophy (a step with which the earlier philosopher, Rene Descartes, is most associated), but also as the object of philosophy. It is the human knower, with all his or her limitations, who is both the arbiter of true knowledge and the object of knowledge. This turn to self sits very uneasily with any kind of attempt to retain orthodox doctrine. Metaphysics is endangered. Kant's God is little more than a postulate for morality. If one feels morality is justified without God then Kant's theology is swiftly rendered redundant. His philosophical position hardly depends on his theology.

Hick's theology draws out the consequences of this quasi-secular philosophy. One particular Christian doctrine that is trimmed and, eventually, discarded is the doctrine of revelation. Like Kant, Hick has no place for the possibility of revelation in the strong sense of information from God providing knowledge otherwise unobtainable.

Models of Revelation

Avery Dulles offers a useful typology to describe various ways Christians have tried to describe divine revelation. In his outline of five models, he identifies Hick as a possible proponent of two of them. The apparent ambiguity is itself an indication of the uncertainty in Hick's own position. He certainly wants to retain some concept of revelation but it is difficult for his epistemology to have any room for it. It appears that Hick continued to use revelation language for rhetorical reasons related to his Christian heritage but that his philosophical position really rules out any proper sense of revelation.

The first model Dulles describes is 'Doctrinal Propositional'. Proponents of this position would include evangelicals and conservative Catholics. It implies a direct, verbal revelation from God whether located in Scripture (evangelicals) or Scripture and tradition (conservative Catholics). Though a Catholic himself, Dulles criticizes this model for being 'highly authoritarian' and not 'favourable to dialogue with other churches and religions'.[1] Hick likewise dismisses this approach to revelation. He does so because it would run counter to his earliest work on the nature of faith.[2]

The second model also lays emphasis on the written Scriptures. In the 'Revelation as History' model, God reveals himself through significant historical events. This might be the specific events recorded in the Bible or a more general sense of global history being revelatory. Wolfhart Pannenberg is representative of this approach. At first glance, Hick does seem to imply that historical events are revelatory. For example, in reference to Old Testament history he writes, 'Jeremiah was conscious of the downfall of the kingdom in the seventh century BCE as God's just disciplining of the erring Israelites.'[3] However, in the context of Hick's epistemology this is not really a description of revelation at all. The religious dimension of the event is not found in the historical incident itself but in the subjective experience of the prophet (religious seeing-as). Where Pannenberg sees the historical event itself as revelatory, Hick only sees history as a context in which we might choose to interpret events as revelatory.[4]

The third model, revelation as 'Inner Experience', departs entirely from any objective sense of revelation. Revelation is a form of personal experience of the divine. Dulles identifies Karl Rahner and Auguste Sabatier as representative theologians, both of whom were greatly influenced by the earlier work of Schleiermacher. Dulles also describes Hick as a representative of this approach: 'The great founders of religions, he [Hick] holds, are persons on whose consciousness the Transcendent has impinged in new ways with special intensity and power. Since the same infinite Spirit presses in continually on every individual, it is possible, Hick contends, for others to find meaning and credibility in what the mystics claim to have experienced.'[5]

Dulles is clearly correct to highlight the universal experience of revelation in Hick's model. Given that revelation needs to be universally accessible it follows that it must have a very personal, subjective nature. Dulles also correctly distinguishes between Hick's primary sense of religious experience in the lives of the mystics and the secondary experience of later followers. However, Hick does not neatly fit this model and so Dulles returns to Hick's work under a fifth model of revelation.

The fourth model of revelation in Dulles' work need not concern us here. Called the 'Dialectical Model', it is found in the great German theologians, Barth and Brunner. Their bold attempt to steer between revelation as either objective event or as personal experience was motivated by a desire to emphasize the absolute uniqueness of God's self-revelation in Christ. The dialectical model tends towards a more exclusivist response to the world religions.[6] Hick would have little sympathy for such a position.

The fifth model described by Dulles is unique in granting to the human subject a creative role in the process of revelation. Described as 'New Awareness', the emphasis is not on the actions of a divine being but on the development of human understanding: 'According to this approach revelation is a transcendent fulfilment of the inner drive of the human spirit toward fuller consciousness.'[7] The history of human involvement in the world has also been a history of developing awareness. Revelation is not new information given to us, but new stages of consciousness in our own development. Dulles identifies Hick as exemplar, noting that his 'recognition of revelation in the non-Christian religions rests on the premise that revelation does not essentially consist in doctrine but in encounter and awareness'.[8]

This fifth model of revelation helpfully captures the sense in which Hick sees religious knowledge as a human journey of discovery rather than a story of divine disclosure. It shares with the third model the sense of revelation as a contemporary experience rather than as a body of knowledge. However, unlike the third model, it does not maintain any kind of unique status for the historic Christian tradition. Revelation is part of progressive discovery: 'It encourages Christians to believe that their own faith could undergo a further development in the direction of universality by appreciating the perspectives of other human faiths.'[9] This model, more than any other, lends itself to pluralism. It allows for fresh discovery and therefore expectation that the encounter between faiths will lead to a new awareness and a new theology.

Dulles provides a helpful framework for understanding how theologians have developed quite different doctrines of revelation. It is interesting that Hick can be loosely placed in two of these models. His sympathies clearly lie with models three and five because they both describe revelation as universally accessible. Dulles can certainly identify statements made by Hick that are suggestive of one or other of these models. However, I would suggest that this is mistaken and results from the ambiguous way Hick uses religious language. The fact is that Hick's philosophical position rules out the possibility of any kind of revelation.

Religion without Revelation

Hick's apparent affinity with the revelation as 'Inner Experience' model is certainly evident in his first published work, *Faith and Knowledge*. Revelation was described as an awareness of divinity and not any kind of objective or verbal declaration. However, his use of the word 'revelation' is ambiguous. Elsewhere, it may be taken to imply a subjective experience, an objective disclosure or some kind of dialectical encounter; 'revelation is only real or actual in so far as it *becomes* so by being responded to' just as religion itself is only real insofar as human beings live it out.[10] Does Hick mean that there is a genuine divine disclosure that only becomes revelation when we choose to respond to it? Or does Hick mean that some other feature of the universe becomes revelation when we choose to make it so? In the course of Hick's work he moves from the former to the latter. His descriptions of revelation move away from any sense of an objective moment to which we respond toward a more general description of how we choose to make sense of anything in the universe.

Hick's account of the axial age in religious development does sound remarkably close to Dulles' fifth model of revelation. During the axial age a major threshold in human awareness was crossed from the identification of self with tribe to the consciousness of individuality. Revelation is closely allied to the evolution of human self-consciousness. Pre-axial consciousness failed to distinguish between self and society, while axial consciousness recognized the individual as part of a web of relationships to other individuals, to society and to the divine. It is unclear in Hick's work whether this divine being instigated this transitional period or whether it is a natural stage in the evolution of consciousness.[11]

In Hick's early work, some of his writings suggest God has an active role in revelation. For example, in *God and the Universe of Faiths* he asks, 'whether we should not expect God to make his revelation in a single mighty act, rather than to produce a number of different, and therefore presumably partial, revelations at different times and places?'[12] This way of phrasing the question assumes that revelation is something God 'does' or 'makes'. Hick poses the question, could God have made a single revelation to everyone or might he have produced many different revelations? Hick rejects the possibility of a universal revelation because of both the physical constraints of communication in the ancient world and also the need to preserve human freedom in interpretation.

The axial age could be understood as a prolonged period of these different, partial revelations around the world. It is significant that the word 'revelation' is absent in Hick's later description of the axial age as found in *An Interpretation of Religion*.[13] Revelation as an active work of the divine being was never really compatible with Hick's belief in the radical religious ambiguity of the universe, so the word is discretely dropped in his later writing. This reflects the superfluous nature of the concept in Hick's work.

In *The Fifth Dimension*, the axial age is described as a period of intense revelatory activity, but the locus of revelation is the human subject herself, not an active divine being: 'Such immensely powerful moments of God-consciousness, or of Transcendence-consciousness, are what we mean by revelation. These primary revelations were so overwhelming that the lives and words of the founders communicated the reality of the Divine or the Transcendent to others, setting in motion major new currents within the stream of human religious experience.'[14]

This description gives no indication of a divine activity behind revelation, only of a growing awareness by people of a supernatural reality. This period of human history is an epoch of new awareness characterized by Dulles' fifth model of revelation. However, we must not be distracted by Hick's use of the word 'revelation'. Hick has developed a theology without revelation. The 'primary revelations' were actually 'moments of God-consciousness'. The revelation itself was a personal experience. The term is more akin to the moment when we grasp something we had not understood before than to the moment when we are given information we did not have before. The reason why Hick's concept of revelation can have no objective content is because of the wider framework of his epistemology. For Hick, revelation does not describe a divine being choosing to speak but a human subject having an insight.

Knowledge without Revelation

Hick's use of Kant's epistemology creates a sharp distinction between the noumenon and its phenomenal manifestations. Kant was nothing if not consistent. In this desire to be consistent, the noumenon can have no causal relationship to phenomena. Causation is a category of the mind, not a reality that we can attribute to the noumenon. The implications are enormous. The noumenon cannot literally cause things to happen. The attempt to smuggle in causality is obvious when words like 'influence' or 'revelation' are used to describe God causing the revelatory experience.

It is very difficult to avoid causal language in describing Kant's view of the relationship between noumenon and phenomena. Even in defence of Kant's position, Nicholas Rescher recognizes the difficulty: 'It is clear that although things-in-themselves somehow 'affect' the sensibility . . . the relationship here at issue is definitely not to be construed in properly causal terms.'[15] Causation is itself a category of the understanding and not something that can be applied to the thing-in-itself. Using words such as 'affect' or 'influence' does not diminish the problem. Such words smuggle in the idea of causality under other names. But neither Kant nor Hick have any right to describe the noumenon causing anything at all. As we have seen, Rescher discusses this problem carefully and, making reference to how Kant resolves the dilemma, provides this summary:

> Kantian noumenal causality is not actual causality at all, in the strict sense in which causality is governed by the specific, experientially constitutive Principle of Causality of the Second Analogy. Rather, it is only analogical causality, governed by a generic and regulative principle of grounding, a Principle of Sufficient Reason, a principle that controls what we must think to be the case, rather than what we claim to know regarding nature.[16]

This helpfully clarifies Kant's own work by affirming a formal connection between noumenon and phenomena. But if it is not causation then what is this formal connection? Whether Rescher's attempt to answer for Kant is persuasive is not the issue of this work. However, for the theology of John Hick there remains a far more pressing problem. If there is no casual connection between the Ultimate Reality and the universe we experience, then the doctrine of creation has no objective meaning; 'In the beginning God created the heavens and the earth' (Gen. 1:1). The noumenon cannot create or reveal or otherwise cause anything in the realm of phenomena.

When considering Kant's epistemology, the problem is the inability of the human mind to penetrate beyond appearances to know the thing-in-itself. Many followers of Kant may be content with the kind of formal resolution given by Nicholas Rescher. However, for theology the problem is the other way around. It is also impossible for the thing-in-itself to reveal itself as phenomena. The barrier is insurmountable from either side. God cannot cause events. The divine cannot speak in words. Revelation is not simply difficult, it is strictly impossible. The price of Hick's use of a Kantian epistemology is that there really is no such thing as revelation. Revelation is not only impossible because we can have no direct knowledge of the divine Reality, but also because the Ultimate Reality cannot, in any way we could know, influence or affect the world of appearances.

A Silence in Heaven

Driven by his desire to avoid privileging any one tradition over another, Hick strenuously avoids granting special place to any specific claim about what God is like. Hick treats the attributes of God as analogous to Kant's categories of the mind. Like Kant's categories of space and time, the images we have of God are useful ways in which religious people structure their concept of God. Kant thought this a solution to Hume's sceptical challenge. Hick finds the same response useful as a solution to the problem of religious diversity. Our metaphysical ideas tell us more about what is going on in our own minds than anything about a world out there.

One of the foundational religious ideas is whether the ultimate divine reality is personal or non-personal. An example of a personal category used by Christians is God as Father. A non-personal example, used by eastern traditions, would be Nirvana as the ultimate state. The Father God and Nirvana are obviously quite different ideas but, according to Hick, they have a similar functional value in enabling us to relate to whatever we consider Ultimate Reality.

The personification of the Ultimate Real is common to the Semitic religions, implying that individuals can be in relationship with the Real. Hick believes that this cannot apply to the noumenon: 'It follows from this that the Real *an sich* cannot be said to be personal. For this would presuppose that the Real is eternally in relation to other persons.'[17] Personality and relationships are categories belonging to human beings and therefore they naturally apply to the phenomena. However, this tells us more about what matters to human beings than anything about the Real. The Real is often conceived in personal terms because knowledge is always subject to the capacity of the knower. Naturally personal beings see God in personal terms, because they are personal beings.

This conclusion makes it difficult to see why the Real can also be understood in impersonal or non-personal terms. Hick has to be able to extend his psychological insight to include this rival point of view and, in doing so, creates a serious obstacle to any form of revelation. A prime example of an impersonal conception of the Real (the impersonae) is the Buddhist goal of Nirvana, which Hick describes as 'the Real experienced as an ineffable egolessness' in which personal identity is extinguished.[18] Other examples include Brahman and Sunyata. For many Christians it sounds as though these non-personal images of the Real are closer to what Hick is describing than Christian orthodox images.

Hick denies that impersonal images are a closer approximation to the Ultimate Real. He recognizes that the Buddhist example might suggest such a conclusion, for he admits, 'Our pluralistic hypothesis runs parallel to this central strand of Mahayana Buddhism.'[19] Indeed, a Christian might even wonder whether Hick could just ditch the pluralist hypothesis in favour of Mahayana Buddhism. However, there is one feature of this school of thought not compatible with philosophical pluralism. Mahayana Buddhism identifies its impersonae with the Real-in-itself. It claims that the impersonal image is the Ultimate Real. Some form of mystical experience provides direct access to the divine. Therefore, other images of the Real are only accorded the status of representations. In effect, every form of Buddhism offers its own kind of exclusivism because it claims to provide a true description of the Real. That description will only be partial, and not the whole truth, but it is still exclusive truth because it does exclude contradictory claims (such as the Ultimate Reality as a personal being).

Hick wants to maintain that the Real truly transcends both personae and impersonae such that all manifestations are only representational. Impersonal images, like Nirvana, are yet more phenomenal manifestations of the noumenal real. Though the phenomena are varied and even contradictory forms, each is interpreted as a representation of the same underlying reality. Pluralism can accord no religion superior epistemic status: the Real is neither personal nor impersonal, but such images all remain useful for us to experience the Real. Hick sounds as though he is offering equal theological opportunities. However, this proposal is not as straightforward as it seems.

The attempt to deny the ultimate status of both the non-personal and personal status of the divine is misleading because these are asymmetrical claims. Denying the personal status of the Ultimate Real would mean denying the absolute attribution of qualities such as love, will, faithfulness and relationship. Hick can deny that the Ultimate Reality is that kind of thing. However, denying the non-personal status of the Real says nothing. It is a double negative. To claim that the Ultimate Real is not non-personal is to say nothing at all. Hick's attempt to rise above the religions leads only to the conclusion that any substantial descriptions of God are wrong. It certainly sounds as though Nirvana, nothingness, is a closer approximation to the way things really are.[20] Writing from an eastern Christian point of view, Ramachandra notes this connection between revelation and the personal nature of God, 'For if we allow for a God who speaks, then the view that all religions are on the same level, as equally flawed human ways of speaking of a transcendent experience, becomes less plausible. So this pluralist scheme is fatally biased against the Semitic traditions and those Indian religious traditions that focus on a personal Deity.'[21]

Hick's analysis of the Real rules out any possibility of meaningful revelation. Descriptions like 'revealer' or 'being able to reveal' are personal attributes which cannot apply to the Real-in-itself. The concept of a revealer assumes, minimally, something capable of relationship and having a will to disclose information. Hick's noumenon, whatever else it is, cannot be a revealer. Consider Brunner's neo-orthodox description of God as revealer and how alien his description would be to Hick's position:

> He [God] can be known as absolute Subject only through the fact that He Himself makes Himself known through His own action: He is not at our disposal as an object of knowledge. He proves Himself as Lord in the fact that He, He alone, gives the knowledge of Himself, and that man has no power at his own disposal to enable him to acquire this knowledge.[22]

Whatever other problems attend the neo-orthodox case, this is a distinctively Christian description of revelation. Revelation is essentially the self-manifestation of the personal God who chooses to make himself known for reasons of his own. If God were not personal then this sense of revelation would be impossible. But what other sense of revelation is there? The sun reveals itself when the clouds part. A problem reveals itself when a car breaks down. But these are analogical senses of revelation. At least in Christian theology, revelation requires a being with the capacity to choose to reveal. Even if we do not accept the assumptions of neo-orthodoxy, 'revelation' in any theistic sense implies qualities of will and ability to communicate absent in non-personal descriptions of the Ultimate Reality. Vinoth Ramachandra points out how profoundly incompatible pluralism is with those religions that emphasize historical revelation: 'For to entertain this possibility one must then be willing to acknowledge the other possibility that this God wills to reveal God's self and enter into personal relationship with us. Hick has effectively excluded any meaningful concept of divine revelation from his "meta-religion" of religions, and so it is doubtful whether any orthodox Jew, Christian or Muslim can subscribe to it.'[23]

Religious pluralism requires a demythologization of the Personal God and with it disappears all possibility of revelation. There is silence in the heavens.

A Mythology of Revelation

Hick clearly considers the various scriptures of the world religions, along with their creeds and confessions, as having value as contexts in which God might be experienced. However, his view of mythology as a type of language use allows him to curtail their value for knowledge.

Myth and metaphor do not inform us about objective reality. They encourage a moral transformation on the part of those who use that language. Its use helps orientate the life of believers toward Reality-centredness. But myth does not disclose anything about reality, a function reserved for factual language use.

The Ultimate Reality is a philosophical and moral presupposition. But according to Hick's position it is not being described by our myths and metaphors. Helpful myths are those that guide our behaviour, not those that disclose reality. This has serious consequences for any claim to revealed knowledge. While revelation might take many forms (dreams, visions, prophecy), for it to be revelation it must be possible to state the content of that revelation, at least partially and with the aid of analogies or metaphors.[24] Yet, according to Hick, informative statements about the Real can be only either formal, logical postulates or mythological claims. Mythological claims do not reveal anything because they are not fact-asserting. They are functional statements used in order to direct our behaviour. This leaves purely formal, logical postulates as the sum total of our actual knowledge about God. However, these are not the results of revelation. Such statements are postulates of human experience, not the result of divine disclosure. They are the conclusions of a religion within the limits of reason alone, making no appeal to supposed revelation.

Hick's distinction between myth and fact necessarily rules out the possibility of revelation. Revelation is simply a word we use to describe the myths and metaphors that help us orientate our lives towards an otherwise unknown divine reality. It yields no new truths and cannot be the result of divine activity.

History without Revelation

A final feature of Hick's philosophy utterly destroys any possibility of revelation. His description of the history of religions, dependent as it is on the dubious perspective of Jaspers, is nothing more than a history of the evolution of human consciousness. This history has no place for the revelatory activity of the Real. It may be the case that a spiritual dimension to the universe is being discerned through that evolutionary process but, if so, such discernment arises through human awareness and discovery, not through divine disclosure. This is why Dulles identifies Hick as representative of his fifth model of revelation.

The idea of an axial age has much against it and little for it. It has to deal with many factors that do not fit Jaspers' apparently simple observation that the world underwent a period of spiritual development *c.* 800–200 BC. The fact is that forms of monotheism appear much earlier, such as Akenhaten's reforms in Egypt *c.* 1400 BC.[25] Even such 'monotheistic moments' can distract us from the suggestion that forms of monotheism are earlier still. Finding such evidence is difficult, because such ancient references become sketchy but 'We can do so by recognizing the vestiges of a monotheistic core in the sense that the gods are traced back to one in the cosmogonies.'[26] Furthermore, anomalous with the axial framework are the influential religious developments that occur much later (Christianity and Islam). These developments are difficult to square with the axial age narrative. In his critical overview of Jaspers' idea and influence, Provan concludes: 'There never was such an entity as an axial age, I suggest. It is a construct that has little to say for itself from the point of view of actual historical data. Only inattention to the past, or indeed downright misrepresentation of it, provides the theory with the air that it needs to breathe in order to stay alive.'[27]

The axial age is useful for those who wish to explain religious development as a particular moment in human consciousness. It is of very little use for those interested in sociology, anthropology or history. Probably fictitious, it is useful as a way of placing religious development as simply one strand of human progress. Inevitably, Hick appeals to it because he wishes to identify the development of religions as part of the growth of human consciousness. However, the word 'revelation' is redundant in this narrative. It is a way of reading history in terms of human awareness punctuated by periods of insight and advance. Like the grand story of evolution in biology, it serves the purpose of explaining apparent leaps forward in development.[28] Nowhere in Hick's account does he need to describe a divine initiative in supplying revelatory content to the human race.

Having surveyed Hick's comprehensive case for religious pluralism, the implications for other theological themes become clear. For a Christian believer these implications are fundamental. Stephen Williams argues that Hick's doctrine of revelation (or non-revelation) rules out the Christian conception of God. Williams points out:

> [Hick] denies that we may validly think of God as personal in any way resembling the tradition. It has been difficult enough for many to swallow the claim that Christians must regard belief that God is personal as an optional belief. One is dealing with a veritable camel if one is to swallow the claim that such belief is no longer optional at all and that effectively impersonal notions of the Real are nearer the mark.[29]

This is fatal for Christian theology, based as it is on a belief in a God who has revealed himself. However, believers of any religious tradition may find parallel problems.[30] Hick's pluralism requires that no revelation in any significant sense can occur. Instead, a transcendent force of some ineffable kind has created humankind (or allowed them to come to be) and then left them to discover their own significance. The world's religions may be regarded as of roughly equal validity because they are of roughly equal invalidity. They all misunderstand the nature of their faiths, mistaking expressions of personal experience for descriptions of objective reality. They are equally ignorant of the transcendent reality about which they claim to speak. Hick may be correct in his arguments but, if so, the believer of any faith needs to recognize where these arguments have taken them. The philosophical pluralist has adopted a view of the universe in which God is notable only for his absence. The object of our worship is our own religious experience, not the divine reality itself. It cannot reveal itself, and we cannot perceive it. This is an account of religion without revelation. It is also a religion without God.

15

Religious Diversity

Hick often presented his case as the 'best' hypothesis. His claim was that though he might be wrong, he challenged anyone to present a better explanation of religious diversity. On the face of it, this is a very honest challenge, but the problem with it as a test is specifying what 'best' might mean. Does it mean the hypothesis best able to resolve conflicts and remove the need for argument? Or could 'best' mean the most coherent and widest explanatory power? Perhaps 'best' simply means what appeals to one's personal priorities and inclination?

Hick's conviction that pluralism represents the best hypothesis reflects his own commitment to a certain Enlightenment tradition of liberalism with its treatment of religion as devoid of revelation or any unique content. I think that evangelical Christian theology offers a better interpretation of religion. It provides a basis for the unique claims of Christian theology and a perspective from which to evaluate rival claims. It also provides a basis from which to respect diversity and live with difference. We can close our study of Hick's work by considering its claims in the light of a different theological perspective. Evangelical theology provides a basis for tolerance and an explanation of diversity. Of course there will be plenty of remaining unanswered questions and areas in which evangelicals will disagree but all the resources are available from this perspective in which to develop a robust and coherent theology of religions.[1]

Inter-Religious Encounter

Hick's proposal is attractive for a number of reasons. His work will obviously appeal to those who are already committed to some form of quasi-Kantian epistemology. However, there is also great appeal to traditional Christians. This appeal owes much to the possibilities pluralism offers for inter-religious co-operation, for pluralists would claim that their way of thinking engenders humility and respect for those of other faiths.

Christians find a strong moral force in the argument that one should approach others in humility, with the expectation that we will learn from them.[2] Even among evangelicals this has led to great debate and diversity. This diversity has stretched the very definition of what it means to be evangelical. While not embracing Hick's pluralism, many have sought to adopt a more inclusivist approach to the role of religion in the providence of God.[3] Clark Pinnock urges such an inclusivist approach by describing Paul's teachable spirit:

> If we hold the Apostle in high esteem, we must take seriously interreligious dialogue as part of the strategy of missions. Paul was prepared to begin the conversation with people to see where it would lead. In dialogue, he was ready to move to their territory, to their comfort zones, to preach Christ to them . . . he was prepared to work with agreements and learn from disagreements.[4]

This is an ambiguous statement. It appeals to our intuitive desire to seek truth wherever it may be found and avoid the arrogance of assuming we are always right. However, Pinnock's brief caricature seems to ignore Paul's strong convictions about the exclusive truth of the gospel (Gal. 1:6–8) and his intense focus on the message of the cross (1 Cor. 2:2). Paul certainly moved into the territory of pagan religion and sought to build bridges with it (Acts 14:14–18; 17:22–34) but these examples ill-fit the contemporary picture of inter-religious dialogue. Schnabel's description of Paul is much closer to the mark:

He was convinced of the truth of his theological affirmations, of the deception of secular religions, of the fact that God now provides salvation only on account of the death and resurrection of Jesus Christ, and of the reality of God's judgement. Paul was a missionary, not a religionist involved in a dialogue that proceeds from the assumption that God is present in all religions, that salvation is possible through all faiths and ideologies, and that God's Spirit is at work in all religions, faiths, and ideologies.[5]

Of course there is no necessary reason why dialogue may not be compatible with polemic, apologetics and debate along with those conversations of mutual learning in the pursuit of truth: 'As they defend the faith, apologists can remain open to learning, growth, and the possibility of revision in their views. But they also live with a sense of loyalty to the truth they have.'[6] However, the contemporary attraction to restate evangelism as dialogue leads to ever more optimistic interpretations of the salvation and knowledge accessible through other religions.[7]

It is important to distinguish this more general cultural shift from the pluralist hypothesis. Religious pluralism is founded upon an 'epistemic' humility. In other words, built into this theory of knowledge is scepticism regarding the validity of religious truth claims. We have seen how Hick outlines three levels of knowledge, each offering an increasing level of ambiguity, ignorance and uncertainty. This mirrors what he believes should be an increasing sense of humility on the part of the believer. For example, in matters of scientific debate – such as the Copernican view of the orbital motion of sun and earth – Hick would argue that there is little need for epistemic humility. We are permitted a sense of absolute conviction regarding this belief, a belief based on natural knowledge.

However, the second and third steps of knowledge are increasingly based on ambiguous data and correspondingly require increasing humility. Some moral claims warrant such universal assent that we have a right to absolute convictions – that murder and rape are wrong. However, many other ethical areas reveal grey areas and on these our convictions are less clear. Historically, Christians have disagreed over divorce and remarriage. Hick refers to euthanasia and abortion as areas of moral debate which cannot be settled definitively. Regarding euthanasia it is a matter of personal choice: 'Each individual, rather than the state or the medical profession, should – in my opinion – have the right to make the final decision in this area.'[8] Hick considers aesthetic judgement to be in a similar epistemological category to moral judgement. While it is possible to speak of broad agreement over what is beautiful or ugly there remains great freedom over such subjective evaluations.

In matters of religious belief the data is at its most ambiguous. Therefore, believers must hold to their faith with a sense of philosophical humility. This is not so much an attitude of mind as a theoretical principle. We simply cannot know for sure. There is no privileged route through revelation or experience. This leads to a certain kind of inter-religious dialogue.

If all dialogue partners share Hick's epistemology then they will all be able to suspend their personal convictions and admit that what they believe is open to doubt. Religious pluralism provides a theoretical framework in which to discuss our differences. Rather than being divided by contrary doctrines, believers may find unity in a common ethical agenda.

A good example of such an agenda is to be found in the 1993 Declaration of the Parliament of the World's Religions. This was a major international assembly of representatives from many religions. Its purpose was to agree upon and commend to the world a statement of common ethics. The declaration is a broad statement of ecological concerns, the importance of community and rejection of corporate greed and social injustice.[9]

The declaration does not mention God and avoids specific language that might privilege one religious group or exclude another. Hans Küng introduces its published form, 'The hope is that this document may set off a process which changes the behaviour of men and women in the religions in the direction of understanding, respect and cooperation.'[10] Disputes over the nature of God were excluded from the discussion at the outset.[11] Indeed, Küng freely acknowledged that 'a consensus can be achieved in matters relating to a global ethic only if... one leaves aside all differences of faith and "dogma", symbols and rites, and concentrates on common guidelines for human conduct'.[12] The Parliament of the World's Religions has privileged a mode of religious speech that must be compatible with all. The question is whether this intention actually helps in the expression of religions or is their distortion. Noting how the Theosophical Society found a happy home in original development of the Parliament of World's Religions, G.K. Chesterton described it as a 'pantheon for pantheists'.[13]

While Küng has argued against Hick's form of religious pluralism, there is no doubt that his pluralist hypothesis would provide exactly the right kind of framework for this type of declaration. For Hick, the specific content of religious belief *must* be laid aside in favour of vague, common values because only when this is done can true co-operation be possible. Hick's own commentary on the global ethic is revealing. He points out that the 'Intermediate Principles' of the declaration are all phrased in terms acceptable to modern, secular liberalism. So where did they come from? They did not come from Christianity so much as Christianity was itself reformed by them: 'During much the greater part of its history Christianity has been neither democratic, nor liberal, nor science-oriented, nor historically minded.'[14] So if Christianity has been so ethically weak, to what may we attribute the moral advance of the modern west? Hick's answer is entirely in keeping with the argument of this book: 'These Intermediate Principles clearly come out of contemporary Western post-Enlightenment culture. Anyone reading them can readily identify their provenance, reflecting as it does the concerns and presuppositions of modernity.'[15]

For all the attention paid to the 'Golden Rule' in the ethical systems of the world religions, it was the Enlightenment age that saw a major move forward in ethical sensitivity and values. Hick sees the adoption of the global ethic as impossible without a prior discovery and acceptance of the Enlightenment approach to religion. For those, like those he calls fundamentalists, unable to accept the epistemology of the Enlightenment, such moral advance is considered to be impossible.

For all the attraction and strengths of the pluralist case for inter-religious encounter it is here that it begins to unravel. The virtues of humility and tolerance entailed by the pluralist hypothesis are more apparent than real. Far from being a philosophy of tolerance, it leads to a serious form of intellectual intolerance.

Humility and Tolerance

Humility is a virtue (Gal. 5:23; Eph. 4:2; 1 Pet. 3:8). The English word finds its etymological roots in the Latin word for 'lowly' or 'earthly'. The New Testament word (*prautès*), 'refers to a trait of character independent of any conditions of poverty . . . political powerlessness or oppression'.[16] In other words, humility is a choice, not a condition. If we are unavoidably in a position of weakness or ignorance then we are not being humble to admit to it. We are simply being honest. The great example of Christian humility is found in the account of Jesus washing the feet of his disciples. By this action he gave an example of his role as a servant of others. Even the proper growth of the church has come through humble service rather than violent oppression or mastery. Humility implies that one freely lays aside rights or privileges in order to put others first and serve them. In no sense have Christians taken the humility of Jesus to imply that he lacked knowledge or insight. It is exactly because of his knowledge and power that Christians have considered this such a profound example of humility. The example of the washing of the disciples' feet is then all of a piece with the incarnation itself, culminating in the cross. Jesus Christ takes upon himself a powerlessness that is chosen not enforced

> who, being in very nature God,
> did not consider equality with God something to be used to his
>   own advantage;
> rather, he made himself nothing
> by taking the very nature of a servant,
> being made in human likeness.

And being found in appearance as a man,
he humbled himself
by becoming obedient to death –
even death on a cross![17]

The Christian church has only really been true to her master when she has been such a servant of others. Humility implies that one freely lays aside rights or privileges in order to put others first and serve them. This is the humility revealed in the incarnation and demanded of those who would follow Jesus. In contrast, Hick's account only appears to commend humility.

Religious believers, of any tradition, may have absolute convictions regarding the truth of their faith and yet exercise profound humility. Thus we must fault the kind of pluralist claim made by Wilfred Cantwell Smith. Regarding the statement 'Without the particular knowledge of God in Jesus Christ, men do not really know God at all' he writes: 'Let us leave aside for the moment any question of whether or not this is true . . . My point here is simply that, in any case, it is arrogant. At least it becomes arrogant when one carries it out to the non-Western or non-Christian world.'[18]

Smith's point is either trivial or false. If he simply means that making an absolute truth claim is necessarily arrogant then that is a trivial point. It would be equally arrogant to claim that 'Without knowledge of the Copernican system, people do not really understand the motion of the planets at all'. There is a trivial sense in which all truth claims are arrogant, and Hick concedes this too. However, if Smith means that whenever the claim is made it always implies a morally abhorrent attitude then his point is false. Lesslie Newbigin defends an orthodox doctrine of the incarnation, but denies the charge of arrogance: 'No human mind can grasp the depth of that mystery. But, having been laid hold of by it, no human being can think of it as merely one among many symbols of an unknowable reality. To affirm that this is the truth, not merely truth for me but truth for all, is not arrogance. It is simply responsible human behaviour.'[19]

If we believe something is true, it is not arrogant to communicate that truth. If we believe something is true and matters for our health and wellbeing, then it is responsible behaviour to communicate that truth. A doctor that fails to prescribe appropriate medication is considered irresponsible.

Furthermore, Hick's form of religious pluralism is built upon its own absolutes. It is not true to claim that religious pluralism means laying aside all personal convictions and treating one's own knowledge as provisional. Hick's pluralism only requires that we do this with regard to our religious beliefs. However, there are a number of other beliefs which Hick does hold to be non-negotiable. Primarily these beliefs are those that represent the achievement of the Enlightenment age in both its scientific methodology and its truncated form of religion. As we have seen, even the Golden Rule is only as filtered through the perspective of modern liberalism. Hick sees no need for humility regarding his essential convictions over epistemology and liberal ethics. The underlying incoherence of the pluralist hypothesis is that it requires intellectual humility regarding all religious positions other than its own. Hick would claim that religious pluralism is exempt from this requirement because it is not itself a religion. This, however, may only be a case of special pleading and reveals a blind spot in the pluralist argument. Even if pluralism is not, in itself, a religion, it so reframes the faith of the enquirer that it becomes a new form of religion. The religion of a 'Christian pluralist' is quite different from the religion of an evangelical Christian. To this religion of Christian pluralism there must be an absolute loyalty. Fundamentalism takes many forms.

It would be better to refrain from applying humility to epistemology. Humility is a virtue and, as a character trait, to be cultivated throughout life whatever our beliefs may be. The way that we share our beliefs and regard other people should be shaped by humility. However, the convictions with which we hold to our beliefs and the manner in which we commend them are distinct issues. The religious pluralist position is itself a case in point. Hick's form of pluralism offers a clear structure of belief including absolute claims regarding what we can and cannot know along with absolute moral demands. However, whether a pluralist is a humble person or not is a separate issue. There is no logical or sociological reason why someone might not be absolutely certain of a truth about God or salvation and yet exemplify humility in their relations to others.

Destroying Diversity

We may press this point regarding tolerance further and ask whether religious pluralism really delivers the tolerant environment for inter-religious engagement that it claims. Hick rejects both exclusivism and inclusivism for being intolerant. Both positions make assumptions about other faiths regarding their erroneous beliefs. Despite appearances, Hick cannot avoid also making such assumptions. Indeed, the philosophy of language embedded in the pluralist hypothesis demands a constant reinterpretation of the claims religious people make. The pluralist interprets the doctrines of all traditions as, substantially, mythological. The pluralist can gently nod as they listen to the voice of the Other, all the while reinterpreting what the Other really means to say in terms of the canons of Enlightenment thought. Father, forgive them, for they do not know what they are talking about. The only religious claims that escape demythologization are those minimal philosophical ones made by the pluralist.

This point leads D'Costa to a devastating exposition of Hick's implicit exclusivism. Describing Hick's treatment of all religious truth claims as mythological (other than those minimal claims made by the pluralist), he writes, 'Such a position has the effect of claiming that there are no true religions, for all misunderstand themselves until they embrace the pluralist hypothesis. They must fundamentally reinterpret their self-understanding in modernity's terms.'[20]

The pluralist hypothesis tolerates no division or dissent. It must always interpret the claims others make in order to fit its own conclusions. In a sense, Hick can point out that this is true of any all-encompassing hypothesis.[21] It is unavoidable that an observer will depart from the self-understanding of those they interpret. But at least the traditional religious believer is explicit about this. A Christian exclusivist will not hide their confidence in the universal application of their faith. They are explicit in their commitment to a meta-narrative. This is not in conflict with the benign context of a multicultural society. D'Costa even argues that within a pluralist academic setting it should be possible, and desirable, to establish 'tradition-specific forms of enquiry',[22] in which specific faith commitments can be a starting point for intellectual enquiry. Traditional believers already bring commitments to their intellectual enquiries but at least they are honest and up front about them. In contrast, the pluralist is reticent about their underlying exclusivism.

Worse still, the pluralist is committed to reinterpreting rival beliefs in order to harmonize them. The exclusivist has no such intention. They can allow rival beliefs to speak for themselves. They may claim that those of other faiths are wrong in their beliefs but they are not committed to saying that those practitioners have misunderstood their own beliefs.

One assumption betrayed in much pluralist rhetoric is that division and disagreement are always a bad thing. The orthodox doctrines of the incarnation and atonement are rejected by pluralists, partly on account of the disagreement they create among religious people. For example, consider these further words of fellow pluralist Wilfred Cantwell Smith: 'Any position that antagonizes and alienates rather than reconciles, that is arrogant rather than humble, that promotes segregation rather than fellowship, that is unlovely, is *ipso facto* un-Christian.'[23] There is a peculiar mix of ambiguous language in this statement. Antagonism, arrogance and segregation would all be un-Christian in matters of personal relationships, justice and racial equality. The virtues of humility and fairness are relevant here. But do they apply to truth itself? Smith applies these attitudes to cover the very things that we believe. His argument is misplaced because truth-claiming necessarily requires some kind of 'segregation'. Truth must be segregated from error. Christian faith must be distinguished from rival or alternative world-views at those points where doctrines diverge.[24]

The pluralist approach to religion is far from tolerant. It assumes the supremacy of a post-Kantian, liberal outlook and interprets all religions from this vantage point. Hick denies the charge that he interprets religions from a neutral position. He claims that he arrives at his position 'inductively', starting with his own Christian experience.[25] This response is beside the point. How he came to hold his position is a separate issue from the validity of that position. Starting from a Christian faith position, Hick was inductively led to an intellectual hypothesis that claims no particular religious affiliation. The only intellectual affiliation evident in this position is a certain kind of post-Kantian liberalism.

Paul Knitter readily admits that his approach to dialogue requires a commitment to a certain kind of Christian pluralism: 'Only if Christians are open to such a possibility (which I will argue below, is for Christians a probability bordering on a necessity) that there *are* many true, saving religions and that Christianity is one among the ways in which God has touched and transformed our world – only then can authentic dialogue take place.'[26]

Knitter's possibility–probability–necessity is an assumption in favour of a pluralist view without which dialogue is not genuine. While writing from the perspective of a theologian in a Christian tradition, the same demand could be made of a practitioner from any religion. Some pluralists have been even more strident in their admission of this point. One educator, influenced by the pluralist case, concedes, 'Pluralism and secularism are two sides of the same coin; education for pluralism means education for secularism.'[27] Few pluralists are quite so candid.

Far from providing a framework in which diverse religions can co-exist in tolerance, respect *and* disagreement, the pluralist hypothesis subjects every religion to this secular agenda. Religious diversity appears to be valued when pluralists engage in dialogue but there is a more fundamental common commitment. Pluralism makes secular assumptions about religion and the kind of tolerance on offer only extends to those who make no absolute claims. It is a sham neutrality. The specific, historical claims of a religion like Christianity must be relativized or rejected in order to pursue the pluralist agenda.

Intolerant Tolerance

The appeal of pluralism lies in its harmonization of religious divergence. The impression is given that ugly conflict can be replaced by benign co-operation through a shared commitment to pluralism.

This appeal is misguided. Tolerance does not require agreement, quite the opposite. Tolerance requires respect where there are deep disagreements. We do not tolerate those with whom we have no differences. Tolerance and respect are required when ideas diverge and intellectual conflicts arise. The irony of the pluralist case is that it assumes social harmony requires creedal harmony. Religious pluralism is intellectual intolerance – it cannot tolerate the possibility that other religions might be genuinely 'other', but instead seeks to reinterpret them, even against their practitioners' self-understanding. Pluralists attempt to remove the grounds of disagreement in order to strike a victory for toleration. But it is a Pyrrhic victory. The price of the pluralist hypothesis is the validity of those very things that distinguish religions and give them their identity. The world religions are reduced to the bland and insipid values of secular modernity with its obvious inability to answer the greatest questions of life. As MacIntyre observes of modernity, 'The facts of disagreement themselves frequently go unacknowledged, disguised by a rhetoric of consensus.'[28] Worse still, those facts are simply jettisoned in the interests of a common core. Pluralism collapses into monism, 'Homogeneity – inappropriate pressure that inhibits others from being their true selves in abiding otherness – and not pluralism is the problem.'[29]

Can a Christian be both exclusivist and tolerant? Is it possible to hold to the traditional, orthodox position on the incarnation, atonement and character of God and still have a coherent view of religious diversity? Christian mission proves that it is. Since the days of the early church, Christianity has engaged with diversity and opposition. Sometimes that engagement has been harmful and coercive. But at other times it has been respectful and tolerant. It is true that in peaceful dialogue the Christian should still seek to communicate and share the good news of Jesus Christ but this is no more intolerant than the pluralist desire to share modern, liberal philosophy. Given this contrast, the missionary seems more honest. It is the pluralist who should admit to an imperialist agenda which represents not the preservation of religions but their secularization.

16

An Evangelical Theology of Religions

In the biographical survey of Hick's career I sought to demonstrate a certain trajectory to his work. His initial commitment to an orthodox Christian theology established certain foundations for his thought. However, he also held a fundamental commitment to the philosophical tradition of the Enlightenment, evident in his epistemology. This is probably not unusual among Christians. After all, a case can easily be made that much of the Enlightenment era was itself a fruit of Christian tradition and thought. In certain respects Christianity and the Enlightenment are compatible.

However, Hick developed a theory of knowledge in which Christian theology was always peripheral. His central commitment was to a largely secular philosophical position in which God's presence is not evident, but a matter of interpretation. This is not to deny that his philosophical work is formidable. Hick is an effective philosopher. The point here is that the philosophical position he develops is inevitably opposed to orthodox theology. His epistemology cannot help but distort Christianity.

It has been my claim that Hick's position has never had to undergo a radical revolution. His life's work has been a matter of his theology catching up with his philosophy. The religious pluralist account, a natural position for anyone who adopts the kind of modernist philosophy espoused by Hick, may well become the most popular account of religions within liberal theological thought. Sceptical of any claims to absolute certainty regarding matters of faith, the position assumes that the most important beliefs will be those based on universally accessible reason, not those based on particular historical events or personalities. This position inevitably jettisons key Judeo-Christian doctrines.

Hick is dependent on a philosophical position that must drastically revise the meaning of Christianity. Having discarded core historic doctrinal claims regarding the incarnation and atonement, he is left with a few simple beliefs compatible with most of the world religions. Three core beliefs survive the pluralist reinterpretation: the existence of some kind of divine reality, the possibility of a continued existence beyond the grave, and the moral value of selfless behaviour. Unsurprisingly, these few beliefs are largely compatible across the religions.

From a Christian point of view, the major weakness that must be identified in this account is the way that it handles historical claims. Christian theology has always put great emphasis on God revealing himself through and even acting within history. Hick, in contrast, has no place for such historical particularities.

As I have sought to show in the body of this work, Hick's treatment of history is a consequence of his epistemology. David Hume had provided a powerful critique of knowledge based on observation and history. Our universal or abstract beliefs go far beyond what historical observation and evidence can really sustain. After him, and largely in response to him, Kant developed a theory of knowledge and religion that did not regard truth as dependent on historical events. Hick's religious pluralism is a natural outcome of this Enlightenment movement.

The Historical Core

The identity and purpose of Jesus of Nazareth lies at the heart of the Christian faith. The Jesus claim is a historical claim. Of course, this can be considered a naive statement in contemporary circles. Indeed, Hick frequently points out that he relies upon New Testament scholarship for his own sceptical view of a high Christology. However, David Nah points out how misleading Hick's summary of this scholarship can sometimes be: 'Although Hick is surely correct about a general agreement that Jesus did not use the christological titles found in the gospels, what Hick so conveniently fails to mention is the other powerful and overwhelming consensus among New Testament scholars that Jesus did make implicit claims about himself that strongly imply virtually the same thing as many of the titles.'[1]

It should be accepted that there is no such thing as a pure, unbiased, historical record. But whoever claimed that there was? In his survey of the New Testament, N.T. Wright dismisses the crude modernist caricature of history as a neutral recording of events; 'There is not, nor can there be, any such things as a bare chronicle of events without a point of view. The great Enlightenment dream of simply recording "what actually happened" is just that: a dream.'[2] This should be non-controversial. All history involves selection and interpretation. New Testament scholarship has often been associated with great scepticism over the historical sources themselves, and Hick himself assumes much of this particular critical scholarship.

However, in commenting on the present scene, Wright indicates a course correction in scholarship. A more positive approach to the relationship of theology and history has led to a renewed quest for the historical Jesus without the naturalistic bias and scepticism of the Enlightenment era. Wright describes it as the prodigal returning home, the tools of historical research now becoming more acceptable in a confessional Christian context.[3] Taking the historical data seriously, and laying aside any naturalistic bias against the possibility of miracles, it becomes evident that Jesus claimed a unique role for himself as the fulfilment of the Jewish expectations. The great biblical themes of worship, temple and sacrifice find their true significance in the life and death of Jesus. 'Jesus, then, believed himself to be the focal point of the people of YHWH, the returned-from-exile people, the people of the renewed covenant, the people whose sins were now to be forgiven. He embodied what he had announced. He was the true interpreter of Torah; the true builder of the Temple; the true spokesperson for Wisdom.'[4]

The Jesus of John Hick's reconstruction marginalizes these unique, tradition-specific characteristics in favour of a portrayal more amenable to pluralism. It is obvious why Hick must do this. Once we accept the historical evidence for Jesus' self-understanding as Messiah we are left with the classic trilemma. Jesus is either psychologically disturbed, of sinister intention or truly God incarnate.[5] Unless we follow the radical line of denying the existence of Jesus, the historical sources demand such a decision. It is not possible to try to unhitch the response of the early church from the claims Jesus made about himself. The historical evidence for Jesus' self-understanding is too strong. Interestingly, much of the 'Third Quest' for the historical Jesus finds this emphasis in the Jewish roots of Jesus.[6] It is the neglect of his Jewish context that led to the humanist reinterpretations of his character common to Protestant Enlightenment scholarship. Rediscovering the Jewish character of the claims of Jesus highlights the problem for religious pluralism.[7] The historical Jesus is a poor candidate as a proponent of religious pluralism.

The historical study of Jesus endorses the general Christian belief that God has acted in history. The Bible as revelation includes a witness to historical events. The very character of the gospels is shaped by historical particularities.[8] This wealth of historical evidence cannot be lightly dismissed. Even if a critic identified contradictions or erroneous details, the fundamentally historical character of the record cannot be ignored.[9]

Hick's sceptical views on the reliability of the gospels are formed from a particularly sceptical tradition on New Testament scholarship. Since the publication of *The Myth of God Incarnate*, New Testament studies have developed a more positive view of their historical value. Richard Burridge laid out the persuasive evidence that the genre of the gospels fits best with ancient Greco-Roman biographies (otherwise known as *bioi*).[10] Various features demonstrate that the gospel writers considered themselves to be writing biography. Their chronological structure, emphasis on final years, description of subject's character and style of prose narrative all indicate that they are to be understood as biographies. Whether they are mistaken or not, the gospel writers themselves thought that they were conveying historical events. These historical intentions demand that we take seriously their claims. They fit with the wider Greco-Roman culture of historical biographies based on eyewitness sources.

Hick's approach to religion fits better with what many would understand to be the traditions of Hindu culture, rather than those of Judeo-Christianity. D'Costa identifies the crucial connection between Christianity and history: 'For the Semitic religions the events of history tend to be all important and decisive. For example, if Jesus did not die on the cross, then by implication the resurrection appearances and the events that followed would be cast in a vastly different light.'[11]

This implication does not trouble Hick. He defines faith as a way of interpreting the universe rather than as a response to public, historic events. Therefore, all events may be reinterpreted as mythological. Whether a core of those myths actually took place or not is an open question, of little consequence to him.[12] However, Hick must still affirm some kind of significance for Jesus, given that he stands in the tradition of Christian theology. What little we can affirm of Jesus, Hick claims, suggests that he would have been a pluralist of sorts. Indeed, all that can be gleaned from the historical evidence is that Jesus would have been admired and considered significant in any religious culture. It just happens that he was admired by a Hellenistic culture and interpreted in corresponding Greek philosophical categories. Had Jesus been admired among those in Hindu cultures then a different theological understanding would have emerged. There would have been no Chalcedonian definition of orthodoxy. D'Costa points out the difficulties in this suggestion: 'It is pure hypothesis that if Christianity had expanded eastwards, Jesus would have been identified as a Bodhisattva or Avatar. In fact, it is interesting to note that when Christianity did spread eastwards at a very early date, if the tradition of St. Thomas' arrival in India is true, no such process occurred.'[13]

Christianity did develop in the east. Hick's hypothesis can be tested. Yet a low Christology did not emerge there. A high Christology, along Chalcedonian lines, has always been part of Christian theology. It is impossible to get behind the historical sources and find a person who fits Hick's reconstruction. Hick's Jesus is pure conjecture, and it is hardly surprising that the character that emerges is one who would support the pluralist hypothesis.

This is not to deny that Christian theology has developed. The question is whether those developments are a legitimate reflection on the original, historical data. In the year following SCM's publication of *The Myth of God Incarnate*, Cambridge University Press published C.F.D. Moule's *The Origin of Christology*. In this important work, Moule demonstrated a fallacious assumption in much liberal critical scholarship. The assumption was the Christology evolved during early church history. This evolutionary paradigm gave the impression that Jesus would not have recognized Chalcedon, that beliefs had changed over time. On the contrary, Moule demonstrates that a high view of Christ is already embedded in the New Testament. Orthodox understanding developed, rather than evolved, in the course of later theological reflection. In particular, Christ is seen as an individual distinct, in important respects, from his followers. According to Moule, the disciples 'attribute to him a unique closeness to God and a divine, creative initiative, which marks him off from their conception of what each believer – precisely because of him and through him – may become.'[14]

Moule's evidence includes the divine title, LORD (Greek: *kurios*), which the Greek-speaking Jews used to translate the Hebrew name for God. In *Koine* Greek, the word might only be a term of respect, but its use in relation to Jesus is highly significant. Some New Testament passages that apply the title to Jesus do so in a way that deliberately echoes the Old Testament background of its use to signify the divine name (e.g. the use made of the title in Phil. 2:6–11 as a reference to Isa. 45:22–4). However, in the self-understanding of Jesus there is a pattern of promise and fulfilment that takes the divine title and attributes in order to fulfil them. In his monumental study, N.T. Wright builds the convincing case that the messianic prophecies point to the coming of the LORD to save and that Jesus consistently identifies these prophecies as fulfilled in his acts: 'Behind the riddle of Jesus' own coming to Jerusalem as Messiah there lay a deeper meaning. Jesus was announcing, and embodying, the return of

YHWH to Zion.'[15] The Jewish background to the self-understanding of Jesus has regained ground again in New Testament studies and its implications are profound. It is even less plausible to make Hick's move to extract Jesus from his cultural context and reconstruct him along liberal Enlightenment lines.

Moule also points to the way worship is offered to Jesus in the New Testament and the claims following his resurrection. All of this evidence belongs to the earliest strands of the New Testament, and it is these that are developed in later church tradition.[16] A high Christology does not simply arise with later reflection but is part of the earliest witness of the New Testament. Paul Barnett provides evidence from the earliest letters of the New Testament and demonstrates that a high Christology was no later ecclesiastical development, but the very cause of the existence of the church.

> [T]he letters point to early and shared convictions of an exalted kind about Jesus. The non-evangelistic nature of the letters indicate that these convictions are shared by both writer and readers . . . The most plausible – *historically plausible* – explanation of the early and exalted view of Jesus is the percussive impact of Jesus the Teacher, risen from the dead, upon his immediate followers, both before and after Easter.[17]

The resurrection of Jesus becomes key in the mature reflection of the first followers. It is the risen Jesus who receives worship from the monotheist Thomas who declares of him, 'My Lord and my God!' (John 20:28). Bauckham identifies the features of Judaism that made this claim intelligible and indicate a high Christology:

> The worship of Jesus serves to focus in conceptuality, as well as making most obvious in religious practice, the inclusion of Jesus in the unique identity of the one God of Jewish monotheism. It was not only the natural religious response of Jewish Christians to the status they perceived the exalted Jesus to have and to the role he played in their religious experience and life. It was also reflectively understood in the context of Jewish monotheistic understanding of God.[18]

Even in this early simple form of worship a Chalcedonian Christology is emerging. There is one God who has been revealed in the exalted Jesus. Without compromise to monotheism, Jesus becomes the object of their worship. A pluralist option was readily available to the Christians in the early church period, and they resisted that option because of their refusal to place Christ alongside other gods. In the words of G.K. Chesterton, if they had not resisted pluralism: 'They would all have been boiled down to one lukewarm liquid in that great pot of cosmopolitan corruption in which all the other myths and mysteries were melting.'[19] Their high Christology prevented Christians embracing Roman pluralism.

In contrast, there is little evidence for the minimalist Christology of Hick, who must rely on an unproven hypothesis of what could lie behind the formation of the New Testament. Hick's dismissal of a high Christology has little to do with exegesis.[20] His rejection of an orthodox Christology has more to do with its implications for religious pluralism than finding the most coherent interpretation of New Testament texts. Commenting on how Hick's Christology developed in the wake of his experience of inter-religious encounter, McCready concludes: 'Hick rejects orthodox Christology because he dislikes its implications, not because he finds it unsupported by facts or logic.'[21]

Revelation and the World Religions

There are a number of related questions which we can do little more than survey here but at least these indicate that Christians have been well aware of them and, among evangelicals, there are answers of increasing sophistication being given.

The orthodox doctrine of the atonement indicates that Jesus is ontologically necessary for salvation, but is he epistemologically necessary for salvation? There is a general knowledge of God known apart from the specific revelation in Christ. Does this general revelation offer a knowledge that could lead to salvation? Or is this only enough knowledge to justify condemnation?

The classic texts on general revelation have received plenty of attention.[22] Whether Psalm 19 or Romans 1 – 2, there is plenty of evidence that biblical writers acknowledged that something of God's nature was being revealed in the created order itself.[23] But what was the nature of this revelation? Did it reveal a knowledge that made salvation possible or only knowledge of God as creator and judge? Speaking to a pagan non-Jewish audience, Paul has no hesitation in appealing to a general revelation, 'He has not left himself without testimony: He has shown kindness by giving you rain from heaven and crops in their seasons; he provides you with plenty of food and fills your hearts with joy.'[24] Calvin recognizes this wider context of God's revealing activity. Not only does God deposit the 'seed of religion' in our minds but he has also sought to 'manifest his perfections in the whole structure of the universe, and daily place himself in our view, that we cannot open our eyes without being compelled to behold him'.[25] Like a mirror, the creation reflects his glory and existence.

But the question remains, what kind of knowledge does this general revelation provide? Paul describes the natural human response as one that will 'suppress the truth' (Rom. 1:18). Calvin notes this propensity in the natural person. Though surrounded and filled with the indications of God's existence and glory, the natural person will deny him, 'Substituting nature as the architect of the universe, he suppresses the name of God.'[26] A central theme of the Old Testament is the idolatry of the nations in contrast with the exclusivism of Israel. The biblical writers frequently indicate their awareness of other religious options and there are many possible explanations for the claim that there are other gods.[27] However, despite the diversity of explanations for idolatry the overwhelming judgement is negative. As Christopher Wright summarizes the Old Testament material, 'While gods and idols may be implements of or gateways to the world of the demonic, the overwhelming verdict of Scripture is that they are the work of human hands, constructs of our own fallen and rebellious imagination.'[28]

But are there indications that general revelation may be received more positively? Clark Pinnock describes the tradition of 'holy pagans' in the Old Testament as examples of this positive response.[29] The list would include Noah, Job, Melchizedek, Jethro and Hiram, king of Tyre. Their positive confessions of faith in the LORD God despite being outside the covenant with Israel might suggest God's saving work through general revelation.

The list is somewhat more problematic than that. There is no reason to think that these biblical characters were considered outside God's special revelation, whether passed on second-hand or given directly through revelation.[30] Hiram was clearly in communication with Solomon (2 Chr. 2:1–12), Noah and Job received direct revelation from God (Gen. 6:13; Job 38ff.), and Jethro, a Midianite priest, is a descendent of Abraham (Gen. 25:1–2). Of Melchizedek much more could be said, but Christians have generally considered him in some way related to the covenant.[31] Daniel Strange finds the theme of 'remnantal revelation' in the example of Melchizedek. His knowledge of *El Elyon*, God Most High, indicates a greater knowledge than that which is displayed in creation, 'Melchizedek is therefore not a recipient merely of general revelation, but of special "remnantal" revelation possibly handed down by oral transmission.'[32] This useful term may well explain a type of knowledge of God distinct from either general or special revelation. There is a knowledge of God passed on like Chinese whispers among the human population, sometimes garbled but other times remaining a valid source of the knowledge of God.

McDermott describes 'types' or pictures of Christ and the atonement scattered among the world religions: 'The Bible itself suggests that there are "little lights" in the religions that help illuminate the realities that the Light of the World more clearly displays.'[33] Perhaps these could serve as a preparation for the gospel? Could they even provide enough knowledge to compel someone without direct knowledge of Christ to repent and believe in him?[34]

From Monotheism to Idolatry

Despite possibilities of wider hope, the biblical picture of a general knowledge of God is rather more pessimistic. What do human beings do with the knowledge of God? Without a special work of divine grace, the biblical picture is one of a natural instinct towards idolatry (Rom. 1:18–32). In his extensive exploration of this theme, Strange notes that whatever is positive in the world religions they cannot be properly understood without the category of idolatry. The many gods of the Old Testament itself indicates that the biblical writers were well aware of religious pluralism. The great confession of ancient Israel was both a statement of monotheism and of monolatry; 'Hear, O Israel: The LORD our God, the LORD is one.'[35] Israel's monotheism recognized that other nations had other gods but denied that they were worthy of worship. There was One God who the Israelites should worship, 'You shall have no other gods before me.'[36] In fact, such rival gods were considered idols (Jer. 16:20; Ps. 96:4–5).

The generally negative tone of this assessment does not prevent evangelicals from developing a theology of religions that creates space for dialogue and learning. Strange has developed a formidable overview of a contemporary subversive fulfilment approach to pluralism. Without conceding that general revelation provides saving knowledge of God, there is no reason to think that God has no purpose in religion: 'Recognising this divine work means it is not possible to give a blanket or simplistic singular negative purpose to non-Christian religions.'[37] All history and culture are in some way swept up in God's purposes. Theologically, the Christian has every reason to be optimistic that religions serve some kind of function. Christ fulfils the deepest aspirations and longings of all people. Negatively, even the rebellion against God expressed in human culture raises questions which can only be finally answered in God. 'Or, to put all this a little more poetically, we might say that non-Christian religions are not glorious, and yet God can be glorified through them, are not truthful, and yet God can teach us truth through them, and are not salvific, and yet serve God's purposes in salvation.'[38]

Christianity and Pluralism

Hick is right that the sticking point for an evangelical theology of religions will be the identity of Christ. The historic core of Christianity revolves around claims made about a real person who reveals the real God and offers atonement for sin. If religion conveys truth about God, it will be in spite of our natural propensity to idolatry and not through it. If salvation is possible without explicit knowledge of Christ it will not be through religion or general revelation in itself but through some implicit knowledge of Christ mediated through some other means of grace.

Hick's theological revolution is propelled and shaped by his philosophical scepticism. His commitment to naturalism rules the miracles of Jesus out of court. His epistemology relativizes the significance of any particular historical events. In their place, he seeks universally binding truths that can be discerned by reason. It is interesting how Hick frames his case with a Christian audience. Contributing to an evangelical publication on the world religions, he describes a wider salvation as an implication of the teaching of Jesus:

> But can it possibly be the will of the loving heavenly Father of Jesus' teaching that only that minority of men and women who have the luck to be born into a Christian part of the world can enter eternal life? This would not be the work of a God of limitless and universal love, who values all human beings equally, but an arbitrary cosmic tyrant.[39]

How can the teachings of Jesus be compatible with exclusivist models of salvation? These questions, often asked by Hick, bring together the essential contradiction in Hick's work. Growing from a Christian theological framework, Hick was motivated by vision of a God of love who is then made obsolete by his later theology. Hick denied that there was a logical relationship between his earlier doctrine of God and his later pluralist vision, 'I didn't reach the pluralist hypothesis from the idea of a God of love, although that is a very good way of presenting it to Christians, but from the ground up by starting with observable human life.'[40] However, while Hick may claim that the pluralist hypothesis is reached in this inductive way, the fact is that he had already come to hold a universalist position because of certain key Christian convictions.

Why should the Ultimate Real be a God of universal love rather than a cosmic tyrant? Why should the Ultimate Real be a loving heavenly Father rather than an impersonal absolute? Without a high Christology, Hick's concept of God cannot sustain the grand pluralist vision of a universe underlain by a transcendental loving purpose.

Writing before *An Interpretation of Religion* was published, Chester Gillis commented, 'Hick's conception of theocentrism is based upon his understanding of God, and his understanding of God is a particular one which derives from the manifestation of God in Christ.'[41] The original impetus for the pluralist hypothesis lay with Hick's conception of an impartial and all-loving God. Where does this concept of God come from if not from the Judeo-Christian tradition?

If Jesus Christ is himself the supreme revelation of God then we are able to speak in personal terms of the character and values of God. Describing God as love, John writes, 'This is how God showed his love among us: He sent his one and only Son into the world that we might live through him. This is love: not that we loved God, but that he loved us and sent his Son as an atoning sacrifice for our sins.'[42] Hick's weaker theocentrism would make this difficult to sustain. Without a high Christology, the Christian understanding of the love of God is brought into question. Worse still, without a concept of God as personal the very notion of a loving God is rendered meaningless. Like Gillis, D'Costa also identified this trajectory to Hick's work even before the publication of *An Interpretation of Religion*: 'I believe that Hick severs the ground from under his Copernican feet. This is so because in arguing for the Copernican revolution on the premise of a God of universal love, such a position entails precisely that one form of revelation of God is definitive and normative compared to others.'[43]

The very ground upon which Hick presented the pluralist hypothesis, with its optimistic perspective of a cosmos in which a divine presence wills the eternal happiness of individual souls, was already undermined by his departure from Christian orthodoxy. His low Christology and dismissal of historic revelation removed the foundations from that type of cosmic optimism. But the problem only got worse with the publication of the more developed case for pluralism in *An Interpretation of Religion*. As we have already seen, the very possibility of revelation is disabled by the pluralist hypothesis. Without revelation there is no basis for such a specific claim to the love and gracious will of the divine being. The purely formal, logical descriptions with which Hick is left, compatible as they are with any form of religion, simply cannot sustain ideas such as the divine having personal will, loving relationships or benign purposes for individual souls.

Conclusion

We have traced Hick's epistemology from its development as part of a Christian world-view to its use in the pluralist hypothesis. Here is the essential weakness. Hick's epistemology is incompatible with the Christian faith. It is a philosophical construct borne out of the Enlightenment and fundamentally in opposition to the possibility of a personal God of love who has revealed himself in the historic incarnation. While Hick's epistemology has not had to undergo any radical revision, his theology has been changed out of all recognition.

Of course, defenders of Hick will make a distinction here between his theology and his philosophy. Some claim that Hick functions as both a personal believer and as a more formal philosopher. His philosophical position is a second-order discourse, to be distinguished from his personal faith. But such a distinction is beside the point. Hick's epistemology is devoid of the possibility of revelation. This 'interpretation' of religion is a radical revision of any personal faith commitment. Without a God who reveals, there is nothing significant that can be said about the character or purpose of the Ultimate Real. Whatever claims are made about history – an Egyptian exodus or a Jerusalem resurrection – are reduced to vague historical possibilities that cannot have a bearing on the most important matters of faith. Truths of history are uncertain, only the truths of reason demand loyalty.

The consequence of this is obviously a minimalist theology – and it is hardly surprising that it may provide some lowest common denominator found in any religion. Hick finds among the world religions a vague 'god' without substance that is neither personal nor non-personal, neither good nor evil, neither existing nor non-existing. This 'god' reveals nothing, never intervenes and is inaccessible to prayer. Such a god is compatible with all because it is specific to none. It is true that this reinterpretation of religion provides a way forward where doctrinal disputes seem to generate impassable barriers. But it is a way forward to agnosticism, a god without form and a salvation for all because it promises nothing to anyone.

Appendix

John Hick and Chris Sinkinson Interview with Justin Brierley: One Truth or Many?

Justin Brierley: In February 2011 I invited Professor John Hick, Emeritus Professor of Theology at Birmingham University, to take part in a radio dialogue about his studies in religious pluralism. Almost exactly a year later, he passed away, aged ninety.

At the time we spoke, the intellectual capacities that had led to his status as 'the greatest living philosopher of global religion' (the words of Keith Ward) were in no way diminished. During his career, Hick set the benchmark for contemporary studies in religious pluralism, publishing seminal books such as *God and the Universe of Faiths*.

His own journey was illustrative of how his thinking developed on the subject. Hick entered ministry in the Presbyterian Church as an evangelical Christian, having been converted as a young adult. That stance began to change during the 1950s as he questioned various key orthodoxies such as the deity of Christ, eventually leading to heresy proceedings against him in the 1960s (but overturned soon after). In particular, his developing theological view that Christianity is but one among a number of equally valid religious expressions of God drew criticism from others in the church.

When the Presbyterian Church became part of the United Reformed Church, Hick found his home there for a long time, until the last few years of his life when he transferred his membership to the Quakers. John Hick was never afraid to change his mind, a trait that would come to be respected even by those who disagree with his theology.

Chris Sinkinson is an Old Testament and apologetics scholar, and a tutor at Moorlands Bible College, whose doctorate was a detailed

critique of Hick's religious pluralism. In common with Hick, he was
converted in late teens to an evangelical faith, but he has never been
tempted in the pluralistic direction that Hick's theological journey
took him on.

They joined me for a dialogue on whether all paths lead to God.

**Justin Brierley: John, are you a very different believer today from
the one you began as?**

John Hick: Yes. When I came to Birmingham University I became
aware first-hand of people of other faiths, because Birmingham is a
very multifaith city. As chair of the city's community relations committee, part of my job was to visit places of worship – so I was in
mosques, synagogues, Sikh gurdwaras and Hindu temples, as well as
Christian churches.

The externals are very different, such as the way in which the building was furnished, the language used and the way in which God was
thought of and referred to. But it struck me that the same thing was
going on in all of them as in the Christian churches – namely human
beings coming together under the influence of some ancient tradition
which enabled them to open their minds and spirits upwards.

I've also spent quite a lot of time in India with Hindus and Sikhs
and in Sri Lanka with Theravada Buddhists and in Japan with Zen
Buddhists. As a result of all this experience, it became fairly clear to
me that there are many paths to God.

JB: Chris, how has your experience as a Christian led you to think
about other faiths?

Chris Sinkinson: I was mostly exposed to world religions when
I was at university, especially during my doctorate at Bristol where
there is a strong inter-religious community. The question of whether
all paths lead to God was one I faced as an undergraduate and a student in philosophy and religion. When I came across John Hick it
was tremendously helpful, not because of the answers that he gave – I
still don't agree with John – but for the questions he asked. He has

always asked the right questions. But my experience of other faiths did not lead me to think we should adopt pluralist views.

JB: Isn't it arrogant to claim that Jesus is the only way to God?

CS: This assertion is often made – that an evangelical or an orthodox Christian view is arrogant. First, there is moral arrogance, which is wrong. I don't think Jesus would have encouraged being disrespectful or dismissive. Then there is intellectual arrogance. At that level it would be true that I want to assert my claims with conviction, but so does Professor Hick. John makes a very persuasive claim towards religious pluralism, and at an intellectual level one could even describe it as an 'arrogant' claim to make, as it concerns the beliefs of millions of people all across the world down through history.

JB: So John, is it arrogant for you to claim to see the bigger picture, where Chris doesn't?

John Hick: I think this whole question of arrogance is an unnecessary one. If you say 'two plus two equals four' you are saying that anyone who is saying that this is not the case is mistaken. Really the issue is whether Jesus is the 'only way', based on the quote from John's Gospel, that he is 'the way, the truth, and the life' – and I say that it isn't true and that Jesus didn't say it. That isn't to say that it isn't in John's Gospel. Modern New Testament scholarship has shown that John's Gospel was the latest of the gospels to be written, and that they were the words of a later Christian being put into Jesus' mouth some seventy years after his death.

CS: C.S. Lewis makes the comment that we should be careful of statements along the lines of what scholarship concludes. After all, scholarship is a moving target and grows in its interpretation of the material. There is plenty to show that the gospels can be trusted and that they are very reliable first-century records of eyewitness accounts. Studies clearly show that the earliest strands of the New Testament are in the letters of Paul, who himself quotes earlier traditions. That earlier material has the highest Christology of all about Jesus and who he was.

JB: Chris, you are an 'exclusivist' – does that mean you don't think people of other religions will be saved?

CS: I would certainly want to hold an exclusivist position because I do believe the world religions have to be respected as independent and distinct from the Christian faith and God is not mediating salvation through them. However it does not follow that God cannot in some way make the means of salvation available by general revelation or direct grace into the lives of those who have never heard. So I would be quite optimistic that clearly those who have never heard – children dying in infancy, those who were sometimes considered Old Testament saints who did not know of Christ directly but who knew him implicitly – are saved. So though I would hold an exclusivist position – salvation comes exclusively through the work of Christ – that could be mediated in some way by God's revelation and common grace.

John Hick: That seems to me a very strange thing to believe. If you look around the world, it is true of the majority of human beings that the religion which they adhere to depends on where they were born and by whom they were brought up. So anybody born to a Hindu family in India is extremely likely to become a Hindu, or in a Muslim context is extremely likely to become a Muslim and so on. Now, it would be very odd indeed if salvation is only available in one faith, even though it were in some mysterious, surreptitious way made available in some diluted form to people of other faiths.

JB: That doesn't strike you as the way that a just and loving God would act?

John Hick: It seems impossible, or that it is stretching the idea of a loving God very far indeed.

Here is an analogy. Let's think of God as the sun, at the centre of the universe, and the earth and the other planets revolve around it. Now according to exclusivism, the life-giving warmth of the sun falls only directly on the earth and not on the others. Or in a financial analogy, the wealth of divine grace falls only on Christians and trickles down in a diluted form to people of other faiths. This could be the case – but it seems extremely odd.

CS: I can understand why you would see this as an odd position. In many respects the message of Christ can be a scandal, it can cause offence. But the fact of this phenomenological point – that children may have the religion of their parents or culture – doesn't in itself have any logical effect on whether Christianity or exclusivism is true or not. It's not a logical point being made, is it?

John Hick: Well, it does put the burden of proof on the exclusivist Christian and that is an uphill task.

JB: John, you have also used the analogy of there being 'one light and many lampshades' to describe God's presence in all religions.

John Hick: The Sufi poet, Rumi, said: 'The lamps are many but the light is one', and that is a very good way of expressing the pluralist point of view. There is just one light, which lights many lamps, and those lamps are the religions. Many religious people of every faith affirm that there is an ultimate transcendent reality and our English word for this is 'God'. God is the 'Ultimate Reality'. But there are different concepts which have formed in the traditions that explore this Ultimate Reality. They have developed on the basis of religious experience, but also all sorts of cultural factors. On the one hand we have this 'Ultimate Reality' in itself and on the other hand different human awareness of it.

CS: But, John, you would say that there are some religions that are essentially atheistic, such as Zen Buddhism. I worry about the use of your term 'Ultimate Reality' which, although it speaks of your consistency, is such a lowest common denominator definition of the ultimate object of our worship, that it becomes empty of content. And in the past you have even described this Ultimate Reality as 'beyond good and evil, beyond personal and non-personal and beyond loving and hating'.

John Hick: It is true that the Ultimate Reality is not in itself a loving God but it is expressed in many penultimate realities which are loving, such as the Christian faith. But I think we have to accept that, even as the most profound Christian and other thinkers have said in the past, God in God's fullness is beyond our understanding. It cannot be limited by any human definition – God is the ultimate mystery, in fact. He is beyond human definition. This means that you cannot even say that God, in God's ultimacy, is a loving person.

JB: Christianity is about God becoming personal in Jesus Christ. But doesn't your view make God ultimately rather impersonal?

John Hick: Christianity is one of these totally valid and very valuable paths to the ultimate, to God. But it isn't the only one. Also the concept of a loving God was not the only way of appealing to some people in the world. It doesn't appeal to Buddhists. They do not affirm the ultimate as a person, but as a benign Ultimate Reality in which we can rely and rest. Buddhism is much older than Christianity, and equally as valid and profound.

CS: It is one thing to say we don't have an exhaustive knowledge of God; it's another to say that our understanding of God could be compatible with a contradiction. You have been accused of being a 'transcendental agnostic' – because the 'Ultimate Real' in itself is beyond language, beyond words, so therefore we have to be agnostic about what the Ultimate Real is.

JB: John, are you saying that the different religions are wrong about their conceptions of God, whereas your definition of an 'Ultimate Reality' is right?

John Hick: They are all right.

JB: Can they all be right?

John Hick: They all have their authentic paths to the Ultimate that they follow and can lead to their ultimate good. In that way they are all right.

JB: Chris, do you think John's pluralism is beneficial in terms of practical interfaith dialogue?

CS: This isn't a personal comment about John, who has done great work in anti-Semitism in the 1960s, not to mention his work on interfaith relations. But I am concerned that the cash value of the religious pluralist position is that the only way in which we can create a tolerant society is by coming to an agreement at a philosophical level.

John Hick: No, that is not the only way. We have a relatively tolerant society in this country now. What it amounts to in practice is that, if you are living next to a Muslim, you respect their beliefs without enquiring too much into them.

CS: But John, the Muslim friends I know are absolutely persuaded by the truth of Islam and we have some lively chats but we are still friends.

John Hick: I am not for a moment suggesting that Muslims don't have very emphatic beliefs; they certainly do. But it seems obvious to me that if you believe all these religions are paths to God, this must make for mutual tolerance.

CS: It's only tolerant on the grounds that you have reinterpreted those religions within your own framework. I don't agree with my Muslim friends but I do want to respect them as well as being a good witness in my faith, and I'd humbly admit I may be wrong on various things. Yet all of that comes from the fact that we fundamentally disagree. Your position is to commend living alongside each other by reinterpreting what they are saying or doing to fit with your philosophical position.

John Hick: No, it's not. I take them as unitary positions, which have their own validity in that they do lead to salvation, to human ultimate wellbeing. But there are many different kinds of Christian – you are an evangelical and I am a Quaker. Quakers do not emphasize beliefs, they emphasize life; for them, the reality of their faith is in the way they live.

JB: An atheist might see religious diversity as evidence that there is no God at all. Why do you come to the conclusion that there is nevertheless this 'Ultimate Reality', John?

John Hick: Ultimately it is a matter of religious experience. I practise a form of meditation every day; I concentrate on my breathing and sometimes there is an experience of being part of the universe – a universe that is good and benign and that you are free and liberated, or in Christian language you are 'saved'. So it is based on experience.

CS: I too practise a form of meditation, although I meditate on the word of God, his breath, his word. I do think that our experience can be deeply misleading. But if our faith is rooted in revelation then our experience should not be responding to what we think or feel, or how we respond to our breathing, but to what God has said and what he has spoken.

Justin Brierley presents the faith discussion show, Unbelievable, *on Premier Christian Radio.*

This article was published in the February 2013 edition of Reform.

Endnotes

1. John Hick's Religious Journey

[1] Demonstrated in Alister McGrath, *The Twilight of Atheism: The Rise and Fall of Disbelief in the Modern World* (London: Random House, 2004).

[2] John Hick, *God Has Many Names* (London: Macmillan, 1980), p. 1.

[3] John Hick, *The Fifth Dimension* (Oxford: Oneworld, 1999), p. 161.

[4] John Hick, *An Autobiography* (Oxford: Oneworld, 1999), p. 31.

[5] Hick, *Autobiography*, p. 29.

[6] Hick, *Autobiography*, p. 33.

[7] Hick, *God Has Many Names*, p. 2.

[8] John Hick, *Disputed Questions* (London: Macmillan, 1992), p. 139.

[9] Hick, *Autobiography*, p. 69.

[10] Such as the discussion found in Thomas Aquinas, *Summa Contra Gentiles*, Book 1, chs 6–8.

[11] In C.S. Lewis' influential popular presentation of the moral argument he points out that even when protagonists differ over what might be a moral course of action they still tend to appeal to command standards such as what is 'fair', Lewis, *Mere Christianity* (Glasgow: Collins, 1986), p. 18.

[12] Hick, *Faith*, p. 216.

[13] A.J. Ayer, *Language, Truth and Logic* (London: Victor Gollancz, 1946).

[14] Brian Magee, *Talking Philosophy: Dialogues with Fifteen Leading Philosophers* (Oxford, OUP, 2001), p. 107.

[15] Hick, *Faith*, pp. 177–8.

[16] See e.g. Alvin Plantinga and Nicholas Wolterstorff, eds, *Faith and Rationality* (Notre Dame: University of Notre Dame Press, 1983).

[17] John Hick, 'The Christology of D.M. Baillie', *SJT* 11 (1958): pp. 1–12.

[18] Hick, *Autobiography*, p. 116.

[19] John Hick, *Problems of Religious Pluralism* (London: Macmillan, 1985), p. 2.

[20] Hick, *Autobiography*, p. 124.

2. Questioning Orthodoxy

[1] Augustine, *On Genesis* (New York: New City Press, 2006).

[2] John Hick, *Evil and the God of Love* (London: Macmillan, 1977), pp. 284–5.

[3] Hick, *Evil and the God of Love*, p. 377.

[4] Hick, *Evil and the God of Love*, p. 380.

[5] It seems odd in this particular text that Hick dismisses Origen in a passing footnote as another representative of the Augustinian view of evil (Hick, *Evil and the God of Love*, p. 53).

[6] Mark Scott, '"Suffering and Soul-Making": Rethinking John Hick's Theodicy', *JR* 90/1 (2010): pp. 313–34.

[7] Irenaeus, *Against Heresies* 5.23.1.

[8] Irenaeus, *Against Heresies* 5.27.1.

[9] Origen, *Principles*, 3.1.13.

[10] Scott, 'Suffering', p. 323.

[11] John Hick, *An Autobiography* (Oxford: Oneworld, 1999), p. 160.

[12] John Hick, *Disputed Questions* (London: Macmillan, 1992), p. 141.

[13] John Hick, *God and the Universe of Faiths* (London: Macmillan, 1988), p. 108.

[14] Hick, *God and the Universe of Faiths*, p. 111.

[15] Hick, *God and the Universe of Faiths*, p. 115.

[16] See Richard Baukham, *Jesus and the God of Israel* (Milton Keynes: Paternoster, 2008).

[17] For a discussion of the history and significance of this pronouncement see Francis A. Sullivan, *Salvation Outside the Church?* (London: Geoffrey Chapman, 1992); and Gavin D'Costa, *John Hick's Theology of Religions* (Lanham: University Press of America, 1987), pp. 73–90.

[18] Hick, *God and the Universe of Faiths*, p. 122.

[19] The typology is generally credited to Alan Race who used it to catalogue various theologians in Alan Race, *Christians and Religious Pluralism* (London: SCM Press, 1983). The categories work fairly well, demonstrated in the exchange between theologians of each position as seen in Gavin D'Costa, Paul Knitter and Daniel Strange, *Only One Way? Three Christian Responses on the Uniqueness of Christ in a Religiously Plural World* (London: SCM Press, 2011). However, they can also distort the discussion as indicated by Terry C. Muck, 'Theology of Religions after Knitter and Hick: Beyond the Paradigm', *Interpretation* 61/1 (2007): pp. 7–22.

[20] See the historical overview by David Hilborn and Don Horrocks, 'Universalistic Trends in the Evangelical Tradition: An Historical

Perspective' in *Universal Salvation? The Current Debate* (ed. Robin Parry and Chris Partridge; Carlisle: Paternoster, 2003), pp. 219–44.

[21] Loraine Boettner, *The Reformed Doctrine of Predestination* (Grand Rapids, MI: Eerdmans, 1957), p. 120.

[22] Küng reflects on this influential claim in the introduction to a later work, see Hans Küng et al., *Christianity and the World Religions* (London: SCM Press, 2nd edn, 1993).

[23] Karl Rahner, *Theological Investigations*, vol. 6 (London: SCM Press, 1969), p. 391.

[24] A point repeated by Hick in the dialogue that we had shortly before his death (see Appendix).

[25] See, e.g., Clark Pinnock, *A Wideness in God's Mercy* (Grand Rapids, MI: Zondervan, 1992).

[26] Norman Anderson, *Christianity and the World's Religions* (Leicester: IVP, 1984), pp. 174–5. Tiessen describes the position as 'accessibilism' and suggests it is based on both an agnosticism regarding what Scripture does not clearly say and 'hopefulness that God's saving work is even greater than the awareness of any of us' (Terrance L. Tiessen, 'The Salvation of the Unevangelised in the Light of God's Covenants', *EQ* 36/3 (2012): p. 249.

[27] The sharp-minded and sharp-witted Calvinist Baptist preacher, Charles Haddon Spurgeon, was practically a universalist as regards those dying in infancy (Sermon No. 411, 29 September 1861; http://www.ccel.org/spurgeons/sermons52.txt). 'Would your God cast away an infant? If yours could, I am happy to say he is not the God that I adore.' Given this conviction, Spurgeon confidently asserted that the majority of the human race would be saved because the majority would be made up of those saved in infancy, 'I do not see how it is possible that so vast a number should enter heaven, unless it be on the supposition that infant souls constitute the great majority.' Spurgeon held to a Calvinist doctrine of election but did not envisage only a small minority of the human race in heaven.

[28] Hick, *God and the Universe of Faiths*, p. 131.

[29] Julius J. Lipner, 'Does Copernicus Help? Reflections for a Christian Theology of Religions', *RelS* 13 (1997): p. 257.

[30] Hick, *God and the Universe of Faiths*, p. 132.

[31] Arguably all forms of Buddhism are properly categorized as atheist (see Paul Williams, *The Unexpected Way: On Converting from Buddhism to Catholicism* (Edinburgh: T&T Clark, 2002) pp. 25ff.). Netland uses the case study of Shinto to make this point against Hick's pluralism in

Harold A. Netland, *Dissonant Voices: Religious Pluralism and the Question of Truth* (Leicester: IVP, 1991), pp. 93–111.

[32] Gemma Lavender, "Is there a centre of the universe?", spaceanswers.com (accessed 28 Jan. 2013).

[33] Gavin D'Costa, 'John Hick and Religious Pluralism: Yet Another Revolution' in *Problems in the Philosophy of Religion* (ed. Harold Hewitt; London: Macmillan, 1991), pp. 3–16.

3. The World Religions

[1] John Hick, ed. *The Myth of God Incarnate* (London: SCM Press, 1977), p. ix.

[2] Jude 3.

[3] Hick, *Myth*, p. 62.

[4] Epistle of Ignatius to the Ephesians 7.2 in *Ante-Nicene Fathers: Volume 1* (Peabody, MA: Hendrickson, 1885 [fifth printing, 2012]).

[5] John Hick, *Evil and the God of Love* (London: Macmillan, 1977), p. 172.

[6] One of his last publications continues to explore this theme: John Hick, *The New Frontier of Religion and Science: Religious Experience, Neuroscience and the Transcendent* (Basingstoke: Palgrave Macmillan, 2010). See especially pp. 191–200.

[7] John Hick, *Death and Eternal Life* (London: Collins, 1976), p. 456.

[8] Hick, *Death and Eternal Life*, p. 446.

[9] John Hick, *An Autobiography* (Oxford: Oneworld, 1999), p. 276.

[10] Hick, *Autobiography*, p. 251.

[11] Hick describes attendance of around fifty.

[12] This important element of his epistemology was developed after the publication of *Faith and Knowledge* (London: Macmillan, 2nd edn, 1988), and is found in 'Religious Faith as Experiencing-as' in *A John Hick Reader* (ed. Paul Badham; London: Macmillan, 1990), pp. 34–48. This essay was first published in 1969.

[13] Hick, *New Frontier*, pp. 182–4.

4. Consistent Faith

[1] John Hick, *Faith and Knowledge* (London: Macmillan, 2nd edn, 1988), Preface to the 2nd edn.

2   Hick, *Faith and Knowledge*, Preface to the reissue of the 2nd edn.
3   This is the primary defence made of Hick's work offered by Chester Gillis who writes; 'I think that much of the criticism of Hick's pluralistic hypothesis has understood his effort to be a Christian theology of religions. This is not what it is.' Chester Gillis, 'John Hick: Theologian or Philosopher of Religion?' in *Religious Pluralism and the Modern World: An Ongoing Engagement with John Hick* (ed. Sharada Sugirtharajah; Basingstoke: Macmillan, 2012), p. 137.
4   Gerard Loughlin, 'Prefacing Pluralism: John Hick and the Mastery of Religion', *Modern Theology* 7 (1990): p. 30.
5   Gavin D'Costa, 'John Hick and Religious Pluralism: Yet Another Revolution' in *Problems in the Philosophy of Religion* (ed. Harold Hewitt; London: Macmillan, 1991), p. 7. For a detailed response to Hick's eschatology and its development see T. Mathis, *Against John Hick* (Boston: University Press of America, 1985).
6   Loughlin, 'Prefacing Pluralism', p. 37.
7   John Hick, 'A Response to Gerard Loughlin', *Modern Theology* 7 (1990): p. 57.
8   Hick, 'Response', p. 61.
9   Hick, 'Response', pp. 61–2.
10 Hick, 'Response', p. 62.
11 Philip L. Barnes, 'Continuity and Development in John Hick's Theology', *SR* 21/4 (1992): p. 395.
12 Barnes, 'Continuity', p. 396.
13 Barnes, 'Continuity', p. 400.
14 David S. Nah, *Christian Theology and Religious Pluralism: A Critical Evaluation of John Hick* (Eugene, OR: Pickwick, 2012), p. 34.

5. On Knowing God

1   The staged dialogue found in one of his final publications continues this apologetic strand to his work. Responding to Richard Dawkins, Hick comments that the existence of God is 'not a scientific hypothesis. That's his [Dawkins'] most fundamental error.' John Hick, *Between Faith and Doubt* (Basingstoke: Palgrave Macmillan, 2010), p. 55.
2   Paul Helm, *The Varieties of Belief* (London: George Allen & Unwin, 1973), p. 154.
3   John Hick, *Faith and Knowledge* (London: Macmillan, 2nd edn, 1988), p. 13.

[4]   Hick, *Faith*, p. 22.

[5]   Perhaps most clearly expressed by Cornelius Van Til in *Christian Apologetics* and developed by John Frame in, for example, *Apologetics to the Glory of God*. Interestingly, such a Reformed approach to apologetics parts company with the classical apologetics of later Thomists. However, a unifying thread to these varied forms of apologetics is that they can all be characterized as intellectualist. They relate faith to specific doctrines rather than to experience. Christopher Sinkinson, *Confident Christianity* (Nottingham: IVP, 2012), pp. 47–63.

[6]   Hick, *Faith*, p. 30.

[7]   Hick, *Faith*, p. 95.

[8]   Hick, *Faith*, p. 98.

[9]   Hick, *Faith*, p. 111.

[10] Hick, *Faith*, p. 115.

[11] Hick, *Faith*, p. 115.

[12] Hick, *Faith*, p. 135.

[13] Hick, *Faith*, p. 135.

[14] Hick, *Faith*, p. 142; cf. Ludwig Wittgenstein, *Philosophical Investigations* (Oxford, Blackwell, 1967), pp. 193–213.

6. A Faith for All People

[1]   Richard Swinburne, *Faith and Reason* (Oxford: Clarendon Press, 1983), p. 63.

[2]   John Hick, *Faith and Knowledge* (London: Macmillan, 2nd edn, 1988), p. 156.

[3]   Hick, *Faith*, p. 156.

[4]   Hick, *Faith*, p. 107.

[5]   Hick, *Faith*, p. 139.

[6]   Hick, *Faith*, p. 140.

[7]   Hick, *Faith*, p. 216. This work includes a defence of the orthodox doctrine of the incarnation, pp. 219–28.

[8]   Hick, *Faith*, p. 241.

[9]   Hick, *Faith*, p. 2.

[10] Paul Helm, *The Varieties of Belief* (London: George Allen & Unwin, 1973), p. 156.

[11] John Hick, *An Interpretation of Religion* (London, Macmillan, 1970), p. 137.

[12] Hick, *Interpretation*, p. 157.

[13] Hick, *Interpretation*, p. 135.

[14] John Hick, *Between Faith and Doubt* (Basingstoke: Palgrave Macmillan, 2010), p. 60.

[15] John Hick, *The New Frontier of Religion and Science: Religious Experience, Neuroscience and the Transcendent* (Basingstoke: Palgrave Macmillan, 2010), p. 143.

[16] John Hick, *The Fifth Dimension* (Oxford: Oneworld, 1999), p. 29.

[17] Hick, *Interpretation*, p. 102.

[18] Hick, *Interpretation*, p. 114.

[19] Hick, *Interpretation*, p. 124.

7. Sceptical Faith

[1] John Hick, *An Interpretation of Religion* (London, Macmillan, 1970), p. 129.

[2] John Hick, *An Autobiography* (Oxford: Oneworld, 1999), p. 251.

[3] John Hick, *Problems of Religious Pluralism* (London: Macmillan, 1985), p. 50.

[4] A point consistently levelled against Hick's case over the years. See e.g. D.B. Forrester, 'Professor Hick and the Universe of Faiths', *SJT* 29 (1976): p. 72; Harold A. Netland, *Dissonant Voices: Religious Pluralism and the Question of Truth* (Leicester: IVP, 1991), pp. 240–49; and Schubert M. Ogden, 'Problems in the Case for a Pluralistic Theology of Religions', *JR* 69 (1988): pp. 504–7.

[5] Raimon Panikkar, *The Intra-religious Dialogue* (New Jersey: Paulist Press, 1999), p. 71.

[6] In Gavin D'Costa, 'John Hick and Religious Pluralism: Yet Another Revolution' in *Problems in the Philosophy of Religion* (ed. Harold Hewitt; London: Macmillan, 1991); Emi Mase, 'Does Hick's Post-Copernican Pluralism in *An Interpretation of Religion* lead to Agnosticism?' (unpublished MA thesis, University of Bristol, 1994); and also developed by Gavin D'Costa, *The Meeting of Religions and the Trinity* (Edinburgh: T&T Clark, 2000). Peter Byrne identified earlier expressions of Hick's pluralist case as a form of agnosticism in 'John Hick's Philosophy of World Religions', *SJT* 35 (1982): p. 292.

[7] Terence Penelhum, *God and Skepticism* (Netherland: D. Reidel, 1983), p. 4.

[8] Penelhum, *God and Skepticism*, p. 6.

[9] Penehlhum, *God and Skepticism*, p. 9.

[10] The structure of Hick's argument in *Interpretation*, pp. 73–125.

[11] Penelhum, *God and Skepticism*, p. 10.

[12] Terence Penelhum, 'Reflections on the Ambiguity of the World' in *God, Truth and Reality: Essays in Honour of John Hick* (ed. Arvind Sharma; London: Macmillan, 1993), p. 172. This relates to his account of scepticism in Penelhum, *God and Skepticism*, pp. 111–12.

[13] Paul Helm, *The Varieties of Belief* (London: George Allen & Unwin, 1973), p. 152.

[14] John Hick, *God Has Many Names* (London: Macmillan, 1980), p. 223.

[15] John Hick, ed. *The Myth of God Incarnate* (London: SCM Press, 1977), p. 172.

[16] John Hick, *God and the Universe of Faiths* (London: Macmillan, 1988), p. 163.

[17] Hick, *Interpretation*, p. 216.

[18] John Hick, *The Metaphor of God Incarnate* (London: SCM Press, 1993), p. 18.

[19] John Hick, *Faith and Knowledge* (London: Macmillan, 2nd edn, 1988), p. 134.

[20] John Hick, 'Rational Theistic Belief without Proofs' in *A John Hick Reader* (ed. Paul Badham; London: Macmillan, 1990), p. 59.

[21] Hick, 'Rational Theistic Belief', p. 55.

[22] More accurately, there is a distinction between the work of David Hume and classical scepticism (see Paul Helm, *Belief Policies* [Cambridge: CUP, 1994], pp. 159–63) but that need not concern our more general description of Hick's epistemology.

[23] Hick, 'Rational Theistic Belief', p. 58.

[24] Hick, 'Rational Theistic Belief', p. 59.

[25] Hick, *Interpretation*, p. 221.

[26] Hick, *Interpretation*, p. 222.

8. Immanuel Kant and Religious Knowledge

[1] John Hick, 'Ineffability', *RS* 38 (2000): p. 46.

[2] John Hick, *Faith and Knowledge* (London: Macmillan, 2nd edn, 1988), p. 62.

[3] John Hick, *Philosophy of Religion* (London: Prentice-Hall, 1990), p. 29.

[4] Hick, *Faith*, p. 63. The *Opus Postumum* was Kant's unfinished final work and published after his death in 1804. Despite what Hick takes as hopeful signs in Kant's later work, Michalson points out that the *Opus*

Postumum denies the existence of God as a personal being independent of human moral experience; Gordon E. Michalson, *Kant and the Problem of God* (Oxford: Blackwell, 1999), pp. 32–3.

5   John Hick, *Death and Eternal Life* (London: Collins, 1976), p. 426.
6   Hick, *Death*, p. 435.
7   John Hick, *An Interpretation of Religion* (London, Macmillan, 1970), p. 236.
8   Hick, *Interpretation*, p. 240.
9   John Locke, *An Essay Concerning Human Understanding* (London: Everyman, 1976), p. 33.
10 Hick, *Interpretation*, p. 241.
11 Hick, *Interpretation*, p. 243.
12 E.g. Hick, *Faith*, p. 63.
13 Hick, *Interpretation*, p. 246.

9. The Receding Real

1   Immanuel Kant, *Prolegomena* (trans. Paul Carus; Illinois: Open Court, 1989), p. 7.
2   David Hume, *A Treatise of Human Nature* (Oxford: OUP, 2000), p. 61.
3   Bertrand Russell, *A History of Western Philosophy* (London: George Allen & Unwin, 1984), p. 645.
4   Hume, *Treatise*, p. 144.
5   Norman Kemp Smith, *The Philosophy of David Hume* (London: Macmillan, 1941).
6   John Hick, *An Autobiography* (Oxford: Oneworld, 2002), p. 66.
7   There are two references to Kemp Smith in *An Interpretation of Religion*. The first makes much the same point to the same text as Hick's much earlier reference in *Faith and Knowledge*. The second endorses Kemp Smith's view that Hume was not a sceptic (Hick, *Interpretation*, p. 213).
8   Kant, *Prolegomena*, p. 9. Kant is deliberately playing the boat metaphor that Hume had rather more humorously used (Hume, *Treatise*, pp. 171–2).
9   Kant, *Prolegomena*, p. 55.
10 Immanuel Kant, *Critique of Pure Reason* (trans. and ed. Paul Guyer and Allen W. Wood; Cambridge: CUP, 1998), p. 347.
11 Kant, *Critique,* p. 350.
12 Kant, *Critique,* p. 351.
13 See Terry F. Godlove, *Religion, Interpretation and Diversity of Belief* (Cambridge: CUP, 1989). Godlove suggests that Hick's reading is

dependent on a misunderstanding of Kant which was introduced into
religious studies by Emile Durkheim.

[14] Kant, *Critique*, p. 350.

[15] Other commentators see these commitments as belonging together, such
that Kant should be admired as a devout, orthodox Christian philosopher. For example, Westphal argues that Kant's theism is so important in
all his thought that the thing-in-itself is only properly understood as the
thing-for-God. Therefore, without the God of the Christian faith, Kant's
philosophical position is in ruins. See Merold Westphal, 'In Defence of
the Thing in Itself', *Kant-Studien* (1968): p. 119. While the argument he
presents is plausible I certainly do not find it convincing.

[16] George Schrader, 'The Thing in Itself in Kantian Philosophy' in *Kant: A
Collection of Critical Essays* (ed. Paul Wolff; London: University of Notre
Dame Press, 1968), p. 172.

[17] Schrader, 'Thing in Itself', p. 188.

[18] Nicholas Rescher, *Kant and the Reach of Reason* (Cambridge: CUP, 2000),
p. 23.

[19] Rescher, *Kant*, p. 34.

[20] William L. Rowe, 'John Hick's Contribution to the Philosophy of Religion' in *God, Truth and Reality: Essays in Honour of John Hick* (ed. Arvind
Sharma; London: Macmillan, 1993), p. 22.

[21] A point made by Paul R. Eddy, 'John Hick's Theological Pilgrimage',
in *Proceedings of the Wheaton Theology Conference* (Illinois: Wheaton
College, 1992).

[22] Michalson, *Kant*, p. 53.

[23] Hick, *Interpretation*, p. 246.

[24] Christopher J. Insole, 'Why John Hick Cannot, and Should Not, Stay
out of the Jam Pot', *RS* 38 (200): pp. 27–30.

[25] Hick, *Interpretation*, p. 246.

[26] Anselm, 'St Anselm's Reply to Gaunilo', in *The Ontological Argument*
(ed. Alvin Plantinga; London: Macmillan, 1968), pp. 13–27.

[27] Hick provides a full account of a way of understanding Anselm's argument in *Who or What God?* (ed. John Hick; London: SCM Press, 2008),
pp. 179–194, but his treatment is beside the point if we cannot have a
substantive description of God as found in Anselm.

[28] 'One of the two most powerful cities of modernity is thereby built around
an opaque ring of walls, streams, roofs, and trees whose own center is no
more than an evaporated notion', Roland Barthes, *Empire of Signs* (trans.
Richard Howard; New York: Hill & Wang, 1982), p. 32.

[29] Gerard Loughlin, 'Prefacing Pluralism: John Hick and the Mastery of Religion', *Modern Theology* 7 (1990): p. 51.

10. Reasonable Religion

[1] Margaret Bald, *Banned Books: Literature Suppressed on Religious Grounds* (New York: Facts on File, rev. edn, 2006), pp. 285–6. Interestingly, the Vatican did not ban this work though *The Critique of Pure Reason* was placed on the Index of forbidden books.

[2] Immanuel Kant, *Religion Within the Limits of Reason Alone* (trans. Theodore M. Greene and Hoyt H. Hudson; New York: Harper & Row, 1960), pp. 5–6.

[3] In personal communication Hick told me that he last read Kant's *Religion* when he was a student and not consciously been influenced directly by that particular volume. My argument is not that Hick directly reworks Kant's explanation of religion. What I do argue is that a shared general epistemology leads them both to similar conclusions about religion.

[4] Kant, *Religion*, pp. 5–6.

[5] John Calvin, *Institutes of the Christian Religion* 1.2 (trans. Henry Beveridge; Massachusetts: Hendrickson, 2008), p. 289.

[6] Kant, *Religion*, p. 111.

[7] Gordon E. Michalson, *Kant and the Problem of God* (Oxford: Blackwell, 1999), pp. 103–4.

[8] Kant, *Religion*, p. 41.

[9] Kant, *Religion*, p. 46.

[10] Mark Johnson, *Moral Imagination* (London: University of Chicago Press, 1993), p. 25.

[11] Kant, *Religion*, p. 108.

[12] Michalson, *Kant*, p. 26.

[13] Kant, *Religion*, p. 56.

[14] Charlotte Allen, *The Human Christ* (Oxford: Lion, 1998), p. 123.

[15] Kant, *Religion*, p. 69; see also pp. 119–20.

[16] Drayton C. Benner, 'Kant's demythologisation of Christian theories of atonement in *Religion within the Limits of Reason Alone*', *EQ* 79/2 (2007): p. 103.

[17] Kant, *Religion*, p. 79.

[18] Joseph Runzo, *World-Views and Perceiving God* (London: Macmillan, 1993), p. 102.

[19] Kant, *Religion*, p. 94.

[20] Kant, *Religion*, p. 98.

[21] Wilfred Cantwell Smith, *The Meaning and End of Religion* (Minneapolis: Fortress Press, 1991), esp. pp. 170–92.

[22] Kant, *Religion*, pp. 95–6.

[23] Kant, *Religion*, p. 100.

[24] Kant, *Religion*, p. 102.

[25] See Paul Lawrence Rose, *The German Question/Jewish Question: Revolutionary Anti-Semitism in Germany from Kant to Wagner* (Princeton, NJ: Princeton University Press, 2006), pp. 93ff.

[26] Kant, *Religion*, p. 116.

[27] The problem of anti-Semitism in the Christian relationship to the Jewish people remains crucial to understanding the current political situation of the state of Israel. However, this debate now has the added complication of a response to land as well as a people. See Gary M. Burge, *Whose Land? Whose Promise?* (USA: Pilgrim Press, 2003), pp. 233–59.

[28] Kant, *Religion*, p. 117.

[29] Kant, *Religion*, p. 112.

[30] Kant, *Religion*, p. 112.

[31] Immanuel Kant, *The Conflict of the Faculties* (trans. Mary J. Gregor; New York: Abaris Books, 1979), p. 95.

[32] For example, see Richard S. Levy, *Antisemitism: A Historical Encyclopaedia of Prejudice and Persecution*, vol. 1 (California: ABC-CLIO, 2005), p. 396. It is fair to emphasize that Kant's thoughts reflected the German culture of the time and that there is little evidence for personal animosity to Jewish people who were among Kant's friends.

11. Hick's Debt to Kant

[1] John Hick, *An Interpretation of Religion* (London: Macmillan, 1970), p. 149.

[2] Pelagius, *Pro libero arbitrio* in *Documents of the Christian Church* (ed. Henry Bettenson; Oxford: OUP, 1967), p. 53.

[3] Michalson, *Kant*, p. 115.

[4] Immanuel Kant, *Religion Within the Limits of Reason Alone* (trans. Theodore M. Greene and Hoyt H. Hudson; New York: Harper & Row, 1960), p. 112.

[5] Hick, *Interpretation*, p. 312.

6 John Hick, 'Jesus and the World Religions' in *The Myth of God Incarnate* (ed. John Hick; London: SCM Press, 1977), p. 178.

7 John Hick, *The Metaphor of God Incarnate* (London: SCM Press, 1993), p. 115.

8 Hick, *Metaphor*, p. 116.

9 John Hick, *The Rainbow of Faiths* (London: SCM Press, 1995), pp. 130–31.

10 Kant, *Religion*, p. 100.

11 Hick, *Metaphor*, p. 149.

12 Kant, *Religion*, p. 132.

13 Richard Burridge, *Four Gospels, One Jesus?* (London: SPCK, 2000), p. 176.

14 Kant, *Religion*, p. 94.

15 Hick, *Interpretation*, p. 365.

16 Hick, *Interpretation*, p. 365.

17 John Hick, *Who or What is God? And Other Investigations* (ed. John Hick; London: SCM Press, 2008), pp. 150–55.

18 Hick, *Interpretation*, p. 23.

19 John Hick, *The New Frontier of Religion and Science: Religious Experience, Neuroscience and the Transcendent* (Basingstoke: Palgrave Macmillan, 2010), p. 4.

20 Kant, *Religion*, p. 116.

21 While the theory has come to dominate many scholarly circles, it has always been subjected to intense criticism. The important response of Jewish theologian, Umberto Cassuto, in a series of lectures originally published in 1941, provides perfectly adequate reasons for such verbal variations as El and YHWH. The rabbis had always been quite familiar with such Hebrew variations but had never seen the complex source theory that the liberal German theologians were so readily discovering. See Umberto Cassuto, *The Documentary Hypothesis* (Jerusalem: Shalem Press, 2006), pp. 18–31. A major embarrassment for the entire concept is that two hundred years of textual studies have assembled vast numbers of early manuscripts, including the Great Isaiah scroll of Qumran and still not found any material evidence for the source theory.

22 Karl Jaspers (1883–1969) was a significant German-Swiss philosopher and psychologist who continued in the tradition of Kant. His work on the development of religion is highly speculative. See Karl Jaspers, *The Origin and Goal of History* (trans. Michael Bullock; London: Routledge, 1953), esp. pp. 51–60. For a comprehensive critique see Iain Provan, *Convenient Myths: The Axial Age, Dark Green Religion and the World that*

Never Was (Waco, TX: Baylor University Press, 2013). Hick probably contributed more than most scholars of religion to ensuring the preservation of this highly dubious notion. We will return to it in Chapter 14.

23 Hick, *Interpretation*, p. 33.

24 Kant, *Religion*, p. 118.

25 Kant, *Religion*, p. 156.

26 Eddy, 'Religious Pluralism and the Divine: Another look at John Hick's Neo-Kantian Proposal', *RS* 30 (1994): p. 467. See also Gavin D'Costa, 'John Hick and Religious Pluralism: Yet Another Revolution', in *Problems in the Philosophy of Religion* (ed. Harold Hewitt; London: Macmillan, 1991), p. 4; Gerard Loughlin, 'Noumenon and Phenomena', *RS* 23 (1987): pp. 497–8; and Vinoth Ramachandra, *The Recovery of Mission* (Carlisle: Paternoster, 1996), pp. 117–25.

12. The Enlightenment Tradition

1 E.g. Diogenes Allen, *Christian Belief in a Postmodern World* (Louisville, KY: Westminster/John Knox, 1989), p. 37; Hans Küng, *Does God Exist?* (London: SCM Press, 1991), pp. 5ff.; J. Richard Middleton and Brian J. Walsh, *Truth is Stranger than it Used to Be* (London: SPCK, 1995), p. 41; Lesslie Newbigin, *The Gospel in a Pluralist Society* (London: SPCK, 1989), p. 28.

2 Ernest Gellner demonstrates the significance of this in *Reason and Culture* (Oxford: Blackwell, 1992), pp. 1–22.

3 Immanuel Kant, *On History* (New York: Library of Liberal Arts, 1963), p. 3.

4 Indeed, the entire period can be categorized as a crisis of authority, Alister McGrath, *The Intellectual Origins of the European Reformation* (Oxford: Blackwell), pp. 12–28.

5 Kant, *History*, p. 3.

6 Kant, *History*, p. 9.

7 Alasdair MacIntyre, *Three Rival Versions of Moral Enquiry* (London: Duckworth, 1990), p. 9.

8 David F. Wright, 'Gifford Lectures' in *New Dictionary of Theology* (ed. Sinclair B. Ferguson and David F. Wright; Leicester: IVP, 1989), pp. 268–9.

9 MacIntyre, *Three Rival Versions*, p. 14.

[10] Paul Badham, 'John Hick's *An Interpretation of Religion*' in *Problems in the Philosophy of Religion* (ed. Harold Hewitt; London: Macmillan, 1991), p. 86.

[11] *Encyclopaedia Britannica 1*, viii (9th edn, 1873). Cited in MacIntyre, *Three Rival Versions*, p. 19.

[12] MacIntyre, *Three Rival Versions*, p. 19.

[13] Alasdair MacIntyre, *Whose Justice? Which Rationality?* (London: Duckworth, 1988), p. 6.

[14] Robert Cook, 'Postmodernism, Pluralism and John Hick', *Themelios* 19/1 (1993): pp. 10–12.

[15] John Hick, 'Readers' Responses', *Themelios* 19/3 (1994): pp. 20–21.

[16] D.A. Carson, *The Gagging of God* (Leicester: IVP, 1996), p. 147.

[17] A point influentially made by Russell 'He nowhere proves that thoughts need a thinker, nor is there reason to believe this except in a grammatical sense' (Bertrand Russell, *A History of Western Philosophy* [London: George Allen & Unwin, 1984]), p. 550. The *cogito ergo sum* 'has provided philosophers with ample shooting-practice' (Colin Brown, *Philosophy and the Christian Faith* [Leicester: IVP, 1968]), p. 51.

[18] MacIntyre, *Whose Justice?*, p. 336.

13. The Myth of Religious Pluralism

[1] Friedrich Nietzsche, *The Twilight of the Idols/The Anti-Christ* (London: Penguin, 1990), pp. 79–80.

[2] Nietzsche, *Twilight of the Idols*, p. 49.

[3] Alasdair MacIntyre, *Whose Justice? Which Rationality?* (London: Duckworth, 1988), p. 350.

[4] Thomas S. Kuhn, *Structures of Scientific Revolutions* (London: University of Chicago Press, 1970), p. 152.

[5] Paul Williams' remarkable story of his conversion from Buddhism to Christianity while the Co-director of Buddhist Studies at Bristol University would be a striking example in *The Unexpected Way: On Converting from Buddhism to Catholicism* (Edinburgh: T&T Clark, 2002).

[6] Richard Dawkins, *The God Delusion* (London: Bantam Press, 2006), p. 187.

[7] Gavin D'Costa, *John Hick's Theology of Religions* (Lanham: University Press of America, 1987), p. 9.

[8] Stanley J. Grenz and Roger E. Olson, *20th Century Theology* (Carlisle: Paternoster, 1992), p. 44.

[9] Friedrich Schleiermacher, *The Christian Faith* (Edinburgh: T&T Clark, 1960), pp. 133–4.

[10] Rudolph Otto, *The Idea of the Holy* (London: OUP, 1950).

[11] George Lindbeck, *The Nature of Doctrine* (London: SPCK, 1984). Lindbeck's categories for understanding theology are useful for this study of Hick. His own position, in his rejection of what he calls cognitive-realism, is problematic. Without some objective event or experience how did beliefs ever begin? Lindbeck analyses how he considers beliefs to function in the present experience of a believer but not how they origi-nated. See Alister E. McGrath, *The Genesis of Doctrine* (Grand Rapids, MI: Eerdmans, 1997), pp. 14–34.

[12] Lindbeck, *Nature of Doctrine*, p. 23.

[13] Lindbeck, *Nature of Doctrine*, p. 49.

[14] A point made by Hick in an early article on pluralism, 'On Grading Religions', where he affirmed that religious phenomena can 'in princi-ple be assessed and graded' (John Hick, *Problems of Religious Pluralism* (London: Macmillan, 1985), p. 86), though in practice this is compli-cated by the fact that a religion in its totality cannot be graded. In a later work, Hick simply conceded that 'no overall ranking is realistically possible' (John Hick, *The New Frontier of Religion and Science: Religious Experience, Neuroscience and the Transcendent* [Basingstoke: Palgrave Macmillan, 2010], p. 148).

[15] Chester Gillis, 'John Hick: Theologian or Philosopher of Religion?' in *Religious Pluralism and the Modern World: An Ongoing Engagement with John Hick* (ed. Sharada Sugirtharajah; Basingstoke: Macmillan, 2012), p. 137.

[16] Sharada Sugirtharajah, ed., *Religious Pluralism and the Modern World: An Ongoing Engagement with John Hick* (Basingstoke: Macmillan, 2012), p. 148.

[17] David Cheetham, *John Hick: A Critical Introduction and Reflection* (Farnham: Ashgate, 2003), p. 144.

[18] Cheetham, *John Hick*, pp. 159–69.

[19] John Hick, *The Rainbow of Faiths* (London: SCM Press, 1995), p. 136.

[20] John Hick, *God and the Universe of Faiths* (London: Macmillan, 1988), pp. 22–3.

[21] John Hick, 'Jesus and the World Religions' in *The Myth of God Incarnate* (ed. John Hick; London: SCM Press, 1977), p. 178.

[22] Hick, 'Jesus', p. 178.

[23] John Hick, *An Interpretation of Religion* (London: Macmillan, 1970), p. 348.

[24] Hick, *Interpretation*, p. 348.

[25] For example, in John Hick, *The Metaphor of God Incarnate* (London: SCM Press, 1993), pp. 160–62; and in *Who or What is God? And Other Investigations* (ed. John Hick; London: SCM Press, 2008), pp. 75–76.

[26] John Hick, *The Fifth Dimension* (Oxford: Oneworld, 1999), p. 230.

[27] Hick, *Fifth Dimension*, pp. 230–31.

[28] Hick, *Who or What is God?*, p. 116.

[29] I. Howard Marshall, 'Myth' in *New Dictionary of Theology* (ed. Sinclair B. Ferguson and David F. Wright; Leicester: IVP, 1989), p. 450.

[30] Chester Gillis, *A Question of Final Belief* (London: Macmillan, 1989), p. 165.

[31] Hick, *Interpretation*, p. 349.

[32] As demonstrated in the brief overviews provided by John H. Walton, *The Lost World of Genesis One* (Downers Grove, IL: IVP, 2009); and Tremper Longman III, *How to Read Genesis* (Downers Grove, IL: IVP, 2005). For example, see also Augustine, *On Genesis* (New York: New City Press, 2006).

[33] Longman, *How to Read Genesis*, p. 62.

[34] Alastair McKitterick, 'The Language of Genesis' in *Should Christians Embrace Evolution?* (ed. Norman C. Nevin; Nottingham: IVP, 2009), pp. 27–42.

[35] Hick, *Who or What is God?*, p. 76.

[36] Zoltán Kövecses, *Where Metaphors Come From: Reconsidering Context in Metaphor* (Oxford: OUP, 2015), p. 4, who considers the important role of our context as embodied creatures in the way we form our metaphors.

[37] Hick, *Interpretation*, p. 246.

[38] John R. Holmes, 'Mythopoeia' in *J.R.R. Tolkien Encyclopedia: Scholarship and Critical Assessment* (ed. Michael D.C. Drout; London: Routledge, 2013), p. 451.

[39] Holmes, 'Mythopoeia', p. 451.

[40] Terence Hawkes, *Metaphor* (London: Methuen, 1984), p. 11.

[41] Gillis, *Question*, pp. 141–3.

[42] Janet Martin Soskice, *Metaphor and Religious Language* (Oxford: Clarendon Press, 1988), p. 112.

[43] Soskice, *Metaphor and Religious Language*, p. 145.

[44] Ian G. Barbour, *Myths, Models and Paradigms* (London: SCM Press, 1974), p. 24.

[45] Examples of attempts at a modernist theology without Kant's anti-supernatural perspective would include John Locke, *The Reasonableness*

of Christianity as Delivered in the Scriptures (Bristol: Theommes Press, 1997); and William Paley, *Natural Theology.*

14. The Unknown God of Pluralism

[1]   Avery Dulles, *Models of Revelation* (London: Gill & Macmillan, 1992), pp. 50–51.

[2]   As seen in John Hick, *Faith and Knowledge* (London: Macmillan, 2nd edn, 1988), pp. 11–31.

[3]   John Hick, *An Interpretation of Religion* (London: Macmillan, 1970), p. 155.

[4]   Pannenberg himself is highly critical of John Hick's pluralism, Wolfhart Panneberg, 'Religious Pluralism and Conflicting Truth Claims' in *Christian Uniqueness Reconsidered* (ed. Gavin D'Costa; New York: Orbis), pp. 96–106.

[5]   Dulles, *Models*, p. 70.

[6]   E.g. Hendrick Kraemer, *Religion and the Christian Faith* (London: Lutterworth, 1956). In a typical discussion of Barth's work he is categorized as a religious exclusivist, see Race, *Christians and Religious Pluralism* (London: SCM Press, 1983), pp. 11–17.

[7]   Dulles, *Models*, p. 98.

[8]   Dulles, *Models*, p. 107.

[9]   Dulles, *Models*, p. 111.

[10]   John Hick, 'The Outcome: Dialogue into Truth' in *Truth and Dialogue* (ed. John Hick; London: Sheldon, 1974), p. 145.

[11]   Hick is dependent for this account of history on the work of the German theologian, Karl Jaspers. Jaspers' account certainly gives the impression that a traditional view of God is redundant. Indeed, we are on the verge of a new age, according to Jaspers, as a result of the revolution in science and technology. See Karl Jaspers, *The Origin and Goal of History* (trans. Michael Bullock; London: Routledge, 1953), pp. 81–8. There is compelling evidence that the axial age is a figment of academic imagination. Provan gives good reason to dismiss Jaspers' construct, though he also notes Hick's cautious use of this dubious idea, Iain Provan, *Convenient Myths: The Axial Age, Dark Green Religion and the World that Never Was* (Waco, TX: Baylor University Press, 2013), pp. 29–31.

[12]   John Hick, *God and the Universe of Faiths* (London: Macmillan, 1988), p. 136.

[13]   Hick, *Interpretation*, pp. 12, 21–33.

[14] John Hick, *The Fifth Dimension* (Oxford: Oneworld, 1999), p. 78.

[15] Nicholas Rescher, *Kant and the Reach of Reason* (Cambridge: CUP, 2000), p. 26.

[16] Rescher, *Kant*, p. 34.

[17] Hick, *Interpretation*, p. 264.

[18] Hick, *Interpretation*, p. 287.

[19] Hick, *Interpretation*, p. 292.

[20] Defences of Hick's claims make reference to Hick as a theological realist but can this really bear the freight that Graham Adams suggests: 'Hick is indeed committed to theistic realism: God *is* real' (Graham Adams, *Christ and the Other: In Dialogue with Hick and Newbigin* (Farnham: Ashgate, 2010), p. 101? I do not deny that Hick is a realist but I cannot see any reason to defend this as 'theistic' realism. What is really there may be closer to a non-personal force than anything remotely theistic. I think the evidence is that Hick is an epistemological realist but not a theistic realist.

[21] Vinoth Ramachandra, *Faiths in Conflict?* (Leicester: IVP, 1999), p. 127.

[22] Emil Brunner, *Revelation and Reason* (London: SCM Press, 1947), p. 24.

[23] Vinoth Ramachandra, *The Recovery of Mission* (Carlisle: Paternoster, 1996), pp. 124–5.

[24] A point argued in Paul Helm, *The Divine Revelation* (London: Marshall, Morgan & Scott, 1982), pp. 21–7. Or for a more fluid proposal see John Goldingay, *Models for Scripture* (Carlisle: Paternoster, 1994), pp. 299–313.

[25] The 'Amarna' theology of Akenhaten, by any account, represents a significant religious development. That it can be called monotheism is demonstrated by Hoffmeier, *Akhenaten and the Origins of Monotheism* (Oxford: OUP, 2015), pp. 193–210.

[26] John Walton, *Ancient Near Eastern Thought and the Old Testament* (Nottingham: Apollos, 2007), p. 93.

[27] Provan, *Convenient Myths*, p. 39.

[28] For biology the equivalent would be the Cambrian 'explosion' and the impression of sudden leaps forward described as 'punctuated equilibria'. Many evolutionary biologists dismiss this narrative as a misleading example of assuming that, because the fossil record shows leaps forward, this is actually what happened. Perhaps such leaps tell us more about the nature of fossilization than anything about organic evolution. Likewise, the story of history told by Jaspers may say more about the records that have survived than anything about the development of religious thought.

[29] Stephen Williams, 'The Trinity and "Other Religions"' in *The Trinity in a Pluralistic Age* (ed. Kevin J. Vanhoozer; Grand Rapids, MI: Eerdmans, 1997), p. 38.

[30] Gavin D'Costa provides a very helpful account of the way in which Radhakrishnan's neo-Hindu philosophy must be distinguished from Hick's pluralism. Though appearing similar to Hick's pluralist case, Radhakrishnan argues that there may be direct mystical apprehension of the Absolute. While this is a non-personal divine reality, Radhakrishnan is still claiming a direct knowledge which is strictly ruled out by Hick's epistemology. See Gavin D'Costa, *The Meeting of Religions and the Trinity* (Edinburgh: T&T Clark, 2000), p. 63.

15. Religious Diversity

[1] Recent examples must include Harold Netland, *Encountering Religious Pluralism: The Challenge to Christian Faith and Mission* (Leicester: IVP, 2001); and Daniel Strange, *'For Their Rock Is Not as Our Rock': An Evangelical Theology of Religions* (Nottingham: IVP, 2014).

[2] A good example of this from a traditional perspective is Claire Disbrey, *Listening to People of Other Faiths* (Oxford: BRF, 2004).

[3] These various positions are surveyed in John Sanders, *No Other Name* (Grand Rapids, MI: Eerdmans, 1992).

[4] Clark Pinnock, *A Wideness in God's Mercy* (Grand Rapids, MI: Zondervan, 1992), p. 131. An evangelical interaction with Pinnock's position on the world religions is to be found in *Reconstructing Theology: A Critical Assessment of the Theology of Clark Pinnock* (ed. Tony Gray and Christopher Sinkinson; Carlisle: Paternoster, 2000), pp. 155–265.

[5] Eckhard J. Schnabel, 'Other Religions: Saving or Secular?' in *Faith Comes by Hearing* (ed. Christopher W. Morgan and Robert A. Peterson; Nottingham: Apollos, 2008), p. 121.

[6] David K. Clark, *Dialogical Apologetics: A Person-Centered Approach to Christian Defence* (Grand Rapids, MI: Baker, 1993), p. 119.

[7] While not stating a clear position, Rob Bell probes the apparent narrow-mindedness of those who would hold a position that would entail Gandhi being in hell. His alternative is to propose that evangelicals should embrace universal salvation. Rob Bell, *Love Wins* (London: HarperCollins, 2011), pp. 1–3.

[8] John Hick, *The Fifth Dimension* (Oxford: Oneworld, 1999), p. 252.

[9] First held in Chicago in 1893, the Parliament of the World's Religions is generally considered the first formal meeting of the interfaith movement.

[10] Küng, Hans, and Karl-Joseph Kuschel, *A Global Ethic* (London: SCM Press, 1993), p. 8.

[11] Küng and Kuschel, *Global Ethic*, p. 61.

[12] Küng and Kuschel, *Global Ethic*, p. 65.

[13] G.K. Chesterton, *The Everlasting Man* (London: Hodder & Stoughton, 1947), p. 206.

[14] John Hick, *Who or What is God? And Other Investigations* (ed. John Hick; London: SCM Press, 2008), p. 158.

[15] Hick, *Who or What*, pp. 158–9.

[16] M.A. Reid, 'Humility' in *New Dictionary of Christian Ethics and Pastoral Theology* (ed. David J. Atkinson and David H. Field; Leicester: IVP, 1995), p. 470.

[17] Phil. 2:6–8. Hick dismisses the significance of such passages with his observation that they present an 'objectively undecidable issue', John Hick, *The Metaphor of God Incarnate* (London: SCM Press, 1993), p. 44.

[18] Wilfred Cantwell Smith, *Patterns of Faith around the World* (Oxford: Oneworld, 1998), p. 135.

[19] Lesslie Newbigin, 'Religion for the Marketplace' in *Christian Uniqueness Reconsidered* (ed. Gavin D'Costa; New York: Orbis, 1990), pp. 138–9.

[20] Gavin D'Costa, *The Meeting of Religions and the Trinity* (Edinburgh: T&T Clark, 2000), p. 46.

[21] John Hick does so in 'The Possibility of Religious Pluralism: A Reply to Gavin D'Costa', *RS* 33/2 (1197): pp. 161–6.

[22] Gavin D'Costa, *Theology in the Public Square: Church, Academy and Nation* (Oxford: Blackwell, 2005), p. 37.

[23] Smith, *Patterns*, p. 135.

[24] Alvin Plantinga and Nicholas Wolterstorff provide a cogent defence of epistemic exclusivism and also considers the positive contribution pluralism may make to it. In our encounter with other religious options we may become more convinced of the truth of our own, 'knowledge of the facts of pluralism could initially serve as a defeater, but in the long run have precisely the opposite effect.' Alvin Plantinga and Nicholas Wolterstorff, 'A Defense of Religious Exclusivism' in *The Rationality of Belief and the Plurality of Faith* (ed. Thomas D. Senor; Ithaca and London: Cornell University Press, 1995), p. 215.

[25] John Hick, *The Rainbow of Faiths* (London: SCM Press, 1995), p. 50.

[26] Paul Knitter, *One Earth, Many Religions* (Maryknoll, NY: Orbis, 1995), p. 30.

[27] J. Rosario Narchison, 'Theological Education for Pluralism in India' in *Pluralism and the Religions* (ed. John D'Arcy May; London: Cassell, 1998), p. 67.

[28] Alasdair MacIntyre, *Whose Justice? Which Rationality?* (London: Duckworth, 1988), p. 2.

[29] Esther L. Meek, 'Honouring True Otherness in a Still-Antipluralist Culture', in *The Gospel and Pluralism Today: Reassessing Lesslie Newbigin in the 21st Century* (ed. Scott W. Sunquist and Amos Young; Downers Grove, IL: IVP, 2015), p. 131.

16. An Evangelical Theology of Religions

[1] David S. Nah, *Christian Theology and Religious Pluralism: A Critical Evaluation of John Hick* (Eugene, OR: Pickwick, 2012), p. 136.

[2] N.T. Wright, *The New Testament and the People of God* (London: SPCK, 1992), p. 82.

[3] N.T. Wright, *Jesus and the Victory of God* (London: SPCK, 1996), p. 27.

[4] N.T. Wright, *Jesus and the Victory of God*, p. 538.

[5] Famously stated by C.S. Lewis, *Mere Christianity* (Glasgow: Collins, 1986), p. 52.

[6] Craig S. Keener, *The Historical Jesus of the Gospels* (Grand Rapids, MI: Eerdmans, 2009), p. 34.

[7] In turn, this helps us read the entire New Testament in a properly Hebraic-Jewish context such as Brad H. Young, *Paul the Jewish Theologian: A Pharisee among Christians, Jews, and Gentiles* (Massachusetts: Hendrickson, 1997).

[8] Many detailed examples are to be found in Richard Bauckham, *Jesus and the Eyewitnesses: The Gospels as Eyewitness Testimony* (Grand Rapids, MI: Eerdmans, 2006). The numerous place and people names clearly reflect first-century historical context. The contrast between the canonical gospels and the later gnostic gospels is striking on this point.

[9] Once we lay aside a bias against the possibility of the miraculous, it is difficult to ignore the implications of this evidence even for the claims regarding the empty tomb (cf. Michael R. Licona, *The Resurrection of Jesus: A New Historiographical Approach* [Nottingham: Apollos, 2010]). The basic historical nature of the resurrection claims were evident to Jewish theologian Pinchas Lapide, even though he denied that the evidence led to the conclusions drawn by Christians. Lapide, *The Resurrection of Jesus: A Jewish Perspective* (Eugene, OR: Wipf & Stock, 1982), p. 153.

[10] 'While they may well form their own subgenre because of their shared content, the synoptic gospels belong within the overall genre of *bioi*.' Richard A. Burridge, *What Are the Gospels? A Comparison with Graeco-Roman*

Biography (Michigan: Eerdmans and Michigan: Dove, 2nd edn, 2004), p. 212. It is interesting to note that one feature of Greco-Roman biography not shared by the gospel writers is the propensity to interpret physical characteristics as a guide to inner character. See also Richard A. Burridge, *Four Gospels, One Jesus?* (London: SPCK, 2000).

[11] Gavin D'Costa, *John Hick's Theology of Religions* (Lanham: University Press of America, 1987), pp. 106–7.

[12] The conclusion of John Hick, *An Interpretation of Religion* (London: Macmillan, 1970), pp. 372–6.

[13] D'Costa, *John Hick's Theology of Religions*, p. 121.

[14] C.F.D. Moule, *The Origin of Christology* (Cambridge: CUP, 1978), p. 103.

[15] N.T. Wright, *Jesus and the Victory of God*, p. 642.

[16] Phil. 2:6–11; Col. 1:15–20; 1 Cor. 15:3–8.

[17] Paul W. Barnett, *Jesus and the Logic of History* (Leicester: Apollos, 1997), p. 56.

[18] Richard Bauckham, *Jesus and the God of Israel* (Milton Keynes: Paternoster, 2008), p. 181.

[19] G.K Chesterton, *The Everlasting Man* (London: Hodder & Stoughton, 1947), p. 206.

[20] Hick is generally approving of Moule's scholarship, as he is of James Dunn, but dismissive of their conclusions. See John Hick, *The Metaphor of God Incarnate* (London: SCM Press, 1993), pp. 28–39.

[21] Douglas McCready, 'The Disintegration of John Hick's Christology', *JETS* 39/1 (1996): p. 270.

[22] A comprehensive survey is provided by Bruce Demarest, *General Revelation: Historical Views and Contemporary Issues* (Grand Rapids: Zondervan, 1982). For a critical assessment of inclusivist views see Daniel Strange, 'General Revelation: Sufficient or Insufficient?' in *Faith Comes By Hearing: A Response to Inclusivism* (ed. Christopher W. Morgan and Robert A. Peterson; Nottingham: Apollos, 2008), pp. 40–77.

[23] 'Part of the meaning of the goodness of creation in the Bible is that it witnesses to the God who made it, reflecting something of his character.' Christopher J.H. Wright, *Old Testament Ethics for the People of God* (Leicester: IVP, 2004), p. 106.

[24] Acts 14:17.

[25] John Calvin, *Institutes of the Christian Religion* 1.5.1 (trans. Henry Beveridge; Massachusetts: Hendrickson, 2008), p. 16.

[26] Calvin, *Institutes*, 1.5.4, p. 18.

[27] Christopher J.H. Wright, *The Mission of God: Unlocking the Bible's Grand Narrative* (Downers Grove, IL: IVP, 2006), pp. 136–88. Briefly, I provide

my own popular level summary in Christopher Sinkinson, *Time Travel to the Old Testament* (Nottingham: IVP, 2013), pp. 109–30.

28 Christopher J.H. Wright, *Mission of God*, p. 187.

29 Clark Pinnock, *A Wideness in God's Mercy* (Grand Rapids, MI: Zondervan, 1992), pp. 92–106.

30 A point discussed in relation to Pinnock's work in Christopher Sinkinson, 'Clark Pinnock and the World Religions', in *Reconstructing Theology: A Critical Assessment of the Theology of Clark Pinnock* (ed. Tony Gray and Christopher Sinkinson; Carlisle: Paternoster, 2000).

31 Daniel Strange, *'For Their Rock Is Not as Our Rock': An Evangelical Theology of Religions* (Nottingham: IVP, 2014), pp. 196–202.

32 Strange, *For Their Rock*, p. 201.

33 McDermott, Gerald R. *Can Evangelicals Learn from World Religions? Jesus, Revelation and Religious Traditions* (Downers Grove, IL: IVP, 2000), p. 114.

34 From an evangelical perspective such possibilities are explored by the contributors to John Sanders, ed., *What About Those Who Have Never Heard?* (Downers Grove, IL: IVP, 1995), and a cautious suggestion is offered by Norman Anderson, *Christianity and the World Religions* (Leicester: IVP, 1984). The possibility of salvation among the evangelized is generally held to be an open question but few have given it the extensive explanation provided by Terrance L. Tiessen, *Who Can Be Saved? Reassessing Salvation in Christ and World Religions* (Leicester: IVP, 1984). A robust rebuttal of the wider hope position is found in Daniel Strange, *The Possibility of Salvation Among the Unevangelised: An Analysis of Inclusivism in Recent Evangelical Theology* (Carlisle: Paternoster, 2002).

35 Deut. 6:4.

36 Deut. 5:7.

37 Strange, *For Their Rock*, p. 306.

38 Strange, *For Their Rock*, p. 307.

39 John Hick, 'Response to R. Douglas Geivett and W. Gary Phillips' in *Four Views on Salvation in a Pluralistic World* (ed. Dennis L. Ockholm and Timothy R. Philips; Grand Rapids, MI: Zondervan, 1996), p. 250.

40 Christopher Sinkinson, 'John Hick: Religion for the Modern World?' in *Getting Your Bearings: Engaging with Contemporary Theologians* (ed. Philip Duce and Daniel Strange; Leicester: Apollos, 2003), pp. 61–2.

41 Chester Gillis, *A Question of Final Belief* (London: Macmillan, 1989), p. 171.

42 John 4:9–10.

43 D'Costa, *John Hick's Theology of Religions*, p. 102.

Bibliography

John Hick

Hick, John. 'The Christology of D.M. Baillie'. *Scottish Journal of Theology* 11 (1958): pp. 1–12.

_____. 'Theology and Verification'. *Theology Today* 27/2 (1960).

_____. *Arguments for the Existence of God* (London: Macmillan, 1970).

_____. *Death and Eternal Life* (London: Collins, 1976).

_____. *Evil and the God of Love* (London: Macmillan, 1977).

_____. *God Has Many Names* (London: Macmillan, 1980).

_____. *The Second Christianity* (London: SCM Press, 1983).

_____. 'On Grading Religions', in *Problems of Religious Pluralism* (London: Macmillan, 1985).

_____. *Faith and Knowledge* (London: Macmillan, 2nd edn, 1988).

_____. *God and the Universe of Faiths* (London: Macmillan, 1988).

_____. *An Interpretation of Religion* (London: Macmillan, 1989).

_____. *Philosophy of Religion* (London: Prentice-Hall, 1990).

_____. 'Rational Faith as Experiencing-as'. Pages 34–48 in *A John Hick Reader* (ed. Paul Badham; London: Macmillan, 1990).

_____. 'Rational Theistic Belief without Proofs', in *A John Hick Reader* (ed. Paul Badham; London: Macmillan, 1990).

_____. 'A Response to Gerard Loughlin'. *Modern Theology* 7 (1990): pp. 57–66.

_____. *Disputed Questions* (London: Macmillan, 1992).

_____. *The Metaphor of God Incarnate* (London: SCM Press, 1993).

_____. 'Readers' Responses'. *Themelios* 19/3 (1994): pp. 20–21.

_____. *The Rainbow of Faiths* (London: SCM Press, 1995).

_____. 'Response to R. Douglas Geivett and W. Gary Phillips'. Pages 246–50 in *Four Views on Salvation in a Pluralistic World* (ed. Dennis L. Ockholm and Timothy R. Philips; Grand Rapids, MI: Zondervan, 1996).

_____. 'The Possibility of Religious Pluralism: A Reply to Gavin D'Costa'. *Religious Studies* 33/2 (1997): pp. 161–6.

_____. *The Fifth Dimension* (Oxford: Oneworld, 1999).

_____. 'Ineffability'. *Religious Studies* 38 (2000): pp. 35–46.

_____. *An Autobiography* (Oxford: Oneworld, 2002).

_____. *Who or What is God? And Other Investigations* (London: SCM Press, 2008).

_____. *Between Faith and Doubt* (Basingstoke: Palgrave Macmillan, 2010).

_____. *The New Frontier of Religion and Science: Religious Experience, Neuroscience and the Transcendent* (Basingstoke: Palgrave Macmillan, 2010).

Hick, John, ed. *Truth and Dialogue* (London: Sheldon, 1974).

_____. *The Myth of God Incarnate* (London: SCM Press, 1977).

Secondary Texts

Adams, Graham. *Christ and the Other: In Dialogue with Hick and Newbigin* (Farnham: Ashgate, 2010).

Allen, Charlotte. *The Human Christ* (Oxford: Lion, 1998).

Allen, Diogenes. *Christian Belief in a Postmodern World* (Louisville, KY: Westminster/John Knox, 1989).

Anderson, Norman. *Christianity and World Religions* (Leicester: Inter-Varsity Press, 1984).

Anselm, 'St Anselm's Reply to Gaunilo'. Pages 13–27 in *The Onto-logical Argument* (ed. Alvin Plantinga; London: Macmillan, 1968).

Atkinson, David J., and David H. Field, eds. *New Dictionary of Christian Ethics and Pastoral Theology* (Leicester: Inter-Varsity Press, 1995).

Augustine. *On Genesis* (New York: New City Press, 2002).

Ayer, A.J. *Language, Truth and Logic* (London: Victor Gollancz, 1946).

Badham, Paul. 'John Hick's *An Interpretation of Religion*'. In *Problems in the Philosophy of Religion* (ed. Harold Hewitt; London: Macmillan, 1991).

Badham, Paul, ed. *A John Hick Reader* (London: Macmillan, 1990).

Bald, Margaret. *Banned Books: Literature Suppressed on Religious Grounds* (New York: Facts on File, rev. edn, 2006).

Barbour, Ian G. *Myths, Models and Paradigms* (London: SCM Press, 1974).

Barnes, Philip L. 'Continuity and Development in John Hick's Theology'. *Studies in Religion* 21/4 (1992): pp: 395–402.

Barnett, Paul W. *Jesus and the Logic of History* (Leicester: Apollos, 1997).

Barthes, Roland. *Empire of Signs* (trans. Richard Howard; New York: Hill & Wang, 1982).

Baukham, Richard. *Jesus and the Eyewitnesses: The Gospels as Eyewitness Testimony* (Grand Rapids, MI: Eerdmans, 2006).

_____. *Jesus and the God of Israel* (Milton Keynes: Paternoster, 2008).

Bell, Rob. *Love Wins* (London: HarperCollins, 2011).

Benner, Drayton C. 'Immanuel Kant's Demythologization of the Christian Theories of the Atonement in *Religion within the Limits of Reason Alone*'. *Evangelical Quarterly* 79/2 (2007): pp. 99–111.

Bettenson, Henry, ed. *Documents of the Christian Church* (Oxford: Oxford University Press, 1967).

Boettner, Loraine. *The Reformed Doctrine of Predestination* (Grand Rapids, MI: Eerdmans, 1957).

Brown, Colin. *Philosophy and the Christian Faith* (Leicester: Inter-Varsity Press, 1968).

Brunner, Emil. *Revelation and Reason* (London: SCM Press, 1947).

Burge, Gary M. *Whose Land? Whose Promise?* (USA: Pilgrim Press, 2003).

Burridge, Richard A. *What are the Gospels? A Comparison with Graeco-Roman Biography* (Michigan: Eerdmans and Michigan: Dove, 2nd edn, 2004).

Byrne, Peter. 'John Hick's Philosophy of World Religions'. *Scottish Journal of Theology* 35 (1982): pp. 289–301.

Calvin, John. *Institutes of the Christian Religion* (trans. Henry Beveridge; Massachusetts: Hendrickson, 2008).

Carson, D.A. *The Gagging of God* (Leicester: Inter-Varsity Press, 1996).

Cassuto, Umberto. *The Documentary Hypothesis* (Jerusalem: Shalem Press, 2006).

Cheetham, David. *John Hick: A Critical Introduction and Reflection* (Farnham: Ashgate, 2003).

Chesterton, G.K. *The Everlasting Man* (London: Hodder & Stoughton, 1947).

Clark, David K. *Dialogical Apologetics: A Person-Centered Approach to Christian Defence* (Grand Rapids, MI: Baker, 1993).

Cook, Robert. 'Postmodernism, Pluralism and John Hick', *Themelios* 19/1 (1993): pp. 10–11.

D'Costa, Gavin. *Christianity and World Religions: Disputed Questions in the Theology of Religions* (Oxford: Wiley-Blackwell, 2009).

_____. 'John Hick and Religious Pluralism: Yet Another Revolution'. Pages 3–16 in *Problems in the Philosophy of Religion* (ed. Harold Hewitt; London: Macmillan, 1991).

____. *John Hick's Theology of Religions* (Lanham: University Press of America, 1987).

____. *The Meeting of Religions and the Trinity* (Edinburgh: T&T Clark, 2000).

____. *Theology in the Public Square: Church, Academy and Nation* (Oxford: Blackwell, 2005).

D'Costa, Gavin, ed. *Christian Uniqueness Reconsidered* (New York: Orbis, 1990).

D'Costa, Gavin, Paul Knitter and Daniel Strange. *Only One Way? Three Christian Responses on the Uniqueness of Christ in a Religiously Plural World* (London: SCM Press, 2011).

Dawkins, Richard. *The God Delusion* (London: Bantam Press, 2006).

Demarest, Bruce. *General Revelation: Historical Views and Contemporary Issues* (Grand Rapids, MI: Zondervan, 1982).

Disbrey, Claire. *Listening to People of Other Faiths* (Oxford: Bible Reading Fellowship, 2004).

Drout, Michael D.C., ed. *J.R.R. Tolkien Encyclopedia: Scholarship and Critical Assessment* (London: Routledge, 2013).

Dulles, Avery. *Models of Revelation* (London: Gill & Macmillan, 1992).

Eddy, Paul R. 'John Hick's Theological Pilgrimage'. In *Proceedings of the Wheaton Theology Conference* (Illinois: Wheaton College, 1992).

____. 'Religious Pluralism and the Divine: Another Look at John Hick's Neo-Kantian Proposal'. *Religious Studies* 30 (1994): pp. 467–78.

Ferguson, Sinclair B., and David F. Wright, eds. *New Dictionary of Theology* (Leicester: Inter-Varsity Press, 1989).

Forrester, D.B. 'Professor Hick and the Universe of Faiths'. *Scottish Journal of Theology* 29 (1976): pp. 65–72.

Gellner, Ernest. *Reason and Culture* (Oxford: Blackwell, 1992).

Gillis, Chester. 'John Hick: Theologian or Philosopher of Religion?' In *Religious Pluralism and the Modern World: An Ongoing Engagement with John Hick* (ed. Sharada Sugirtharajah; Basingstoke: Macmillan, 2012).

_____. *A Question of Final Belief* (London: Macmillan, 1989).

Godlove, Terry F. *Religion, Interpretation, and Diversity of Belief* (Cambridge: Cambridge University Press, 1989).

Goldingay, John. *Models for Scripture* (Carlisle: Paternoster, 1994).

Gray, Tony, and Christopher Sinkinson, eds. *Reconstructing Theology: A Critical Assessment of the Theology of Clark Pinnock* (Carlisle: Paternoster, 2000).

Grenz, Stanley J., and Roger E. Olson. *20th Century Theology* (Carlisle: Paternoster, 1992).

Hawkes, Terence. *Metaphor* (London: Methuen, 1984).

Helm, Paul. *Belief Policies* (Cambridge: Cambridge University Press, 1994).

_____. *The Divine Revelation* (London: Marshall, Morgan & Scott, 1982).

_____. *The Varieties of Belief* (London: George Allen & Unwin, 1973).

Hilborn, David, and Don Horrocks. 'Universalistic Trends in the Evangelical Tradition: An Historical Perspective'. Pages 219–44 in *Universal Salvation? The Current Debate* (ed. Robin Parry and Chris Partridge; Carlisle: Paternoster, 2003).

Hoffmeier, James K. *Akhenaten and the Origins of Monotheism* (Oxford: Oxford University Press, 2015).

Holmes, John R. 'Mythopoeia'. Page 451 in *J.R.R. Tolkien Encyclopedia: Scholarship and Critical Assessment* (ed. Michael D.C. Drout; London: Routledge, 2013).

Hughes, Dewi Arwel. *Has God Many Names?* (Leicester: Apollos, 1996).

Hume, David. *A Treatise of Human Nature* (Oxford: Oxford University Press, 2000).

Insole, Christopher J. 'Why John Hick Cannot, and Should Not, Stay out of the Jam Pot'. *Religious Studies* 38 (2000): pp. 25–33.

Jaspers, Karl. *The Origin and Goal of History* (trans. Michael Bullock; London: Routledge, 1953).

Johnson, Mark. *Moral Imagination* (London: University of Chicago Press, 1993).

Kant, Immanuel. *The Conflict of Faculties* (trans. Mary J. Gregor; New York: Abaris Books, 1979).

_____. *Critique of Pure Reason* (trans. and ed. Paul Guyer and Allen W. Wood; Cambridge: Cambridge University Press, 1998).

_____. *On History* (New York: Library of Liberal Arts, 1963).

_____. *Prolegomena* (trans. Paul Carus; Illinois: Open Court, 1989).

_____. *Religion Within the Limits of Reason Alone* (trans. Theodore M. Greene and Hoyt H. Hudson; New York: Harper & Row, 1960).

Keener, Craig S. *The Historical Jesus of the Gospels* (Grand Rapids, MI: Eerdmans, 2009).

Kemp Smith, Norman. *The Philosophy of David Hume* (London: Macmillan, 1941).

Knitter, Paul F. *One Earth, Many Religions* (Maryknoll, NY: Orbis, 1995).

Kövecses, Zoltán. *Where Metaphors Come From: Reconsidering Context in Metaphor* (Oxford: Oxford University Press, 2015).

Kraemer, Hendrick. *Religion and the Christian Faith* (London: Lutterworth, 1956).

Kuhn, Thomas S. *The Structure of Scientific Revolutions* (London: University of Chicago Press, 1970).

Küng, Hans. *Does God Exist?* (London: SCM Press, 1991).

Küng, Hans, and Karl-Josef Kuschel. *A Global Ethic* (London: SCM Press, 1993).

Küng, Hans, et al. *Christianity and the World Religions* (London: 2nd edn, SCM Press, 1993).

Lapide, Pinchas. *The Resurrection of Jesus: A Jewish Perspective* (Eugene, OR: Wipf & Stock, 1982).

Lavender, Gemma. 'Is there a Centre of the Universe?'", spaceanswers. com (accessed 28 January 2013).

Levy, Richard S. *Antisemitism: A Historical Encyclopaedia of Prejudice and Persecution*, vol. 1 (California: ABC-CLIO, 2005).

Lewis, C.S. *Mere Christianity* (Glasgow: Collins, 1986).

Lindbeck, George. *The Nature of Doctrine* (London: SPCK, 1984).

Licona, Michael R. *The Resurrection of Jesus: A New Historiographical Approach* (Nottingham: Apollos, 2010).

Lipner, Julius J. 'Does Copernicus Help? Reflections for a Christian Theology of Religions'. *Religious Studies* 13 (1977): pp. 243–58.

Locke, John. *An Essay Concerning Human Understanding* (London: Everyman, 1976).

_____. *The Reasonableness of Christianity as Delivered in the Scriptures* (Bristol: Theommes Press, 1997).

Longman III, Tremper. *How to Read Genesis* (Downers Grove, IL: InterVarsity Press, 2005).

Loughlin, Gerard. 'Noumenon and Phenomena'. *Religious Studies* 23 (1987): pp. 493–508.

_____. 'Prefacing Pluralism: John Hick and the Mastery of Religion'. *Modern Theology* 7 (1990): pp. 29–55.

MacIntyre, Alasdair. *Three Rival Versions of Moral Enquiry* (London: Duckworth, 1990).

_____. *Whose Justice? Which Rationality?* (London: Duckworth, 1988).

Magee, Brian. *Talking Philosophy: Dialogues with Fifteen Leading Philosophers* (Oxford: Oxford University Press, 2001), p. 107.

Markham, Ian S. *Plurality and Christian Ethics* (Cambridge: Cambridge University Press, 1994).

Marshall, I. Howard. 'Myth'. Pages 449–51 in *New Dictionary of Theology* (ed. Sinclair B. Ferguson and David F. Wright; Leicester: Inter-Varsity Press, 1989).

Mase, Emi. 'Does Hick's Post-Copernican Pluralism in *An Interpre-tation of Religion* Lead to Agnosticism?' (unpublished MA thesis, University of Bristol, 1994).

Mathis, T. *Against John Hick* (Boston: University Press of America, 1985).

McCready, Douglas. 'The Disintegration of John Hick's Christology'. *Journal of the Evangelical Theology Society* 39/1 (1996): pp. 257–70.

McDermott, Gerald R. *Can Evangelicals Learn from World Religions? Jesus, Revelation and Religious Traditions* (Downers Grove, IL: InterVarsity Press, 2000).

McGrath, Alister E. *The Genesis of Doctrine* (Grand Rapids, MI: Eerdmans, 1997).

____. *The Intellectual Origins of the European Reformation* (Oxford: Blackwell, 1987).

____. *The Twilight of Atheism: The Rise and Fall of Disbelief in the Modern World* (London: Random House, 2004).

McKitterick, Alastair. 'The Language of Genesis'. Pages 27–42 in *Should Christians Embrace Evolution?* (ed. Norman C. Nevin; Nottingham: IVP, 2009).

Meek, Esther L. 'Honouring True Otherness in a Still-Antipluralist Culture'. In *The Gospel and Pluralism Today: Reassessing Lesslie Newbigin in the 21st Century* (ed. Scott W. Sunquist and Amos Young; Downers Grove, IL: InterVarsity Press, 2015).

Michalson, Gordon E. *Kant and the Problem of God* (Oxford: Blackwell, 1999).

Middleton, J. Richard, and Brian J. Walsh. *Truth is Stranger than it Used to Be* (London: SPCK, 1995).

Morgan, Christopher W., and Robert A. Peterson, eds. *Faith Comes by Hearing* (Nottingham: Apollos, 2008).

Moule, C.F.D. *The Origin of Christology* (Cambridge: Cambridge University Press, 1978).

Muck, Terry C. 'Theology of Religions after Knitter and Hick: Beyond the Paradigm'. *Interpretation* 61/1 (2007): pp. 7–22.

Nah, David S. *Christian Theology and Religious Pluralism: A Critical Evaluation of John Hick* (Eugene, OR: Pickwick, 2012).

Narchison, J. Rosario. 'Theological Education for Pluralism in India'. In *Pluralism and the Religions* (ed. John D'Arcy May; London: Cassell, 1998).

Netland, Harold A. *Dissonant Voices: Religious Pluralism and the Question of Truth* (Leicester: Inter-Varsity Press, 1991).

_____. *Encountering Religious Pluralism: The Challenge to Faith and Mission* (Leicester: Inter-Varsity Press, 2001).

Nevin, Norman C., ed. *Should Christians Embrace Evolution?* (Nottingham: Inter-Varsity Press, 2009).

Newbigin, Lesslie. *The Gospel in a Pluralist Society* (London: SPCK, 1989).

_____. 'Religion for the Marketplace'. In *Christian Uniqueness Reconsidered* (ed. Gavin D'Costa; New York: Orbis, 1990).

Nietzsche, Friedrich. *The Twilight of the Idols/The Anti-Christ* (London: Penguin, 1990).

Ogden, Schubert M. 'Problems in the Case for a Pluralistic Theology of Religions'. *Journal of Religion* 69 (1988): pp. 493–507.

Otto, Rudolf. *The Idea of the Holy* (London: Oxford University Press, 1950).

Panikkar, Raimon. *The Intra-Religious Dialogue* (New Jersey: Paulist Press, 1999).

Pannenberg, Wolfhart. 'Religious Pluralism and Conflicting Truth Claims'. Pages 96–106 in *Christian Uniqueness Reconsidered* (ed. Gavin D'Costa; New York: Orbis, 1990).

Parry, Robin, and Chris Partridge, eds. *Universal Salvation? The Current Debate* (Carlisle: Paternoster, 2003).

Penelhum, Terence. *God and Skepticism* (Netherlands: D. Reidel, 1983).

_____. 'Reflections on the Ambiguity of the World'. In *God, Truth and Reality: Essays in Honour of John Hick* (ed. Arvind Sharma; London: Macmillan, 1993).

Pinnock, Clark. *A Wideness in God's Mercy* (Grand Rapids, MI: Zondervan, 1992).

Plantinga, Alvin, and Nicholas Wolterstorff. 'A Defense of Religious Exclusivism'. In *The Rationality of Belief and the Plurality of Faith* (ed. Thomas D. Senor; Ithaca and London: Cornell University Press, 1995).

Plantinga, Alvin, and Nicholas Wolterstorff, eds. *Faith and Rationality* (Notre Dame: University of Notre Dame Press, 1983).

Provan, Iain. *Convenient Myths: The Axial Age, Dark Green Religion and the World that Never Was* (Waco, TX: Baylor University Press, 2013).

Race, Alan. *Christians and Religious Pluralism* (London: SCM Press, 1993).

Rahner, Karl. *Theological Investigations*, vol. 6 (London: SCM Press, 1969).

Ramachandra, Vinoth. *Faiths in Conflict?* (Leicester: Inter-Varsity Press, 1999).

_____. *The Recovery of Mission* (Carlisle: Paternoster, 1996).

Rescher, Nicholas. *Kant and the Reach of Reason* (Cambridge: Cambridge University Press, 2000).

Reid, M.A. 'Humility'. Page 470 in *New Dictionary of Christian Ethics and Pastoral Theology* (ed. David J. Atkinson and David H. Field; Leicester: InterVarsity Press, 1995).

Rose, Paul Lawrence. *The German Question/Jewish Question: Revolutionary Anti-Semitism in Germany from Kant to Wagner* (Princeton, NJ: Princeton University Press, 2006).

Rowe, William L. 'John Hick's Contribution to the Philosophy of Religion'. In *God, Truth and Reality: Essays in Honour of John Hick* (ed. Arvind Sharma; London: Macmillan, 1993).

Runzo, Joseph. *World-Views and Perceiving God* (London: Macmillan, 1993).

Russell, Bertrand. *A History of Western Philosophy* (London: George Allen & Unwin, 1984).

_____. *Why I Am Not a Christian* (London: George Allen & Unwin, 1975).

Sanders, John. *No Other Name* (Grand Rapids, MI: Eerdmans, 1992).

Sanders, John, ed. *What About Those Who Have Never Heard?* (Downers Grove, IL: InterVarsity Press, 1995).

Schleiermacher, Friedrich. *The Christian Faith* (Edinburgh: T&T Clark, 1960).

Schnabel, Eckhard J. 'Other Religions: Saving or Secular?' In *Faith Comes by Hearing* (ed. Christopher W. Morgan and Robert A. Peterson; Nottingham: Apollos, 2008).

Schrader, George. 'The Thing in Itself in Kantian Philosophy'. In *Kant: A Collection of Critical Essays* (ed. Paul Wolff; London: University of Notre Dame Press, 1968).

Scott, Mark. '"Suffering and Soul-Making": Rethinking John Hick's Theodicy'. *Journal of Religion* 90.1 (2010): pp. 313–34.

Senor, Thomas D., ed. *The Rationality of Belief and the Plurality of Faith* (New York: Cornell University Press, 1995).

Sinkinson, Christopher. 'Clark Pinnock and the World Religions'. In *Reconstructing Theology: A Critical Assessment of the Theology of Clark Pinnock* (ed. Tony Gray and Christopher Sinkinson; Carlisle: Paternoster, 2000).

_____. 'Confessing Christ in a Pluralist Culture'. In *Grace and Truth in a Secular Age* (ed. Timothy Bradshaw; Cambridge: Eerdmans, 1998).

_____. *Confident Christianity* (Nottingham: Inter-Varsity Press, 2012).

_____. 'In Defence of the Faith: Clark Pinnock and the World Religions'. In *Reconstructing Theology: A Critical Assessment of the Theology of Clark Pinnock* (ed. Tony Gray and Christopher Sinkinson; Carlisle: Paternoster, 2000).

_____. 'John Hick: Religion for the Modern World?' In *Getting Your Bearings: Engaging with Contemporary Theologians* (ed. Philip Duce and Daniel Strange; Leicester: Apollos, 2003).

_____. *Time Travel to the Old Testament* (Nottingham: Inter-Varsity Press, 2013).

Smith, Wilfred Cantwell. *The Meaning and End of Religion* (Minneapolis: Fortress Press, 1991).

_____. *Patterns of Faith around the World* (Oxford: Oneworld, 1998).

Soskice, Janet Martin. *Metaphor and Religious Language* (Oxford: Clarendon Press, 1988).

Strange, Daniel. *'For Their Rock Is Not as Our Rock': An Evangelical Theology of Religions* (Nottingham: Inter-Varsity Press, 2014).

_____. 'General Revelation: Sufficient or Insufficient?' Pages 40–77 in *Faith Comes By Hearing: A Response to Inclusivism* (ed. Christopher W. Morgan and Robert A. Peterson; Nottingham: Apollos, 2008).

_____. *The Possibility of Salvation among the Unevangelised: An Analysis of Inclusivism in Recent Evangelical Theology* (Carlisle: Paternoster, 2002).

Sugirtharajah, Sharada, ed., *Religious Pluralism and the Modern World: An Ongoing Engagement with John Hick* (Basingstoke: Palgrave Macmillan, 2012).

Sullivan, Francis A. *Salvation Outside the Church?* (London: Geoffrey Chapman, 1992).

Sunquist, Scott W., and Amos Young, eds. *The Gospel and Pluralism Today: Reassessing Lesslie Newbigin in the 21st Century* (Downers Grove, IL: Inter-Varsity Press, 2015).

Swinburne, Richard. *Faith and Reason* (Oxford: Clarendon Press, 1983).

Tiessen, Terrance L. 'The Salvation of the Unevangelised in the Light of God's Covenants'. *Evangelical Quarterly* 36/3 (2012): pp. 231–49.

_____. *Who Can Be Saved? Reassessing Salvation in Christ and World Religions* (Leicester: Inter-Varsity Press, 2004).

Walton, John H. *Ancient Near Eastern Thought and the Old Testament: Introducing the Conceptual World of the Hebrew Bible* (Nottingham: Apollos, 2007).

_____. *The Lost World of Genesis One* (Downers Grove, IL: InterVarsity Press, 2009).

Ward, Keith. *Religion and Revelation* (Oxford: Clarendon Press, 1994).

_____. *A Vision to Pursue* (London: SCM Press, 1991).

Westphal, Merold. 'In Defence of the Thing in Itself'. *Kant-Studien* (1968): pp. 118–41.

Williams, Paul. *The Unexpected Way: On Converting from Buddhism to Catholicism* (Edinburgh: T&T Clark, 2002).

Williams, Stephen. 'The Trinity and 'Other Religions''. In *The Trinity in a Pluralistic Age* (ed. Kevin J. Vanhoozer; Grand Rapids, MI: Eerdmans, 1997).

Wittgenstein, Ludwig. *Philosophical Investigations* (Oxford: Blackwell, 1967).

Wright, Christopher J.H. *The Mission of God: Unlocking the Bible's Grand Narrative* (Downers Grove, IL: InterVarsity Press, 2006).

_____. *Old Testament Ethics for the People of God* (Leicester: Inter-Varsity Press, 2004).

Wright, David F. 'Gifford Lectures'. Pages 268–9 in *New Dictionary of Theology* (ed. Sinclair B. Ferguson and David F. Wright; Leicester, Inter-Varsity Press, 1989).

Wright, Nigel Goring. *Disavowing Constantine: Mission, Church and the Social Order in the Theology of John Howard Yoder and Jürgen Moltmann* (Carlisle: Paternoster, 2000).

Wright, N.T. *Jesus and the Victory of God* (London: SPCK, 1996).

_____. *The New Testament and the People of God* (London: SPCK, 1992).

Young, Brad H. *Paul the Jewish Theologian: A Pharisee among Christians, Jews, and Gentiles* (Massachusetts: Hendrickson, 1997).

Index

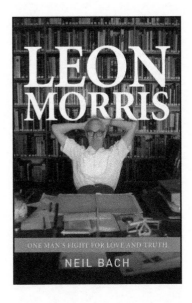

Leon Morris

One Man's Fight for Love and Truth

Neil Bach

Leon Morris's story needs to be told. In this unique and long-awaited work Neil Bach shows Leon Morris as a prodigious and original thinker from the wrong side of the world who restored the credibility of evangelical scholarship and the centrality of the cross. Many of us have been nurtured by his enormously helpful books on the cross, but few know about the obstacles that had to be overcome. The author gives us a life of Leon Morris which is true to the man, unflinching in its evaluation of his work and inspiring in its conclusions. The book claims what evangelicals have widely acknowledged: Leon Morris was, and remains, Australia's most influential international scholar and pastor.

978-1-84227-986-1

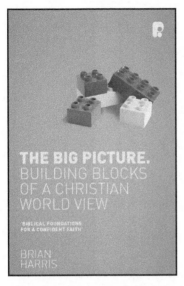

The Big Picture

Building Blocks of a Christian World View

Brian Harris

The Big Picture is an accessible and stimulating exploration of the big building blocks of the Christian faith. Harris's take on the big building blocks of Christian faith is refreshing and will be appreciated by all who would like to think through different ways to follow Jesus the Christ in an ever-changing context.

'Skilfully bringing together biblically-informed theology and the everyday world, Brian Harris unpacks themes of grace, creation and Christian hope in an engaging conversational manner. The result is a book that empowers us to live out our faith wherever we are.'
Stephen Garner, Laidlaw College, Auckland, New Zealand

978-1-84227-856-7

The Tortoise Usually Wins

Biblical Reflections on Quiet Leadership for Reluctant Leaders

Brian Harris

The Tortoise Usually Wins is a theological exploration of the theory of quiet leadership aimed at those who reluctantly accept the mantle of leadership, but who often make a significant difference.

'Books on leadership are today two a penny. Just occasionally, however, one of these books might stand head and shoulders above most of the others, and to my delight *The Tortoise Usually Wins* falls into that category. I can see many church leaders benefitting from this book. I warmly commend this unusual book.'
Paul Beasley-Murray, Senior Minister, Central Baptist Church, Chelmsford; Chair of Ministry Today UK

978-184227-787-4

We trust you enjoyed reading this book
from Paternoster. If you want to be informed
of any new titles from this author and other
releases you can sign up to the Paternoster
newsletter by contacting us:

By post:
Paternoster
PO Box 6326
Bletchley
Milton Keynes
MK1 9GG

E-mail:
paternoster@authenticmedia.co.uk

Follow us: